Welcome to

THE EVERYTHING® PARENT'S GUIDES

As a parent, you're swamped with conflicting advice and parenting techniques that tell you what is best for your child. THE EVERYTHING® PARENT'S GUIDES get right to the point about specific issues. They give you the most recent, up-to-date information on parenting trends, behavior issues, and health concerns—providing you with a detailed resource to help you ease your parenting anxieties.

THE EVERYTHING® PARENT'S GUIDES are an extension of the bestselling Everything® series in the parenting category. These family-friendly books are designed to be a one-stop guide for parents. If you want authoritative information on specific topics not fully covered in other books, THE EVERYTHING® PARENT'S GUIDES are the perfect resource to ensure that you raise a healthy, confident child.

THE EVERYTHING® PARENT'S GUIDE TO Children with Asperger's Syndrome

Dear Reader,

When I was a little boy, I loved *The Wizard of Oz* more than anything. At every opportunity, I would endlessly recite related facts and statistics, or I would draw my favorite characters over and over again. However, as I grew, my passion remained constant while the interests of my peers became typical of preteens and adolescents. As you can imagine, this led to a number of social conflicts and challenges.

When I was growing up, there was no such term as "Asperger's syndrome," at least not that anyone actively applied to my way of being. Fortunately, that has changed and today's parents desire information about Asperger's syndrome more than ever before.

The Everything® Parent's Guide to Children with Asperger's Syndrome is a fresh, basic introduction for parents of children newly diagnosed with Asperger's.

I am grateful to many parents, kids, educators, and caregivers who have validated the contents of this book. And, along the way, I've had the good fortune to meet more than a few really cool little boys as equally passionate about *The Wizard of Oz* as I was!

Best wishes,

William Stillman

CHILDREN WITH ASPERGER'S SYNDROME

Help, hope, and guidance

William Stillman

Adams Media
Avon, Massachusetts

For Jay, my ally and protector

• • •

Publishing Director: Gary M. Krebs
Managing Editor: Kate McBride
Copy Chief: Laura MacLaughlin
Acquisitions Editor: Kate Burgo
Development Editor: Karen Johnson Jacot
Production Editors: Jamie Wielgus, Bridget Brace

Production Director: Susan Beale
Production Manager: Michelle Roy Kelly
Cover Design: Paul Beatrice, Matt LeBlanc
Layout and Graphics: Colleen Cunningham Rachael Eiben, John Paulhus, Daria Perreault, Erin Ring

• • •

An Everything® Series Book.
Everything® and everything.com® are registered trademarks of F+W Publications, Inc.

Published by Adams Media, an F+W Publications Company
57 Littlefield Street, Avon, MA 02322 U.S.A.
www.adamsmedia.com

ISBN: 1-59337-153-5

Printed in Canada.
J I H G F E D C B A

Library of Congress Cataloging-in-Publication Data
Stillman, William
The everything parent's guide to children with Asperger's syndrome / William Stillman.
p. cm.
(An everything series book)
ISBN 1-59337-153-5
1. Asperger's syndrome. 2. Asperger's syndrome--Patients--Family relationships.
3. Parents of autistic children. I. Title: Parent's guide to children with Asperger's syndrome. II. Title. III. Series: Everything series.

RJ506.A9S7595 2004
649'.154--dc22

2004013570

This book is available at quantity discounts for bulk purchases.
For information, call 1-800-872-5627.

As•per•ger's syndrome

(ăs′pər-gərz) ▶ Asperger's syndrome: the natural way by which some perceive the world from an alternate perspective and logic, creating misunderstandings, misinterpretations, and social challenges when one attempts to assimilate with the world at large.

All the examples and dialogues used in this book are fictional and have been created by the author to illustrate disciplinary situations.

Acknowledgments

I am grateful for the generosity and enthusiasm of the following people who helped make The Everything Parent's Guide to Children with Asperger's Syndrome *possible: Debra Andreas; Kate Burgo; June Clark, literary agent extraordinaire; Dr. Michael Glew; Bill Kaiser, Police Training Specialist, Pennsylvania State Police Academy; Trieste Kennedy; Chris Khumprakob; Linda McCormick; Patrick Moore; Angela Uliana-Murphy, Esquire; Jim Murphy; Gina Rattle; Susan Rockwood; Noel Schaefer; Bonnie Schaefer; Richard Shull; Mark Sachnik; Dr. Barney Vincelette; Stephen Shore; and Barbara Scott-Mazza*

• • •

Contents

Introduction

Long ago and far away, kids who drew detailed diagrams of spacecraft, created intricate models of the human digestive system, spent all their free time reading about medieval cathedrals, or enjoyed reciting complex dinosaur names—and preferred those isolated activities over playtime with peers—were labeled. The labels were a reflection of a so-called socially inappropriate desire to be absorbed with things, instead of people. Words often used to describe such kids may have included *gifted, moody, antisocial, irritable, obsessed, geek, brainiac,* or even *stoic*. They may have been thought of as outsiders, with no or few friends. As adults, they may have been considered odd and eccentric, loners or hermits.

Fortunately, today we are shifting our perception of what we now know to be Asperger's syndrome. We are learning more about Asperger's as a milder "cousin" on the autism spectrum. (Some equate Asperger's and the phrase "high-functioning autism.") We are accepting Asperger's as a legitimate framework to describe a unique experience. Slowly but surely, we are moving beyond stereotypes in our collective understanding of children with Asperger's. We are recognizing their different ways of thinking, different ways of perceiving the world, and different ways of being. As we grow in our sensitivity and understanding, we are better able to support and celebrate the child with Asperger's syndrome. Instead of labeling a child as "obsessed," we may now praise her giftedness and balance her needs to find a social niche.

We are learning more and more about autism all the time, but we're only just beginning to scratch the surface of Asperger's syndrome. Asperger's is still a very new consideration for parents and a new diagnosis for many prescribing doctors. There is much to explore on this broad learning curve: social differences, mental health, sensory sensitivities, and coping strategies that will be of lifelong value. Parents may become overwhelmed with clinical information that reinforces their child's perceived deficits—the things they are not expected to be able to do in life. Other areas that may prompt confusion include options regarding learning and educational placement, training and programming, therapies and techniques. Well-intentioned neighbors and family members may offer their perspectives based on what they've heard or read, whether it has any factual basis or not. Considerations for a child's future living arrangements, adult relationships, and viable vocations may create family and marital stress.

Throughout this journey, it will be important for parents to remain grounded in one thought: We are all more alike than different. Understanding the child with Asperger's syndrome is a learning opportunity for parents, siblings, and extended family.

When we foster an appreciation of the unique ways we *all* participate in the world, we are poised to better value those with Asperger's. When we actively project new and positive ways of supporting the child with Asperger's, he will respond in equally positive ways. The result is that a mutual relationship is strengthened tenfold, and a ripple effect occurs.

The Everything® Parent's Guide to Children with Asperger's Syndrome aids parents in making balanced, informed choices about their child and her future. Ideally, this journey is a partnership between parent and child in decision-making and education about Asperger's syndrome. More than ever, a path of opportunity lies before parents of children with Asperger's syndrome.

Foreword

DIANE TWACHTMAN-CULLEN, PH.D.

Needless to say, an *everything* guide to *anything* is a consummately ambitious project! The task is all the more daunting when the subject is as complex and multifaceted as Asperger's syndrome. Hence, you can imagine how delighted I was (okay, surprised too!) to find that *The Everything® Parent's Guide to Children with Asperger's Syndrome* lives up to exactly what it purports to be—a one-stop guide to give parents and other family members help, hope, and guidance. Having said that, don't let the title fool you. This book will also serve as a useful reference guide for school-based personnel.

Readers will not only find a tremendous amount of useful information in this book, they will also find it beautifully organized and categorized for easy access—no small feat for a book as comprehensive as this one. Indeed, it is difficult to imagine a subject that is not addressed in this book.

Parents, especially, will appreciate the upbeat nature of the book, for after giving important background information, the author sets the tone of the book with a chapter devoted to "Positive Perspectives." Fittingly, he concludes with a chapter entitled, "The Rewards of Being an Asperger's Parent." Readers will also find the many examples interspersed throughout the book illuminating and most helpful in understanding the complexities of Asperger's syndrome.

This book provides much-needed information across a variety of subjects and ages, and it does so in an unpretentious and thoughtful manner. Most important, it will become immediately obvious to readers as they embark upon their tour of *The Everything® Parent's Guide to Children with Asperger's Syndrome* that they have signed on with a tour guide who really knows the territory!

Chapter 1

Defining Asperger's Syndrome

Although first defined sixty years ago, Asperger's syndrome has only recently become an accepted diagnosis on the autism spectrum. Asperger's is defined by a series of clinical symptoms that may describe a child's behavior or way of being. Since the early 1990s, the syndrome has slowly but increasingly been identified by pediatric psychiatrists, psychologists, and other physicians. It is useful to understand the background and clinical definition of the term "Asperger's syndrome."

Background and History

Asperger's syndrome was first formally defined in 1944 by Hans Asperger, an Austrian pediatrician. Asperger studied social interactions, communication, and behavior in children with different ways of being. In 1943, he studied a group of children, mostly boys, who had difficulty interacting in socially acceptable ways. The children appeared intrinsic or self-centered—not necessarily selfish, but rather, they preferred to keep to themselves. Another common characteristic was that they were not physically adept, and were rather uncoordinated. Most experienced no cognitive delays and were, in fact, quite articulate, with a strong command of vocabulary. The children engaged in repetitive physical actions, or were fascinated with nuances of timetables or the mechanics of certain objects such as clocks.

Asperger published his findings in a paper titled

"Autistic Psychopathy." By today's standards, the title is alarming and disrespectful but, in using the word "psychopathy," Asperger did not intend to describe mentally ill, violent behavior; he was using the clinically acceptable jargon of the day. Asperger's findings were the first documented collection of traits now used to diagnose Asperger's syndrome.

Unknown to Asperger, a psychiatrist named Leo Kanner was conducting similar research at Johns Hopkins University at about the same time. In 1943, Kanner chose the word "autism" (from the Greek word *autos*, or "self") to describe a group of children who shared like, but stereotyped, personality traits, engaged in solitary actions, and who struggled with expressing communication that was effective, reliable, and understandable. In postwar Austria, Asperger's paper languished while Kanner's research received recognition.

Fact

Hans Asperger's findings were published nearly simultaneously with the research of Leo Kanner, another doctor who, in 1944, first distinguished the traits of autism. The two physicians were unknown to one another. Because Asperger's paper was published in German, and Kanner's in English, Kanner's research received broader distribution and was subsequently popularized. Hans Asperger passed away in 1980 before his research was universally applied.

On the Autism Spectrum

Despite the growing recognition of autism as an acceptable diagnosis during the 1950s and 1960s, Hans Asperger's research went largely unnoticed. Still, there were individuals who experienced autistic-like symptoms but did not have the cognitive differences usually found in those with autism. At the time, such individuals were diagnosed with mental illness or nervous anxiety. Some were institutionalized or imprisoned because of their odd behavior or because they were gullible and easily manipulated into making poor or dangerous choices.

Refrigerator Mother Theory

A popular theory to explain the alleged distance felt between parents, mothers in particular, and their children with autism was similarly applied to those with autistic-like symptoms. It was called "refrigerator mother theory," which referred to the supposed aloofness or indifference shown by mothers unable to connect with their children. This theory reinforced the ridiculous notion that mothers deliberately induced Asperger's in their children. In fact, Asperger's syndrome is no one's fault. During the 1980s, the refrigerator mother theory was on its way out in favor of recognizing a legitimate diagnosis in those with autistic behavior.

Genetics

Some recent theories being researched to explain the prevalence of autism and Asperger's syndrome include genetics, environmental factors (pregnant mothers' exposure to or ingestion of chemical elements), or children's reactions to the mercury preservative in certain childhood vaccinations. There is currently no prenatal or other biological exam to test for Asperger's syndrome.

It wasn't until 1981 that British psychiatrist Lorna Wing revived Hans Asperger's findings in a research paper of her own. This eventually led to the reclassification of autistic experiences in the clinical document titled *Diagnostic and Statistical Manual of Mental Disorders* (or, as it is more commonly referred to, *DSM*).

Asperger's Defined

The *DSM* is published in the United States by the American Psychiatric Association. As of this writing, its fourth edition, published in 1994, is still in effect. This was the first edition of the *DSM* to formally recognize Asperger's syndrome, which was categorized under the general heading Pervasive Developmental Disorders (PDD). In addition to Asperger's, there are several other diagnoses that fall under the PDD heading. These include:

- Autistic disorder (known as autism)
- Rett disorder (or Rett syndrome)
- Childhood disintegrative disorder
- Asperger's disorder (known as Asperger's syndrome)
- Pervasive developmental disorder not otherwise specified (or PDD-NOS)

These are all subcategories of the PDD diagnosis. At present, these experiences are collectively grouped under the PDD heading because of the similarities of symptoms related to challenges in communication, social interaction, and so-called stereotyped behaviors, interests, and activities. Autism is the most prevalent of these experiences, more common than Down syndrome or childhood cancer. Rett disorder is usually found in little girls before the age of four. Childhood disintegrative disorder impacts children before the age of ten. In both circumstances, and for unknown reasons, children experience a loss of previously acquired social skills, language, motor skills, play, and self-care. The category pervasive developmental disorder not otherwise specified (PDD-NOS) is used when a child demonstrates autistic-like symptoms but misses meeting the criteria for the other diagnoses.

Some clinicians consider the term "high-functioning autism" synonymous with Asperger's syndrome. The *DSM* does not presently define this term, so it may or may not apply to a child with Asperger's. It may also be used to describe the child who demonstrates many skills yet still falls within the PDD-NOS range of diagnosis.

PDD-NOS may be used by a physician unaccustomed to diagnosing Asperger's, or it may be used if a doctor wishes to be cautious, to "wait and see" as a child grows and develops. Sometimes, when the PDD-NOS diagnosis is revisited, a child has matured into an official Asperger's diagnosis. However, the *DSM* is a dynamic document, and as the psychiatric field grows and becomes more knowledgeable, reorganization of Asperger's and autistic experiences is inevitable in future, revised editions.

Essential

Asperger's syndrome is now being diagnosed in children as young as three. Little is known about Asperger's at present. There is no single known cause, although there are many theories. It is a neurological condition that primarily creates challenges in understanding social interactions. Asperger's is *not* a disease or chronic mental illness. It is a natural, lifelong experience.

Clinical Criteria

As we've learned, Asperger's syndrome is presently grouped under the diagnostic "umbrella" heading pervasive developmental disorders, along with other disorders with similar symptoms. As currently defined by the *DSM*, a child with Asperger's differs from the child with autism because of the following traits:

- No clinically significant delays in language
- No clinically significant delays in cognitive development
- No clinically significant delays in development of age-appropriate self-help skills
- No clinically significant delays in adaptive behavior (other than social interaction)
- No clinically significant delays in curiosity about the environment in childhood

To qualify for an Asperger's syndrome diagnosis, a child must demonstrate impairment in social interaction, shown by at least two of the following:

- Impairment in the use of nonverbal behaviors (such as eye contact, facial expressions, and gestures) during social interaction
- Lack of development of relationships with peers
- Failure to seek to share enjoyment, interests, or achievements with other people (for instance, by not showing objects of interest to others)
- Failure to reciprocate emotions or social gestures

The child should also demonstrate "restrictive repetitive and stereotyped patterns of behaviors, interests, and activities," shown by at least one of the following:

- Unusually intense preoccupation with one or more stereotyped interests
- Obsessively following specific, nonfunctional routines or rituals
- Repeated motions, such as hand or finger flapping or twisting
- Unusual preoccupation with parts of objects

To qualify as characteristics of Asperger's, these traits must be significant enough to cause great challenges for the child in social, occupational, and other important areas of daily living. Although, increasingly, some children with Asperger's have been diagnosed as young as three, the diagnosis is most often made from age six and up.

These areas and others will be gently and respectfully demystified in the contents of this book. The word "disorder" may not seem like a family friendly way to describe your child's personal Asperger's syndrome experience, but it is currently clinical "shorthand" to summarize it. Please do not be hurt, confused, or upset by this technical jargon. Outside of a doctor's office, you may wish to use the word "difference" or the phrase "different way of being" when you feel the need to describe your child's experience, if at all. Your child's physician, educators, or school psychologist may be able to recommend literature in addition to the *DSM*.

Fact

The *Diagnostic and Statistical Manual* catalogs a wide range of mental health and related experiences. It is the foremost reference guide used by psychiatrists, psychologists, social workers, mental health professionals, therapists, counselors, and nurses, to name a few. It provides a framework to diagnose someone's experience according to symptoms. The first edition was originally published in 1952.

Asperger's and Autistic-like Commonalities

Having just reviewed the clinical criteria for the diagnosis of Asperger's syndrome, you may be filled with many questions and concerns. Some of what was described may match what you know to be true of your child. But you might be surprised to see that other areas weren't included. What about the child who screams and covers his ears when an ambulance goes by, blaring its siren? Or the child who cannot tolerate the taste of Jell-O or pudding in her mouth? These are called sensory sensitivities, a commonality shared with persons with autism but not defined by the *DSM* as clinical criteria.

Your child may vibrate at a different "frequency" than most others. That is, he may be described as "exquisitely sensitive." Because of this, his entire nervous system—his senses and emotions—may be routinely impacted by stimulation others filter out naturally.

Many children with Asperger's share some common sensitivities with people with autism. The most common sensory sensitivities are:

- Auditory (including intolerable noise or frequency levels)
- Smell and taste
- Visual
- Touch

Auditory Sensitivity

The child with exquisitely sensitive hearing may cry and recoil from a variety of sounds. She reacts in this way because in a very real sense, she is physically hurting from the intensity of the noise. The most offensive sounds are those that are not only very loud and startling but also *unpredictable*, meaning there's no telling when or where they will occur with any certainty. The most commonly hurtful, unpredictable sounds for someone with especially sensitive hearing include (in no particular order): dogs barking; babies crying; crowd noises; vacuum cleaners; police, ambulance, and fire engine sirens, or cars backfiring; loud music or television programs not of the child's choosing; public announcement systems and intercoms; people tapping, clicking, or snapping fingers or objects (such as a pencil); and people laughing, talking, or sneezing loudly.

Taste and Smell

Certain smells (especially food scents and perfumes or toiletries) and tastes may also be overwhelming. On occasion, a child may gag and vomit in reaction to the sensation of the smell or texture of foods. Unable to explain herself in the moment, the child may bolt from the environment if the smells or tastes become too much for her to handle.

Visual Sensitivity

Because many people with Asperger's are very visual in how they absorb and process information, they may also become readily overwhelmed by too many visual details in a single environment (think Wal*Mart on a Saturday afternoon). The number of moving, flapping, or spinning objects paired with the vivid mix of colors and combined with too many people cramped together in a single location can push the child with Asperger's into sensory overload. The same is true for many of us!

Light that is too intense can also cause pain and discomfort. Overhead fluorescent lighting is a harsh, abrasive, and unnatural illumination that is especially troublesome for many people with both

Asperger's and autism. In addition to its intensity, fluorescent lighting may flicker and buzz. The flickering and buzzing may go completely unnoticed by others but will become unbearable for the child with heightened sensitivities.

Touch

Finally, the sensation of touch may be equally overwhelming for the child with Asperger's. Being hugged, patted on the head or back, or picked up—especially *unpredictably* and without warning or permission—may cause the child to cry, bite, or even hit. The challenge is that children, particularly small children, often tend to be hugged, patted, and picked up simply because they're adorable. The people doing the touching are well intentioned but don't yet understand that the concept of respecting someone's personal space also applies to children.

The texture of certain clothing fabrics worn against one's skin may create extreme discomfort and physical irritation as well. This unpleasant sensation has been likened to one's flesh being rubbed raw with sandpaper. For some, cotton and natural fiber clothes are a must to ward against the manifestation of skin welts and rashes. Conversely, other children with Asperger's may welcome (and initiate seeking out) the sensory input provided by the deep-pressured touch offered by bear hugs and massage, or burrowing under sofa cushions and mattresses, or self-swaddling in comforters and sleeping bags. The difference here is that these activities occur on the child's terms and at her specifications of endurance.

Other Commonalities

Another commonality children with Asperger's syndrome may have with those with autism is "flat affect" expressions and somewhat different speech patterns. A flat affect refers to facial expressions that are fixed or "artificial" in appearance instead of naturally animated. The child may not laugh or smile unless cued to do so in an appropriate situation, or the child may appear to have a collection of rehearsed or "canned" reactions to match certain circumstances.

(This is actually a real strength, to be discussed further in Chapter 17, under the subheading "Acting and Music.")

The child's way of talking may also seem "flat" and monotone. The child's words may sound robotic and carefully measured. Or there may be a lilting tone to her voice, described by some as "sing-song," in which her speech sounds like it's bouncing up and down when she talks.

Often, the child with Asperger's may find it challenging to demonstrate or understand what others take for granted as a common-sense manner of thought. The child may have a logic all his own that perplexes or exasperates others because it is not representative of the norm. He may not grasp certain social rules or ways of doing things, explained away by others with the phrase "just because."

It is also not uncommon for many children with Asperger's syndrome to have a desire to maintain order, peace, and tranquility. Your child may (from his logic and perspective) initiate great and creative measures to make others happy and content to maintain the status quo, even if it means making decisions that adults may judge as unwise or unacceptable. It may have more to do with desiring to please in order to keep the peace than with being intuitive to others' needs.

It is important to appreciate that none of these reactions are typically "attention-seeking" or deliberately "bad" or noncompliant behaviors. They are a genuine reaction to extreme, hurtful disturbances in the child's immediate environment. For example, one mother assumed her son was engaging her in a power struggle when he refused to wear the new blue jeans he had picked out in the store and that she purchased for him. He complained that they scratched when he wore them. He was speaking truthfully, but mom wasn't listening carefully enough to his words. Washing the new jeans several times to soften them made them physically tolerable, and the conflict was resolved without further incident. This concept of distinguishing an "Asperger's moment" from typical kid behavior will make more sense as you continue reading. Helping the child with Asperger's to cope with his sensory sensitivities will be explored in more detail later in this book.

Fact

Your child *may* have Asperger's syndrome if he or she finds it difficult to make friends; doesn't seem to understand nonverbal communications, like body language or facial expressions; doesn't understand or appears insensitive to others' feelings; is deeply passionate about one or more subject areas; is not physically graceful; has great difficulty accepting change in routine or schedule; or has a different or mechanical-sounding speech patterns.

The *Diagnostic and Statistical Manual* does not presently include any of the previous autistic-like commonalities as clinical criteria for autism or Asperger's syndrome. These attributes, while valid in many children, have become stereotypes when some doctors, journalists, and others generically describe those with Asperger's syndrome. Asperger's is as unique and individual an experience as each individual is unique. You may find that some, all, or none of these nonclinical, autistic-like commonalities make sense when you think about your child's way of being in the world.

Prevalence and Misdiagnosis

There has been a great deal of attention given by the media to the staggering, skyrocketing increase in the numbers of children identified with autism. It has been legitimately described as an epidemic explosion. Fifteen years ago, it was estimated that 1 in 10,000 individuals was autistic. In the 1990s, the estimate narrowed to 1 in 1,000, then 1 in every 500, then 1 in every 250 children. Today, the statistics fluctuate regularly, growing closer and closer all the time. Most recent tallies, such as that proffered by *Time* magazine in 2002, suggest that 1 in every 150 children under the age of ten has autism.

According to a 2002 study commissioned by the California Legislature, during the past fifteen years in the state of California alone, the number of children identified with autism has leapt by 643 percent. Another recent statistic estimated that 1 in every 5 children has either autism, dyslexia, attention deficit hyperactivity disorder, or some form of uncontrollable aggression. In 2003, the federal Centers for Disease Control and Prevention estimated that of the children born daily in the United States, 53 will be diagnosed with autism, or roughly 19,000 infants per year. As noted earlier, this rise is occurring without any single known cause or indicator.

Where does this leave our understanding of the prevalence of Asperger's syndrome? With so much attention being given to young children newly diagnosed with autism, those with Asperger's syndrome are not usually identified and tracked in the same manner by doctors or our education system. We may speculate that there are a number of reasons for this:

- One or both parents may have Asperger's syndrome and do not detect anything out of the ordinary in their child.
- Families who live in isolated or rural areas, or have limited contact with others with similar-aged, typically developing children, may not recognize their child's differences or may be distanced from proper support systems to obtain a diagnosis.
- Family practitioners and other physicians may be unaccustomed to identifying the symptoms of autism, let alone understanding the criteria for Asperger's syndrome. They may have little to no experience with Asperger's or limited resources from which to gather more information.
- The child of school age undiagnosed with Asperger's may be labeled as noncompliant or lazy. Parents and teachers may believe she is simply not applying herself to her full potential.
- The child may be seen as simply quirky or especially gifted, leading to the "Little Professor" moniker that has become a popular way of describing children with Asperger's who present as technically proficient miniature adults.
- The child may have a diagnosis of hyperlexia, an experience that may outwardly present itself as similar to Asperger's in

that the child may be highly fluent. Hyperlexia is marked by a precocious capacity for reading that far exceeds the child's chronological age; however, the child may be unable to comprehend all that has been read. The child may be fascinated with numbers, may need to keep specific routines, and may be challenged in social interactions.

- The child has a "ballpark" diagnosis but, as noted earlier, it is labeled as PDD-NOS or high-functioning autism. As such, it is not specifically identified as Asperger's.

Because the clinical criteria for Asperger's calls for no significant cognitive or developmental delays, it is often undetected until a child is past the age of eligibility for early intervention services. It is also possible for Asperger's syndrome to go undiagnosed altogether, because it can be so subtle. It could also be misdiagnosed as another issue such as a learning disorder, attention deficit disorder, attention deficit hyperactivity disorder, dyslexia, schizophrenia, generalized anxiety disorder, Tourette's syndrome, obsessive-compulsive disorder, oppositional defiant disorder, bipolar disorder, intermittent explosive disorder, or depression—all mental health experiences listed in the *DSM*.

Given all this, what *do* we know about the prevalence of Asperger's syndrome? Like autism, Asperger's knows no social, cultural, or economic boundaries. And, also like autism, it is four times more likely to be found in males than females (again, for reasons presently unknown). Until recently, Asperger's, like the prevalence of autism, was believed to be largely a male experience, but as our culture is becoming more aware and better educated to such social issues, more females with Asperger's are being identified. Conservative estimates conclude that 1 in every 1,000 children has Asperger's syndrome. However, as we've seen with autism, the increasing recognition of Asperger's will surely prompt that statistic to increase in the near future.

CHAPTER 2

Positive Perspectives

The clinical criteria for Asperger's syndrome can be intimidating to parents of children who are newly diagnosed. The diagnostic traits attributed to those with Asperger's can set a negative precedent because of the focus on "disabilities" rather than abilities. It will be important for parents to temper this information with a balanced perspective. The child with Asperger's has much to offer in the form of gifts and talents. The tone with which parents receive these offerings can directly impact the child's self-image.

We're All More Alike

As we enter the twenty-first century, there is a growing emphasis placed upon embracing social and cultural diversity. Increasingly, we are rising to the occasion amidst global adversity. Our politics and entertainment reflect this correct-thinking movement toward valuing individual differences and blending our communities. The time is ripe for positive change, and, more than ever before, people with a variety of different ways of being are poised on the verge of an equal rights movement in keeping with this changing trend.

In essence, we are all more alike than unlike. As human beings, we share greater similarities than differences in the way we live our lives, move through environments, and interact within relationships. And we *all* experience individual autisms—those neurological "blips" that temporarily waylay us without any known cause.

Can't Place Her?

For example, have you ever unexpectedly met someone familiar to you outside of the context in which you know them but cannot think of her name at that moment? You should know the person's name because you've had occasion to interact with her at work, at church, in a class, or some other circumstance. But because you know her by association with a specific environment, your brain has cataloged her face with that situation only. You struggle to make the split-second switch to apply the same information to the new environment (the mall parking lot, for instance).

It can be embarrassing when you fail, and it may only be much later that your brain relaxes and the information comes to you readily. "Of course! Her name was Ellen! Why on earth couldn't I remember that in the first place?" you berate yourself. How frustrating it was at the time, being unable to call up immediate information—information already known to you. This concept of association will be further explored in Chapter 12 when we examine ways in which children with Asperger's commonly think, learn, and process information.

Acting Out of Habit

Here's another example that most people can relate to that sheds light on the neurological workings of people with Asperger's: You may have experienced "gray time" while operating a car—that is, driving along a familiar route and arriving at your destination with absolutely no recall of the drive. Your brain has been on "auto pilot" and you've executed the drive, from start to finish, completely by rote and seemingly without thinking. (This is similar to those occasions when you have been sitting and realize—or someone brings it to your attention—you have been unconsciously tapping your foot, or shaking your leg.) In a twist on this example, you may have had occasion to deliberately deviate from your typical driving route to drop something off or pick something (or someone) up, and, again by rote, you arrive at your destination and realize you've totally forgotten about the change of routine. There has been a misfire in the brain-body connection. You then have to backtrack to make it right, losing additional time and likely escalating your frustration level.

In yet another commonality, have you ever been frustrated at being unable to locate an object and realize you've been holding it in your hand the entire time you've been searching? Both of these examples are the type of neurological experiences people with Asperger's deal with on a daily basis.

Stuck in Your Head

Finally, another neurological blip that underscores the ways we are all more alike than different occurs when you have a song "playing" in your head. It may or may not be a song of your choosing. If it is a song of your choosing, then at first replaying it and, perhaps, singing or moving along to the music, is deliberate and even pleasurable. Later, when you are unable to banish the song from your brainwaves, it becomes a nuisance. It may even derail your thinking and routines. Some of you may have even been awakened in the middle of the night by the song and, patriotic though you may be, hearing "The Star Spangled Banner" playing repeatedly at three o'clock in the morning is not pleasant or desirable.

Similar Habits

Like the person diagnosed with Asperger's syndrome, you may also engage in actions or activities that work for you but may be perceived as eccentric, odd, or peculiar by others. Some of you may have a specific sequence mapped out for the manner in which you grocery shop, run errands, or tend to the yard work. It makes no sense to anyone else but is perfectly logical to you. You may have very precise routines in the way you clean, organize closets, shelves, and cupboards (including arranging canned foods in alphabetical order—labels facing out, of course), or set up your workspace on the job. You may even become distressed or infuriated if anyone "messes" with your system. Your workspace may not be meticulously organized but is instead, to the uninitiated, disheveled in appearance. What no one else may know is that, at any given moment, you can lay your hands on the exact data report in question upon request.

Another example is the way you type at a keyboard. You may be a speed typist, hitting the keys beautifully and by rote, like riding a bicycle. Or you may be someone who was never able to "hardwire" your brain to type with both hands simultaneously. To compensate, you may use one finger on each hand to hunt and peck your way to successful typing. Perhaps you can only use one finger on one hand to type. In the end, isn't the result of the facile typist and the "hunt-and-pecker" typist the same? Does it, then, make any difference how either arrived at the same result? Hold this thought as you broach appreciating your child's unique way of being in the world. This will provide you with the patience to allow your child's unique thought processes to unfold.

Confronting Negative Feelings

When some parents receive their child's diagnosis of Asperger's syndrome, they may despair. On occasion, the family may perceive the diagnosis as hopeless or something that induces shame. Their rationale may be driven by several factors:

- Insensitive presentation by a physician that focuses on disabilities
- Rumors and stereotypes about people with differences, including Asperger's syndrome
- No access to literature or other educational materials that present a balanced perspective
- Projected anxieties about the child's future lack of independence and failure in adult life
- Conflicting pressures about proper childrearing from family, neighbors, or friends
- Conflicting pressures about proper intervention and support from doctors and other professionals
- No previous exposure to people with differences who live well-adjusted, content lives

- Most importantly, no opportunities for contact with families in similar situations who are enjoying their child with Asperger's

Essential

Parents of kids with differences consistently agree that their single greatest resource has been the opportunity to share their story with other parents. The National Parent to Parent Network (*www.P2PUSA.org*) is designed to connect parents with other parents in like circumstances and within geographic proximity. Mothers United for Moral Support, Inc. (MUMS), is another national resource center. The MUMS toll-free phone number is 1-877-336-5333 (*www.netnet.net/mums*).

The media also has a responsibility to endeavor to demonstrate sensitivity when it comes to differences among people, which they rarely do. Instead, it is typical for reporters to widen the gap of our collective differences by using "us and them" language. It fuels the incorrect and improper perception that nondisabled or neurotypical people are superior to those labeled as "poor unfortunates who struggle miserably." One journalist recently described Asperger's syndrome as "a neurological malady that dooms many of its victims to a lonely life and dead-end jobs despite higher-than-average intelligence." It is astounding that in this day and age this actual quote was published as an acceptable description of someone's way of being. Additionally, the journalist has generalized many people with Asperger's syndrome by reducing them to "victims" who are doomed.

Offering Encouragement and Support

When a family believes such hurtful, insensitive stereotypes, the images conjured only reinforce their angst. The child with Asperger's is often inherently gentle and exquisitely sensitive. It is imperative that such negative thoughts and feelings not be projected upon the child or communicated directly in front of him. When this transpires consistently enough, a self-fulfilling prophecy occurs.

If you hear people refer to you only in disparaging, disrespectful terms, you believe it and, eventually, you become it. You reflect back what people project upon you because you believe it is what they expect. After all, it's how you've been defined all along. Being so sensitive, the child with Asperger's may naturally internalize, replay, and agonize over all of this to no end. So you see how easily a vicious cycle can result and even repeat itself over a lifetime.

A chance encounter with a wise stranger prompted Trieste, mom to a young son with Asperger's, to rethink how she perceived her son's differences:

> At an autism conference I attended when my son was very young, I met another parent who shared with me words I have never forgotten. He said, "Don't ever make your child feel bad for who he is." His words were an eye-opener for me, because at the time I was under the impression that the best thing I could do for my son was to eliminate all his "signs of autism" and make him as much like other children as possible. I began to wonder how much of the behavior modification we were constantly doing with him was actually making him feel bad about himself.

Negative thoughts and feelings should be shed in favor of positive perspectives. Your child is a child, first and foremost. A beautiful, entirely unique, magnificently gorgeous human being with as many faults and frailties as gifts and talents; the same is true of us all. In childhood, your son or daughter will rely upon you and your family to provide a solid foundation of self-esteem. Equipped with a strong sense of self-worth—not self-loathing—your child will be better prepared to enter into a life that will likely present many challenges. Much of your time and energy will be expended in raising, counseling, and disciplining your child in ways that she will understand. It is important to try to equalize those occasions by reinforcing your love and appreciation of her gifts and talents.

It is speculated, although not confirmed with certainty, that some of the world's greatest thinkers, innovators, and artists have had Asperger's syndrome. They include a long list of famous personalities: Ludwig van Beethoven, Isaac Newton, Albert Einstein, Thomas Jefferson, Thomas Edison, Vincent van Gogh, Emily Dickinson, Henry Ford, Mark Twain, Alfred Hitchcock, H. P. Lovecraft, Andy Warhol, Charles Schulz, Bill Gates, and Michael Jackson. (On the humorous side, fictional characters dubbed as Asperger's are Bert of "Bert and Ernie" *Sesame Street* fame, Lisa Simpson from *The Simpsons*, Mr. Spock from *Star Trek*, and the U.K.'s Mr. Bean.) Suffice it to say, from an historical perspective, your child with Asperger's syndrome is in outstanding company.

Linda, another mom of a young boy with Asperger's, shares thoughts about giftedness:

> In reading the many books on Asperger's and autism spectrum disorders, I find that so many treat it as a curse. My son is very proud of his different way of viewing the world. He does not care that he is different. He says God makes fewer philosophers than typical thinkers. He is very proud of being one of the special few.

People with Asperger's syndrome who possess great talent tend to fall in a spectrum of pronounced, gifted abilities, as demonstrated by the previous roster of brilliant thinkers and great talents. One end of the spectrum finds those who are naturally gifted at mathematics and numbers, computers and mechanical devices, biology and other sciences. The other end of the spectrum includes the artists, the actors, the authors, and the poets.

Think of the areas in which your child is naturally gifted. Does her comprehension of computer programs exceed that of many adults? Does he enjoy describing the exact alignment of our solar system's planets, identifying each by correct name, placement, and color? Does she assume the personality traits of a favorite cartoon character with uncanny accuracy, down to mimicking lines of dialogue? Or does he have the quiet reverence to render amazing watercolors? These passions are the areas of talent to recognize and encourage as uniquely your child's own.

As you would do for any of your children, at every opportunity, reinforce to your child with Asperger's syndrome how special she is to you. Tell him that you are delighted when he shares his astronomy charts with you. Laugh at her impressions of the Powerpuff Girls and tell her what a terrific actress she is. Highlight your child's gifts when talking with family and friends. Prominently display his works of art. You may be amazed at the long-lasting impact these moments will have as they buoy your child into adolescence and young adulthood.

Essential

Instead of feeling worn out by your child's intense interests, take a moment to indulge him and listen carefully. Or catch your child doing something amazingly gifted and praise her lavishly. Your outpouring of attention and genuine interest will come back to you tenfold.

Positive Philosophies

In viewing your child's Asperger's syndrome in a proactive manner, you will also need to feel grounded in basic, positive philosophies. Because we are all more alike than different, the philosophies will ring true when you reflect upon yourself and your own way of being.

The first philosophy is, "People have good reasons for doing what they do." The second philosophy is, "People are doing the very best they know how to with what they've got."

Your premise as a parent should be to err on the side of caution by approaching situations involving your child's *perceived* wrong-doing from these two perspectives. Here's one example: Upon meeting a greatly overweight man while in the company of his parents and others, a preteenage boy with Asperger's syndrome asked the man in a loud, clear voice how it felt to be "fat." The incident caused some people to conceal smirks while others felt embarrassment at the boy's candor. The gentleman in question surely felt some degree of humiliation as well. In addressing the situation, the (understandably aghast) parent of a typical child might spontaneously scold the child for his insensitive and deliberately rude remark. Instead, now deconstruct the scenario using the previous philosophies.

First, apply the first philosophy. Did the boy have good reasons for doing what he was doing? That is, was his motivation in asking the heavyset man such a blunt and blatant question pure? The answer is yes. The boy was, himself, overweight for his age. In asking the man how it felt to be fat, he was attempting to legitimately glean information that was of importance to him. Why? Because the boy was very cognizant of his own weight as it pertained to his well-being. He was knowledgeable of the inherent health risks and issues that may be associated with being overweight. He was projecting himself into the future by envisioning himself as an overweight adult, not unlike the gentleman he just encountered.

Now apply the second philosophy. Was the boy doing the very best he knew how to in the moment? The parent of a typical child might conclude that the child should have known better to withhold such a crass remark and was deliberately creating an embarrassing scene. However, the boy had never been privately counseled not to make remarks about people's weight in public. Nor had anyone previously told him that the word "fat" was usually highly offensive when used to describe someone, especially if the person had no reason to expect it.

Does this mean that the child with Asperger's is never deliberately a troublemaker? Of course not; kids are kids. Your challenge is to discern what motivates your child with Asperger's syndrome and separate that from jumping to conclusions about typical smart-alecky kid behavior. Follow the path of least resistance by starting with the two positive philosophies. We will explore similar situations in Chapter 4 related to parental discipline.

Comfort Zones

Here are some additional philosophies that will have practical application as you revisit your child's way of being:

- There is safety in sameness and comfort in what is familiar.
- In order to feel safe and comfortable, the child must have control.

Think about the times when your child appeared most content, comfortable, and at ease. Was she enjoying playing a solitary computer game? Was he alone in his bedroom, drawing whales and sharks? Or was he directing the play of his siblings and friends? In these instances—these quiet moments—wouldn't the previous two tenets apply? Was your child engaged in a favored, pleasurable activity? Was it a repetitive activity from which comfort is derived? And during this activity, did your child have control? The response to these questions is likely yes.

Now, reverse the situations and remove the elements of safety, comfort, and control. Say the computer unexpectedly locks up and the video game is interrupted. A sibling won't turn down his music while your child is attempting to concentrate as he executes his marine life drawings with scientific detail. Or a friend decides she doesn't want to be "bossed" by your child and opts out of their playtime. These situations are unexpected and *unpredictable.* One cannot feel safe and comfortable and in control during those occasions when the unpredictable occurs and wins out. When this transpires, your child may feel overwhelmed by the loss of control. This may manifest itself in a variety of undesirable ways or acting-out "behaviors." If the child has good reasons for her behavior and is doing the best she knows how in order to cope with the loss of safety and comfort, then her reaction is a logical progression of that escalation *until she learns other coping strategies.* Until then, it will be critical that you approach interpretation of such situations as objectively as possible by using these positive philosophies first before rushing to judgment. Remember, your child's senses and emotions likely vibrate at a frequency different than most. While feeling safe and comfortable and in control is necessary for us all to be productive, consistent loss of these elements can dramatically unhinge the child with Asperger's. Applying these basic philosophies will serve you well in parenting a child with Asperger's syndrome. They will also enable you to more fully understand the remainder of this book.

It is a myth that all people with Asperger's syndrome want to live in isolation, devoid of meaningful relationships. The child with Asperger's syndrome instinctively wants to be good, wants to fit in, and wants to be just like other kids. He will be best poised to do that if he feels safe and comfortable in knowing there's a place where he is unconditionally loved and understood. Your recognition of Asperger's syndrome as a positive attribute and your appreciation of your child's gifts and talents will make your home and family that very place. Many parents just like you have made this commitment and can readily attest to the profound, loving impact it has made on their lives.

CHAPTER 3

Seeking Diagnosis

Because the symptoms and traits of Asperger's syndrome can be subtle, parents may not recognize any differences in their child until he is age three or older. Pursuing a formal diagnosis is a family's individual decision to make. There are avenues available to aid in this process and a system of community-based and educational services and supports in place to help meet the needs of the child and his family.

Is a Diagnosis Necessary?

Each family is unique and different. The relationships between spouses, children, and extended family can vary drastically. Some families are distant and disconnected from one another. It may be difficult for some family members to outwardly express love and caring. Other families are remarkably and consistently loving and resilient. Still others fall somewhere in between. The dynamics of your family will likely determine how you proceed in seeking a diagnosis of Asperger's syndrome for your child.

Your decision to pursue a formal diagnosis is a personalized and individualized decision to make. There is no "correct" time to form this decision, although many parents agree that they wish to know their child's diagnosis definitively and as early in their child's development as possible.

In observing your child grow and learn, you may have noticed differences in how she is developing when compared with her peers. You may have noticed significant differences in how she interacts with other children. For instance, she may seem not to understand the social rules that other children seem to naturally abide by, such as taking turns in a game. She may play with her toys in ways that are unique but unintended for the toy's purpose, like dismantling the toy to more closely examine its moving parts. The way she talks may sound overly formal, such as addressing you and your spouse as "mother" and "father" instead of mommy and daddy, or inappropriately calling you by your full first name (i.e., "Oh Deirdre, please come help me with my bath now"). She may not be as physically graceful as you might wish for her. Or her temper may be prone to escalate when she loses control of her environment.

Every family is unique, as are the dynamics and interplay of each family member's relationships with one another. In reflecting upon your child's different way of being, be mindful of not ascribing blame to yourself or others for having "caused" Asperger's syndrome in your child. Remember, this was the basis of the now-archaic "refrigerator mother" theory.

Perhaps family, friends, or neighbors have brought some of these issues to your attention. They may wonder or worry if you've witnessed the same differences. When this occurs, it will be important to remember that these people are usually not being nosy, pushy, or humiliating for the sake of making you feel like an inadequate parent. Your concerned family, friends, or neighbors have good reasons for what they're doing, and they are doing the best they know how in the moment. They are merely trying to be helpful in drawing from their own life experiences or those of others they have known.

Try listening to their communications and balancing the information they are sharing with what you know to be true.

As a parent, you know your child best. Is there a ring of truth in the collective observations of all? Are others confirming suspicions you've had but suppressed? If you see your child every day, the observations of the family member, friend, or neighbor who sees the child less frequently should be weighed carefully; your child's different way of being may be more apparent to them than to you. Conversely, if neither you nor your spouse is a stay-at-home parent, then you should accept the observations of your child care or day care professional with similar sincerity. The child care professional can offer you much valuable information about how your child spends his time during the day.

Making the Decision

Most likely, no one at this point will be in a position to suggest Asperger's syndrome as a viable explanation of your child's way of being. So far, you have some questions and concerns about what you are seeing in your child. A place to start might be to compare what you know to be true of your child's development against the *Diagnostic and Statistical Manual* definition of Asperger's syndrome. As you do so, please exercise caution. Specific symptoms in isolation of one another do not a syndrome make.

Remember that the *Diagnostic and Statistical Manual* is a *clinical* document and is not intended to be family-friendly. If the prospect of researching the criteria for Asperger's syndrome in the *DSM* feels a bit daunting, you may access the same or similar information through many of the Web sites listed at the back of this book. They *are* intended to be family- and individual-friendly.

Say your child has a particularly strong affection for watching the same video every day throughout the day and is interested in watching nothing other than this particular video. This may seem to fall under the category of intense preoccupation with an interest. But if you come up short in checking the remaining diagnostic criteria because your child demonstrates no other symptoms of Asperger's, then he simply has a very strong preference for that one video that may pass once he gets his fill of it.

If you are discovering that the criteria for Asperger's might have application for your child, then you are faced with a decision about seeking a diagnosis. You may not wish to pursue a formal diagnosis at this time for one or more of the following reasons:

- You don't believe in labeling people's diversity.
- You'd rather wait to see if anything changes as your child continues developing.
- You don't feel that your child's differences are causing detriments in his life significant enough to obtain a diagnosis.
- You are scared or in denial of the situation.
- You are worried that your child will be stigmatized or singled out.

The benefits of obtaining a diagnosis may be:

- Putting a name and a framework to a collection of symptoms and traits instead of perceiving it all as your child's "bad behavior" or somehow your fault.
- Accessing a system of services and supports designed to give your child a head start in life as early as possible.
- Being able to educate family, friends, and neighbors about your child's unique way of being, when appropriate.
- Being able to educate your child in order to promote self-awareness and self-advocacy, as needed.
- Understanding and appreciating sooner your child's lifelong unique qualities, personal needs, and talents.

Adults with Asperger's syndrome who were never diagnosed as children often ask, "Would it have been helpful to have had the diagnosis as a child?" We are still a long way from being effective in understanding Asperger's in a concerted, global sense, but having this knowledge early on in the lives of many adults might have aided them to:

- Experience greater success in school.
- Be better prepared for higher education, college, or trade school.
- Be better able to initiate and sustain relationships.
- Be better equipped to locate viable employment opportunities that best match skills and talents.
- Avoid struggles with mental health issues, or be better prepared to care for one's mental health.
- Be better prepared to avoid situations in which one may be unwittingly exploited.

Recently, a group of preteens with Asperger's was asked a question: "Is it helpful to know you have Asperger's?" They were unanimous in explaining that it was helpful and cleared up a lot of misperceptions and misinterpretations people had about why they do what they do.

Local Resources for Diagnosis

If you determine that Asperger's syndrome best describes your child's way of being and are interested in pursuing a diagnosis, your first course of action is to seek a referral to the appropriate clinician most qualified to make the diagnosis.

The best place to start is with your child's pediatrician. Your child's pediatrician is not in a position to make an Asperger's diagnosis. You will need to inquire if he or she knows of any pediatric psychiatrist or psychologist who is experienced in seeing kids with autism spectrum differences, or Asperger's specifically. Hopefully the doctor or the nurse practitioner can steer you in the right direction.

If you live in an urban area, there may be a multitude of doctors from which to select. You will need to narrow your range of choices. As autism has become commonplace, you may wish to begin by asking the pediatrician if he or she can tell you of any other patients who have been pleased with particular diagnosing physicians. The pediatrician may or may not be able to share this information based on client confidentiality or conflict of interest outside of a managed care physician's network.

Finding a doctor experienced in ascertaining an Asperger's syndrome diagnosis may prove challenging depending upon your geographic location. Search your library or the Internet for statewide and local resources such as established autism groups in your state. They may be helpful in guiding you.

If you live in a rural area, you should still ask your child's pediatrician for a referral, but there's a greater chance that the doctor may not know of anyone who specializes in making autism or Asperger's syndrome diagnoses. Or, if the doctor does make a referral, depending upon your location you may have to travel a great distance to access a reputable and established medical center with a pediatric psychiatry department.

Preparing for the Appointment

Once you make an appointment with a physician qualified to make an Asperger's diagnosis, it is important to be prepared. When setting up the appointment, ask the receptionist or nurse practitioner what kinds of information the doctor expects to receive from you. Is there a form or forms that may be faxed, e-mailed, or mailed to you in advance to save time and ensure a thorough and complete job?

Be certain to clarify any insurance concerns you may have as well, and ask how the appointment will be billed. Ask for any information about in-office testing or assessment that may be conducted by the doctor. Is there anything you should be prepared for regarding those tests?

Most often, the doctor will conduct an interview to ask specific questions designed to elicit information about your concerns. Depending upon your child's age, the doctor may wish to meet with your child alone to observe or interview her separately. Find out in advance if that is part of the process. Understand that, because of demand and client backlog, it may be several weeks before a qualified physician has room in his or her schedule to see you.

Preparing a psychiatric or psychological appointment for your child may be a very anxious time for you. Be careful of what your child overhears you saying to others. She may be acutely attuned to picking up on your frustrations and anxieties, which may impact her as well. Keep your phone contacts about this topic as private as possible.

Of course, just as you are preparing for this appointment, you will need to help your child to prepare for it as well. Knowledge is power. Your child will do best if she feels safe and comfortable and in control. You may best accomplish this by:

- Explaining that the appointment is with a doctor who only asks questions and does not give shots or ask the child to engage in any other medical-type procedure.
- Sharing with your child your understanding of the structure and sequence of the appointment, including approximate wait time and duration.

- Sharing with your child whatever questions you expect the doctor to ask.
- Getting out a map to show the child exactly where your house is and the route you will take to the doctor's clinic. (Give the child the map or a photocopy and partner with her on driving directions while en route the day of the appointment.)
- Taking your child to the clinic ahead of time to familiarize her with the surroundings and to meet the doctor, if possible. (Take photographs to give to your child well in advance of the appointment.)
- Empowering the child to mark off the days until the appointment on a prominently displayed wall calendar.
- Allowing your child to bring a book or small toy related to her most passionate of interests to defer the tedium of waiting before, during, and after the appointment. (The object of passion will also be a terrific icebreaker by which the doctor can initiate conversation with your child.)

These strategies should help you and your child feel fairly comfortable about the impending appointment.

The Doctor's Visit

During the appointment, it will be important for you to try to stay as focused as possible and to listen carefully to what the doctor is asking. Oftentimes during such a significant time, parents are filled with lots of nervous anxiety, some of which is completely natural. Your anxiety will not be helpful to the doctor if you go overboard. Don't bring stacks of your child's medical, educational, and other records to show the doctor well beyond anything that was requested. Don't digress into lengthy stories intended to highlight one incident in great detail. Be careful not to frequently interrupt in order to press your own agenda, such as pressuring the doctor to make an on-the-spot judgment call.

To be helpful to the doctor, bring exactly what was requested. If you bring additional information, only offer it if you think it's warranted or if it helps to illuminate a specific point. Accept that the doctor may not need it at that time. Be prepared to discuss why you believe your child might have Asperger's syndrome. Talk about specific clinical symptoms—not behaviors. Only tell concise stories that illustrate your rationale. When you talk about symptoms, you're talking the doctor's language. He or she will be far better equipped to discern a diagnosis if you are clear and brief in offering such information. Otherwise, the doctor must sort through a laundry list of descriptive "behaviors," trying to match what you're communicating against the *DSM* criteria. Allow the doctor to guide the interview, and interject with questions only as needed.

Fact

By connecting with other parents—either locally, statewide, or nationally—by phone or e-mail, you may receive valuable information about the diagnostic process for your child. Experiences will vary from person to person, but you will surely obtain valuable "pointers" that may help you feel comfortable in knowing what's best to do and say.

It is unlikely that you will walk away from the appointment with an Asperger's syndrome diagnosis. The doctor will need time to absorb and process all the information he or she has gathered from you. A written summary of the meeting and the doctor's observations and findings will be forthcoming. If several weeks go by and you don't receive such a report, contact the clinic to check on its status.

Intervention

There are other avenues to access information on Asperger's syndrome or community services and supports. Every state's county government system has an office that serves infants and children, adolescents, and adults with a variety of different ways of being, covering autism, intellectual impairment, and mental health issues. (The same or neighboring office may address child welfare, domestic violence issues, and alcohol and substance abuse.) In some areas it is called the Office of Developmental Disabilities. In others, it is known as the county Mental Health–Mental Retardation Office—a title that has become antiquated and offensive (not to mention intimidating) to many parents. That is not to say that such office is in every county; two or more counties may share a hub office. The phone number for your county's local disabilities office is located in the blue pages of your phone directory.

The Early Intervention Program

If your child is younger than five years old, when you call the office, ask for a referral to the Early Intervention Program in order to arrange an assessment of need. Early Intervention is a federally mandated program delivered by every state free of cost to families of children with developmental delays from infancy to school age, or five years old. The Individuals with Disabilities Education Act (or IDEA) stipulates the provisions for delivery of early intervention.

The Early Intervention Office will arrange to have someone come to your home at your convenience to assess your child for developmental delays. If your child qualifies for the program, he may be able to access a variety of professionals and therapists who will educate you about meeting his needs. The challenge in accessing Early Intervention for a child with Asperger's syndrome is that Asperger's is so subtle that kids "fall through the cracks" and go undetected until they are much older than Early Intervention age. Additionally, according to the clinical criteria for Asperger's syndrome, a child should demonstrate *no* cognitive or developmental delays. This would make a child ineligible for Early Intervention.

Your child may experience some physical fine- or gross-motor limitations that could make her eligible for the program, or the Early Intervention representative will support you in accessing any other local resources that may prove helpful. If your child is blind or deaf, she may also qualify for the program, but the services and supports offered will focus on your child's differences and will likely be unable to address Asperger's syndrome.

What are the benefits of the Early Intervention Program?

Early Intervention is a *family-centered* program. The intent of the professionals involved is to work directly with you to accommodate your needs, address your concerns, arrange in-person contact according to your schedule, and link you to other people and opportunities that may prove helpful.

However, one area of developmental delay identified for Early Intervention eligibility is social-emotional development, or how well a child relates to others. If your child's social differences are significant enough to cause you concern and she is within Early Intervention age, you may be able to access certain services and support designed to help engage her socially.

Help from School

Still, the symptoms of Asperger's syndrome may go unnoticed until your child is of school age. If you have not been cognizant of your child's symptoms or you've been in a "let's wait and see" holding pattern, your child's educators may bring it to your attention. They may have noticed your child's distractibility, difficulty in understanding what is expected of him, seeming challenges in social connectedness, and other traits associated with Asperger's. They may recommend a consultation with the school psychologist, who may discuss Asperger's syndrome with you.

The school psychologist will usually be a member of a school team called the Student Assistance Program, or SAP. As a rule, most school psychologists don't make clinical diagnoses such as Asperger's syndrome, but the psychologist can partner with you and the SAP team as part of an assessment process to identify more specific areas of need that interfere with your child's ability to learn.

The school psychologist may assist with observations of your child during the school day or make a referral to a clinician who can make a diagnosis. The school psychologist will then work with the doctor's report to aid the SAP team in supporting your child's social and emotional needs and in making accommodations for your child in the general education curriculum.

If your parental instinct is telling you that your child is struggling socially or academically and you think it is possibly due to Asperger's syndrome, address it with your child's school professionals as soon as possible. Be clear, direct, and concise about what you are thinking, feeling, and seeing, and request their support.

Disclosure and Self-Understanding

So the diagnosis has been made. Now what? Once you obtain an Asperger's syndrome diagnosis for your child, you are faced with another significant hurdle: disclosure. With the advent of diagnosis, you will likely be required to interact with others—family, friends, neighbors, doctors, and educators—for the purpose of discussing the diagnosis. You will need to use discretion with disclosure. Please be mindful of being careless of when, how, and with whom you share information, especially if it occurs in your child's presence. Remember, we're talking about a child, and the child is not defined by the diagnosis. Always remember the concept of the self-fulfilling prophecy. If your child overhears you discussing the diagnosis more often than her gifts and talents and her amazing way of being in the world, she will likely become defined by the diagnosis exclusively. When you appear comfortable readily disclosing sensitive information, you model this behavior for others who think it perfectly acceptable or necessary. And so begins an otherwise avoidable downward, perpetual spiral.

As early as possible, empower your child as the keeper of information. As a parent, you will know best when, where, how, and under what circumstances you broach a discussion about Asperger's syndrome with your child. As with any sensitive discussion, you will want to:

- Follow your child's lead by sharing as much or as little information as needed.
- Balance the discussion by highlighting everything you love about your child.
- Underscore that the diagnosis is just a name—nothing else has changed.
- Be prepared to answer any questions your child may have.
- Give your child the opportunity to write, draw, or otherwise make concrete the information as they envision it.
- Talk about disclosure as the concept of being choosy or very selective about when, where, and with whom personal information is shared.

Regardless of your child's age, he is now your partner in all matters of disclosure. This is the respectful response to supporting the child with Asperger's syndrome. This means that *prior* to arbitrarily sharing personal information about your child's diagnosis, you check with him first to:

- Ask permission to disclose.
- Explain why you believe it is necessary.
- Be open to being flexible if he protests.
- Offer opportunity for compromise.
- Discuss the best, most gentle, most respectful way to disclose the information.

One mother lamented that her child's psychiatrist expects her to disclose sensitive information in front of him, even though her son implores, "No mom, don't! It's embarrassing!" First, how very fortunate she is that her son is self-aware enough to be a good self-advocate at his young age. There *are* ways to privately share information that doctors and others require. For example, information may be faxed, mailed, or e-mailed in advance of appointments instead of openly discussing the most humiliating aspects of one's "perceived" behavior so publicly.

There is power in numbers. If you can establish relationships with other parents, caregivers, and teens and adults with Asperger's syndrome who are also self-advocates, you can advance the respectful concept of "nothing about me without me" in a variety of professional and community-based environments, thus creating positive change in how Asperger's is perceived and discussed by others.

Of her son's control over disclosure, Linda says, "I do not need or have to explain my son's overreactions in a public place. It is really no one's business. I let my son choose whom he tells. Which, as a matter of fact, is practically no one."

Rather than setting aside time for your child to single herself out and reveal her way of being with the entire school class, you may wish to encourage a class-wide discussion of all our collective differences and similarities during which your child shares as much or as little as she wishes.

Still, others do select to disclose information as a personal choice. Bonnie's son Noel wrote a wonderful letter to his classmates. It is a lovely way to conclude this chapter and Noel has given permission for others to use his letter to adapt for their own use.

> I have Asperger's syndrome, which is on the high end of the autistic spectrum. This means that I experience the world very differently than you do.

You're called "neurologically typical," or "NT," because you don't have ASD. Please don't call me "abnormal" or refer to the other kids as being "normal," because you all seem pretty abnormal to me. I am just not typical because I am wired differently. I like my differences. They give me abilities that most NT's don't have.

People, Communication, and My Interests

Being with lots of people and having conversations that interest you and not me are two things I work very hard at. I don't mean to seem rude when I turn the conversation to my interest. If this is getting in the way, you can tell me that we need to switch topics for a while. I learn best when you relate what you are trying to teach me to one of my interests. I know this might seem strange, but this is just the way people with an autistic experience are. Relating information to my interests enables me to keep track of many details.

Social skills do not come naturally to me, so I try to keep learning. I usually like to be around adults more than kids, because they are more interesting. I prefer facts over opinions and feelings.

Remember that I don't automatically understand what is going on in terms of verbal and nonverbal communication. People don't always say what they mean, and they use metaphors or a lot of words to say something. This is not how I communicate. I appreciate it when people notice when something doesn't make sense to me and reword it so that I know what they mean. I may not understand what seems very clear to you. Or I may seem rude—although I don't mean to—in the way I speak because I tend to be very direct. Please have patience with me, and explain clearly to me when my way of relating might cause a problem.

Comments like, "Change your attitude" don't help me much. But if you tell me what behavior is bothering you, then I can understand.

Relating to other people is hard work for me. Like other people with autism, I like to have friends, but I also like to be by myself. It is very important that I am allowed to have some "alone time," especially during the times when I am with other people. I try hard to think of other people's feelings and make eye contact, but this doesn't come naturally to me. So could you have a little patience if I come off sounding rude, and explain to me clearly how I could do it better. As long as I am in the mood for it, I try to fit in around people. But this can really wear me out.

Focusing My Thoughts

Sometimes my thoughts come rushing into my head like an avalanche. I'm not sure which one to hold on to, and I might pick the wrong one, which might make you mad.

This happens especially in the morning and at night. If I seem distracted, you can help by giving me only two or three instructions at a time. When this happens, it's better if you come close to me to tell me rather than call to me across the room. Be clear, and remember that my visual and tactile senses are strong, so maybe you can use this to help me. At home I use a lot of pictures and lists to help keep me focused. Remember, I am trying to do my best.

My Sensory Systems

Most people can think of these five senses: hearing, sight, taste, smell, and touch. Did you know that balance and motion are senses, too? My senses often work pretty differently than yours do.

For example, high-pitched and loud sounds, like the singing at church or a vacuum cleaner, really hurt my ears and can be unbearable. I try to have earplugs with me because this helps. Sometimes I'm asked to talk to audiences and they want to clap to show their appreciation. For me it would be better if you would just pat your arm. Thank you.

Like most people with ASD, I tend to think in pictures. I like bright colors like red and orange. If you want me to remember something, it helps if you can show it to me visually. I like to create pictures, watch cartoons, develop visuals on my PC, and play video games.

I don't eat much, and the food has to be mild. Vanilla milkshakes and pumpkin pie are my favorite foods. I like crunchy foods too, like cereal and carrots. When I get thirsty, this sense can be very strong, so I have learned to carry water with me. When I feel stressed or anxious, I've learned that it helps to drink through a straw or eat cereal. Pretty cool, huh?

Tied in with taste is the sense of smell. Strong smells can make me feel sick. Please don't make me eat foods "to be like everyone else," but also, my mom says I should eat as much as I can, and whenever I can when I am in the mood to eat.

Touch, balance, and motion are three senses that really help me when I feel anxious or uncomfortable. A firm touch from you or a place to swing can really help. Sometimes I hang my head upside down or squeeze a ball when the feeling of people around me is too overwhelming.

Routines and Changes

Change can be hard for people with autism. Some warning or explanation before a new activity helps me a lot. Also, transitions are easier if I am given the schedule ahead of time. It helps me to have it written down so that I can see it.

Time is a strange concept for me. When I'm bored, time seems to go by twice as slow as a snail. But when I am doing something I like, it goes twice as fast as a cheetah. Try to understand that I don't experience time the same way you do.

In Conclusion

Someday I hope to use my knowledge and abilities to invent things that will really help people. Did you know that people like Albert Einstein, Thomas Jefferson, and Marie Curie had Asperger's? Many people think that Bill Gates does, too. I hope to be the next in line of these great scientists and thinkers.

Sometimes I get frustrated because I have to work so hard to fit in and conform to your way of being. But I like myself. God has been good to me by giving me a nice family and letting me be smart. I hope that what I do in the future with my special gifts benefits you someday.

Thank you for your patience and for taking the time to read this. I hope you will be my friend.

Sincerely,

Noel

Chapter 4
Discipline

Disciplining the child with Asperger's syndrome requires some finesse in balancing a number of considerations. As a parent, you have the right to set the same limitations and boundaries as you would for any of your own children. But you also have the responsibility to ensure you are being fair in communicating your parameters so you can expect your child's compliance, within reason. To discipline fairly you will need to first know that you have communicated fully your rules in ways your child understands best.

Your Approach to Discipline

All parents are faced with the task of childrearing to the best of their ability. Loving your child as you do, you want to know you're doing the right thing. Because each child is a unique individual, there is no single method for raising your specific child, only sound generalizations for you to test and apply. Your approach to disciplining your child will likely draw from several things, including your memories of how you were disciplined as a child, strategies, philosophies, and ideas you've read and with which you concur, and personal observations of how your family, friends, and neighbors discipline their own children.

The key to disciplining your child with Asperger's syndrome is to—first and foremost—recall the positive philosophies discussed in Chapter 2:

- Your child has good reasons for doing what he's doing.
- He's doing the very best he knows how to in the moment (and with what he's got available to him).
- He needs to feel safe and comfortable and in control.
- He will become unhinged by anything significantly unpredictable.

Fact

Some parents of kids with Asperger's are accused of being too "soft" with their children. You know your child best. He may be a very sensitive individual, but you have the right as a parent to set realistic expectations of obligations and responsibilities the same as you would for any other child.

Your child's need to feel in control should not be taken to extremes. Parents must set limits and expectations for all children. Having Asperger's syndrome does not give one free reign to be out of control, and that should not be endorsed or indulged by you; you wouldn't allow any of your other children to do everything they want, whenever they please. Before you scold, however, you will also need to be mindful that your child's logic will not necessarily reflect your idea of common sense. For example, imagine a teenager who is driving down the highway and sees a box in the middle of the road. He decides the box must be empty and drives over it, rather than around it. The box isn't empty and damages his car. Even though his logic is questionable, he did not deliberately attempt to damage the car.

Setting Rules

Many parents "fly by the seat of their pants" in setting rules. That is, they assume a child should understand appropriate social behavior under a wide variety of specific circumstances and, when that doesn't occur, they scold in the moment.

For example, suppose you are in attendance at a wedding and your child with Asperger's is bored or distracted. To your chagrin, she insists on telling everyone around her the flight schedule of every major airline departing from your local airport in a loud, clear voice that carries. Your first reaction may be to "shush" her into silence. When that proves ineffective, you may firmly whisper to her to stop. When that doesn't work, you may take hold of her and make a threat, such as the loss of a reward, special privilege, or favored plaything. As a last resort, you may physically remove her from the setting. You have intervened when the situation required it.

However, as the parent of a child with Asperger's syndrome, your approach to discipline should be one of *prevention,* not intervention. After we review steps to ensure prevention, we will revisit this exact scenario.

Essential

Being the parent of a child with Asperger's syndrome may draw upon all your sleuthing skills in discerning the truth when it comes to discipline. Don't be deceived by first impressions of a situation by readily jumping to the conclusion that your child has made a serious error in judgment. Give her time to explain. Was her motive altruistic (though way off base) or was she trying to protect someone else?

Your child with Asperger's syndrome can only know what he knows. Many children with Asperger's interpret information in ways that are very literal and concrete. Remember Tom Hanks as the boy in a man's body in the movie *Big*? At a reception, he drew stares and raised eyebrows by attempting to eat the miniature corn as he would regular corn on the cob. He wasn't trying to be socially inappropriate on purpose. Never having had experience with the social conventions of consuming the mini hors d'oeuvres, he was doing his best in the moment.

Like the parent in the wedding scenario, you may expect your child to automatically "read" your body language and facial expressions of displeasure or to transfer what he's learned in a similar environment to the present situation. It doesn't usually work that way. Most importantly, your child is not consistently misbehaving solely for the sake of "being bad."

Communicating Expectations

In all matters of disciplining the child with Asperger's syndrome, you have the responsibility to be fair in how you communicate rules and expectations. Because your child will be most open to receiving this information in ways that are literal and concrete, this means making it tangible. That is, put it in writing as a simple, bullet-point list. It may even be a partnered agreement that you both review and sign together. This will provide your child with a personal investment in the agreement and give him an incentive to comply. The list of rules becomes your child's property and, depending upon the situation, should be kept in her pocket for ready reference. Be open and flexible enough to listen to her questions. Do not feel personally challenged, or that your child is trying to "outsmart" you. She is merely being direct in asking for clarification of what you're trying to communicate.

Numbering each item on the list may aid your child's recall. You may even wish to decide, in partnership with your child, how many warnings she'll get to stop breaking the rules before you implement your standard means of discipline. This is fair. Now if we revisit the wedding scenario, both you *and* your child are well prepared with regard to your expectations (and those dictated by the environment) prior to going into the situation. Not only is this fair, it is prevention not intervention.

A sample list of rules for the wedding scenario might look like this:

Rules for Going to a Wedding

1. Before the service begins, it is okay to talk with other people, especially people I know.
2. When everyone is sitting down, people will usually be very quiet or whisper. Everyone expects me to be quiet or to whisper, too.
3. If I am not being quiet or if I am whispering too much, Mom or Dad (or spouse) will tell me about it and ask me to stop. They will do this because I am distracting other people who want to see and hear the service.
4. If I get bored during the service, I will think about something else, quietly draw or read, or play a silent game I bring with me.
5. When the service ends and people get up, it is okay to talk in my normal voice again.

The ability to "call up" visual information at will does not necessarily mean your child can do this at your command. This may be confusing because he may recite, on cue, intricate details relative to his most passionate interests but be unable to "replay" concepts you've impressed upon him. Like all kids, your child may need visual reminders and practice to get it down.

When preparing to leave for the wedding, remind your child to bring the rules along (unless she is able to use photographic memory and recite them by rote). On the drive there, review the rules together. When you notice your child becoming restless during the service, she may need reminders about the alternatives you both agreed to. If your child requires a warning, be remindful of the rules and *why* she's getting the warning. You can generalize this positive strategy to numerous and similar social circumstances.

If your child continues to behave improperly, it may be appropriate to discipline at this time. The operative word here is "may," and to further complicate things, there might be mitigating factors to dissuade you from discipline in the moment. These factors will be discussed at the end of this chapter.

Seeing Your Child's Point of View

Again, never assume your child will automatically transfer and apply information previously learned in one environment to a new situation that, in your mind, is remarkably similar. For that child, a new situation is a new situation.

Consider this example: A teenage boy with Asperger's once decided to drive his family's car while his parents were out. His family was preparing to junk the car and had let the insurance on it expire. The young man knew this but took the car out anyway. He believed the worst that might happen would be getting into a minor fender-bender and being held responsible for paying the damage costs, as had been his previous experience with car accidents. When he arrived home, his very upset parents confronted him. They were distraught over the implications of driving without insurance—the potential for a major collision that could've involved serious damage, injury, or death to others and for which they would be held personally responsible. The teenager had no idea of these potential ramifications of his actions. If he had, he likely would not have entertained the notion of taking the car anywhere.

As previously acknowledged, your child with Asperger's syndrome is likely to be very emotionally sensitive. She may tear up and weep at song lyrics or commercials. He may be unable to keep from dwelling on a particularly disturbing news story. Given this, it's important that you never make idle threats in anger or exasperation that have finality to their tone, such as, "I wish you'd just disappear!" "I'm going to call the police to come get you!" or "I'm going to send you far away from here!"

We are all human, and we all say things we don't mean on occasion. However, saying anything along these lines to the child with Asperger's syndrome will have a long-lasting, damaging effect, possibly for the duration of his life. Why? Because, quite simply, he will believe every word of what you're saying as *the truth*. This will perpetuate in undue anxiety, stress, and upset that will persist over time. Your child may take personally criticisms you think mild or trivial. He may cry, pout, or sulk for hours or longer. If you are a parent short on patience and prone to such irrational outbursts, be prepared for your child to withdraw from you more and more until you are shut out completely. Spanking, slapping, hitting, or grabbing will produce results equally as damaging.

Essential

The following ways of disciplining all kids also have application to your child with Asperger's syndrome, but only after you are certain you've effectively communicated your expectations in ways he or she best understands: giving a time-out, temporarily withholding a privilege such as using the phone, computer, or TV; withholding allowance; and grounding.

Being sent to endure a set time limit in a private time-out area (or one's bedroom) or forfeiting certain privileges are acceptable, concrete forms of discipline used for all children with typically positive results.

Knowing When to Discipline

Knowing when, how, and how much to discipline your child with Asperger's syndrome can be quite challenging. You may be filled with worry for your child and her future. You may be learning more about becoming her strongest advocate. In so doing, you will need to find balance in your role as a parent and disciplinarian. There may be a fine line between being an effective parent and being perceived as zealous or coddling of your child.

Your child's diagnosis is a label that describes a sliver of who that individual is as a human being. Your child is many other things; her diagnosis does not exclusively define her (remember the self-fulfilling prophecy). In valuing your child's gifts and talents concurrent with understanding her diagnosis, be cautious about going to extremes. You have every reason to be a strong advocate on behalf of your child and in protection of her rights. But this does not exempt her from being disciplined by you or, where appropriate, by child care or day care providers, or educators.

Overprotectiveness

Some parents can become overprotective. They may make frequent excuses for their child's words or actions. And they may not discipline where most others agree it to be warranted. When this occurs—regardless of the child's way of being—the balance of authority shifts. The child gains more and more control while being protected in a sheltered environment with little to no discipline.

Essential

Remember that kids are kids. You would never do anything to intentionally endanger your child; but, as much as you might wish to keep all your children safe from any harm or wrongdoing, sometimes life's most valuable (and enduring) lessons come courtesy of that famous institution of learning and life experience known as the school of hard knocks.

The Latin root of the word "discipline" means "to teach." Parents who are overprotective and do nothing to discipline their child are teaching some very artificial life lessons that will significantly hinder their child in the real world. One mother openly despaired that she envisions caring for her son with Asperger's syndrome for the rest of her life. This may indeed be the case if she micromanages every aspect of his life.

The Dignity of Risk

There is what is known as the "dignity of risk." It speaks to the luxury we must allow persons with different ways of being to make long- and short-term mistakes, but not without support and guidance. This will be a great challenge to you as a parent who is naturally protective of your child. But it is the only way your child will be able to learn and prepare for greater independence in the future. Disciplining your child should be a teaching and learning opportunity about making choices and decisions. When your child makes mistakes, assure him that he is still loved and valued. In other words, focus on the issue at hand, not the person (i.e., yelling, "How could you be so stupid?" is not an option).

For example, the parents of the teenager who drove the uninsured car should demonstrate their discipline by first discussing his great error in judgment *in addition to* entering into a dialogue about good, better, and best choices in the future. It will be especially helpful—and will maximize the learning opportunity—if, in partnership with the boy, they write it all down to make it as concrete as possible. They may also decide that another form of discipline (such as withholding allowance or grounding him) is an entirely appropriate way to reinforce the seriousness of his actions.

This is not to suggest that they should not have intervened if they had had prior knowledge of his intentions; they certainly should have! But, where possible, look for small opportunities to deliberately allow your child to mess up and make mistakes for which you can set aside discipline-teaching time. It will be a learning process for you and your child.

Meltdowns

Earlier, during discussion of the wedding scenario, it was stated, "If your child continues to behave improperly, it may be appropriate to discipline at this time." The word "may" was emphasized. In addition to being certain that you are communicating your limitations and expectations in as direct, clear, and concrete a way as possible, you will have to take into consideration three other areas before you discipline.

Think of the variety of things that parents and others consider "bad behaviors" in all kids, and especially in kids with Asperger's syndrome or autism. These behaviors include:

- Hitting
- Spitting
- Pulling hair
- Swearing
- Smearing or throwing feces
- Physically harming others, including loved ones
- Kicking
- Biting
- Scratching
- Urinating in places other than the toilet
- Damaging property
- Doing harm to oneself

My child's behavior is sometimes violent. Is this typical?
It is never okay to allow your child to consistently engage in acts of self-injury, property destruction, or physical aggression perpetrated upon others. While misunderstandings or miscommunications may account for some instances, the label "Asperger's syndrome" is not an excuse that should be used for violent, abusive behavior. Chapter 7 will provide lots more detail to help sort this out.

Some of these behaviors are seen from time to time in all kids. Still others are quite extreme, like property damage or self-harm. In isolation, these actions may be rarities. When they happen consistently, they become red flags of a serious nature because it is very unusual for these activities to occur consistently for any child. Let's call these behaviors "junk."

It is important to recognize that these junk behaviors are not "behaviors" but *communications*.

Three Meltdown Triggers

The inability to communicate—to articulately express oneself—in ways that are effective, reliable, and universally understandable is the first meltdown trigger. The other two meltdown triggers fall under the umbrella of communications as well.

The second meltdown trigger is pain and discomfort. That is, severe physical pain and discomfort that is not being communicated in ways that are effective, reliable, and universally understandable.

The third meltdown trigger is mental health issues. That is, significant mental health experiences that are not being communicated in ways that are effective, reliable, and universally understandable.

The latter two areas fall under the communication umbrella because communication is *everything*. If you cannot express your physical or mental pain in the moment, then that obstacle is a communication issue. One or any combination of these three areas, communication, pain, or mental health, is what drives the junk behaviors—not Asperger's syndrome. That's the good news. If you've succumbed to believing stereotypes about Asperger's, then this revelation may come as a surprise to you. Simply because your child has Asperger's, it does not follow that he will automatically manifest some or all of the junk behaviors as a direct result of Asperger's. This is an untruth; otherwise, such behaviors would be listed as Asperger's criteria in the *DSM*. Because your child is inherently gentle and exquisitely sensitive, she may be particularly prone to being vulnerable; she may be more susceptible than neurotypical individuals to experiencing issues of communication, pain, and mental health.

Dealing with the Meltdown Areas

But these vulnerabilities are not directly affiliated with the diagnosis of Asperger's syndrome. They are by-products of the Asperger's experience in some—not all—children. The three meltdown trigger areas—communication, pain and discomfort, and mental health issues—are of such great importance that each topic will be explored in detail in the following three chapters. In order to be an effective parent and disciplinarian of a child with Asperger's syndrome, you will need to comprehend each of these areas fully and place them in the proper context of any given situation. This knowledge will aid you in laying a foundation for prevention in order to minimize your intervention.

Fact

All the resources of your parenting wisdom and expertise may be drawn upon in making respectful speculations about what might be driving a meltdown. Your child may find it extremely difficult or impossible to clearly articulate all the factors and nuances that came to bear upon her loss of control. If you think about the last time you experienced extreme upset, distress, or anger, you may have been similarly challenged and only able to express your motivators in hindsight.

All of parenting is a judgment call. At every moment, you are put in the position of making your very best respectful guess. In striving to be a good parent, you hope that your thinking will be right more often than not. Inevitably, you will make mistakes, and you may hear about them in no uncertain terms direct from your child with Asperger's syndrome. Can you be open to good listening? Can you find it in yourself to recognize that—even as the adult in the relationship—your child was right and you were wrong? If you are able to apologize in those moments in ways that are genuine and sincere, you will be rewarded with a bond. And the bond is one of increasingly mutual respect in the context of your parent-child relationship.

Perhaps the best philosophy to share with your child when it comes to your role as a parent and disciplinarian is this: You may not always get what you want, but, sometimes, you can get what you need.

CHAPTER 5

Communication

As an individual with Asperger's syndrome, one of your child's greatest challenges is in the area of communication. It will be important to grasp how you can communicate in ways that will support your child's ease of understanding. It will be equally important to comprehend how best to assist your child in deciphering communication in everyday conversation. Your child wants to be socially accepted by her peers, and your efforts to foster a mutual comfort level where communication is concerned will be paramount.

How Would You Feel?

In the last chapter, we discussed the three meltdown triggers that typically drive "behaviors" in children with Asperger's and autism. You will recall that the most significant of those three areas was the inability to communicate in ways that are effective, reliable, and universally understandable. When anyone of us is feeling overwhelmed by circumstances that are unpredictable and that spiral out of our control, we may find it very difficult to verbally express ourselves in this situation. For example, think how you would feel if—all in the same morning:

- You oversleep because the alarm didn't go off.
- You have no hot water for a shower.
- You realize you're out of coffee.

- You don't notice that your pants have an obvious fabric snag until you're in the car.
- The entrance to your freeway exit is detoured due to construction.
- You can't find a parking space once at work.

When you finally get inside your workplace, you are likely feeling one or all of the following:

- Angry
- Upset
- Disoriented
- Short-tempered
- Depressed
- Anxious
- Stressed

Upon your arrival at work, what do you instinctively want to do? Find a friend or confidante as soon as possible in order to vent, and tell them about your morning. But where would you start? If you are feeling emotionally stressed or overwhelmed, you may be feeling like a huge, confused mass of all the feelings listed. You may not have the words to describe your frustration, or you may be completely inarticulate in the moment. If you can't get it all out in a way that is effective, reliable, and universally understandable, your frustration will continue to build. Now suppose someone unaware of your experience approaches you and makes a demand that is time-sensitive ("I need this within a half-hour!"). Everything you're feeling will escalate until you release it some way. You may do this by:

- Yelling or screaming
- Swearing
- Throwing something
- Breaking something
- Pulling something off the wall

- Clearing off your desk with a sweep of your arm
- Sitting and crying
- Avoiding the situation by disappearing to the bathroom, lounge, or smoking area
- Going numb and not responding to anything

Fortunately, such overwhelming experiences are rarities for most of us. But isn't it curious how many of these reactive behaviors are similar to the list of Asperger's syndrome "junk behaviors" outlined in the last chapter? If anyone accused you of being unprofessional or even violent in manifesting such behaviors, wouldn't you defend yourself by explaining they were communications of your tremendous angst, that you were coping the best way you knew how? Fortunately, this scenario played out over the course of a few hours one morning. But you may use it as an analogy to understand how most kids with Asperger's feel in trying to cope and get through each day when it comes to navigating communication.

Essential

Sometimes you may find that parenting a child with Asperger's who is overwhelmed means simply abandoning all expectations of trying to understand what just happened in favor of providing a gentle hug or allowing your child to have a good cry or personal space to temporarily shut down. You may find that these unspoken communications that you provide will have as much, if not more, impact than your verbal communications in the moment.

Your child may be quite challenged in her ability to process receptive language, that is, understanding what others are communicating. You may be frustrated by her apparent unawareness of the social repercussions of interrupting or saying something with brutal directness. Conversely, her idea of communication to others, or expressive language, may be skewed from what is considered the norm. Let's examine both perspectives.

Communicating Visually

It is important to understand how your child with Asperger's syndrome thinks and processes information. According to a number of self-advocates with Asperger's, we may speculate that many individuals with Asperger's are visual thinkers. This means, quite literally, they think in constant streams of images and movies—not Hollywood movies, but life-event "memory" movies. This way of thinking is very different from most others. You may think in pictures too, perhaps more so if someone specifically directs you to do so by saying, "Picture this," or "Imagine this." It may be an unnatural way of thinking for you without putting forth great effort, but it is a flowing, seamless, and natural manner of thought for many people with Asperger's or even autism.

Fact

As a fun little role-reversal exercise, set aside time for a game with your child. Request that he describe the rules to his favorite video or computer game (or some other element related to his passions). Ask that he read up to four paragraphs, plowing right through without pause, while you listen *silently*. Once he is finished, you draw exactly what he has described, and see how close you get in accuracy. It may be eye-opening for you!

If you were to think exclusively in imagery, and you were in conversation with someone, then you'd likely require some process time to mentally "call up" pictures and movies based upon your life experiences in order to follow what the person is saying. If you are discussing something relatively familiar or even appealing, then the flow of pictures may be effortless. But what if your communication partner is relating new information for which you have no prior knowledge or experience? You would have to be especially attentive and try to listen very carefully to make sure you understood clearly. Concurrently, you would be attempting to call up or form mental images to equate what you think the person is telling you (which is perfectly obvious to them).

Extra Processing Time

Now, given a similar situation, what if you are a child with Asperger's and your communication partner is your parent or other adult in authority? If the adult doesn't "get" the way you think, you will be set up for failure when given multipart, verbal instruction. As a society, we have been conditioned to communicate with lightening-fast speed and to expect the same in return. But the child with Asperger's will need *process time* to catalog the sequence of steps being communicated *and* make a facsimile image or movie of each that most closely approximates what he thinks the adult is trying to say.

If you're communicating something new and different to the child, then assimilating the information and translating it into images and movies will take time. Your challenge as a parent is to slow down and carefully measure the amount of information dispensed to avoid confusion. If your child is unable to visualize what you verbally communicate, he is less likely to retain it.

You've experienced something similar when you've been lost and stopped to ask for directions. You may have quickly learned that you asked for more than you bargained for if the person who gave you directions slowly built, layered, and embellished the information until you could not keep track of the list of verbal information. Apply this scenario to the child with Asperger's syndrome and you can understand how easy it would be to blame her inability to correctly follow through on noncompliance, or "bad," behavior.

Because your child may be a pleaser or have a flat affect, you may be unable to tell through body language or facial expressions if she understands—even if she says she does. If you wish to be certain *you've* communicated in ways that are effective, reliable, and universally understandable, take a few moments and go through these steps:

- Rethink what you intend to communicate. Can it be simplified?
- Before giving your child instruction, ask her to prepare to make pictures or movies of what you're conveying. Check back on this during your communication by saying something like, "Can you see it?" or "Do you see what that's supposed to look like?"
- Slow the pace of your instruction—especially if it's about something new and different.
- Allow for process time in between steps of instruction. Given how we've been conditioned to interact with others, this will be tough to do, but necessary.
- Ask your child if she's ready for more.
- After you've finished talking, give your child a chance to ask clarifying questions.
- Ensure your child's understanding of what you've communicated by asking her to describe what you've just said.

Like the driving directions scenario, be cautious about overloading your child with too much information all in one shot. As your child's parent, you will be able to best gauge how much or how little your child can absorb at once.

Eye Contact

Be advised that many children with Asperger's will not be as successful as they could be when given instruction if they are required to make direct eye contact concurrent with your delivery of instruction. Many parents command direct eye contact of their neurotypical children by saying something to the effect of, "Look at me when I'm talking to you." Society has ingrained in us the belief that if you make direct eye contact in conversation, you are listening carefully and paying close attention. The twist is that for the child with Asperger's syndrome, the opposite may very well be true.

In some cultures it is a show of respect not to make eye contact while in conversation with others. The next time someone does not make direct eye contact with you, try to pay attention to the thoughts that enter your mind. You may find that some or all of your negative thoughts are socially conditioned.

The child with Asperger's who is across the room from you and appears not to be listening may be taking in nearly all—if not everything—you are saying, as opposed to the child who is compelled to make direct eye contact to "prove" he is paying attention. Why would this be so? Remember that your child is likely extremely visual in how he assimilates and absorbs information. When you speak, your face is in constant motion and there are many, many visual detractors, such as your eyes and glasses, your hair, your jewelry, your mouth, saliva, tongue, and teeth, and your clothing, not to mention other contributing factors like your breath and cologne.

Your child will be tremendously challenged to pay attention and listen if he is distracted by one, some, or all of these visual details. Your child will be faced with complying with the social expectation of making direct eye contact everyday outside his own home. Reflect carefully upon your ability to be flexible where direct eye contact is concerned, especially when giving directions. Your child may surprise you. If you feel that direct eye contact is non-negotiable in your family, then find compromise in:

- Seeking opportunities to make direct eye contact attractive or appealing, such as holding some favored item up near your face, while requesting eye contact

- Accepting your child's need to make fleeting eye contact, look away, then look back
- Accepting your child's "ballpark" approximation of direct eye contact if he stares at your ears, mouth, or some area of your face *other* than your eyes while you are talking
- Accepting your child's need to look away from your eyes in order to formulate a thoughtful, intelligent, and articulate response to you

Creating Trust

Your child may be very dependable. That is, she does what she says she's going to do when she says she's going to do it. Because your child likely interprets others' communications in a very literal sense, she will expect you to do the same. In communicating with your child, it will be important that you do what you say you're going to do by keeping your promises—you'll be held to it! If you consistently overlook, cover up, or excuse your broken promises, you are chipping away at any trust your child has placed in you, and your relationship will grow ever distant.

If you must break a promise, apologize to your child as soon as possible and let her know precisely when you will fix the situation or make it right. If you approach such interactions in this respectful manner—and follow through as you said you would—your chances of being forgiven are far greater than if you do nothing.

Fact

How often have you said to your child, "When I say no, I mean *no*"? The child with Asperger's says what he means and means what he says with the same definitiveness. That is, no means no and yes means yes. Your child's anxiety and frustration will likely escalate if you repeatedly ask the same question or ask him to change his mind without explanation.

Helping Your Child Crack the "Social Code"

Now that we've talked about the way your child will best receive information, let's explore how she may best express communication. As you've just learned, your child may be very literal in her way of being and in everything she does and says. Part of her challenge in making sense of social interactions is to assume some flexibility and understanding when others are not as rigid.

Casual Promises That Confuse

People commonly make promises they have absolutely no intention of keeping. People say things all the time that *sound* friendly and sincere—and they may be genuine in the moment—but they get distracted, forget, or get involved in other things and never follow through. Some of these popular idioms include such "catch phrases" as, "I'll call you in a few days," "Let's do lunch real soon," or "I'll stop by to see you in a couple of weeks." They haven't intentionally mislead you, and most people shrug them off when these social dates don't come to fruition if they haven't already interpreted them as weightless, social conventions. They are in the same vein as asking, by rote, "How are you?" without really expecting to hear a rundown of how someone *actually* is.

Meanwhile, the person with Asperger's is waiting for the other party to come through and make good on the promise. With each day that passes with no communication, the person becomes more hurt, confused, or upset. Some folks probably forget making such comments as soon as they say them, or would be a bit surprised to be called on the carpet about them. You will need to counsel your child in this peculiar nuance of neurotypical behavior, especially as he enters his teen years—a time when people rely less on their parents and interact with greater social freedom.

Subtleties of Language

Another great challenge your child may grapple with is in understanding the flow of typical, everyday conversations. The language most people are accustomed to using may get "lost" on the child with

Asperger's syndrome. This is because everyday interactions are peppered with subtleties including:

- Slang (Example: "He lost his head!")
- Sarcasm (Example: "You're such a hottie!" but meaning just the opposite.)
- Innuendo (Example: "They slept together last weekend.")
- Double-entendre (Example: "She's all that and a bag of chips!")
- Irony (Example: "Be sharp or you'll be flat.")

Essential

As a child, do you remember making up words to bridge your confusion when you didn't understand all of what others were saying during the National Anthem, the Pledge of Allegiance, or the Lord's Prayer? In hindsight, how many of the phrases you *thought* people were reciting were nowhere close to the actual language? Now reflect upon how it might feel to think the way you did then when trying to assimilate everyday conversation.

Most people learn to understand these subtleties by osmosis—simply by experiencing a reasonably typical upbringing in which they've automatically inferred meaning into previously unfamiliar idioms. They use body language and other cues to interpret the real meaning of the words. Many children with Asperger's are not privy to this "social code" and require your gentle coaching to decipher it.

We all occasionally need such clarifications because we are all more alike than different. For instance, if someone said to you, "Duck," would you know how to interpret it? Would you look around for a bird, or would you physically lower your head to avoid being hit by something? Based on your past experience, the chances of being struck might seem higher than your chances of seeing the bird, and therefore you might "duck" your head. But it was a split-second judgment call.

Here are two different, real-life scenarios involving boys with Asperger's that illustrate how slang is frequently misinterpreted. In the first situation, a mother kept her distance in observing her young son's interaction with a baker when placing the order for his birthday cake. The boy responded well to questions such as, "What flavor icing would you like?" and "What flavor cake would you like?" But when the baker asked, "And what would you like your cake to *say*?" the very surprised boy exclaimed, "Are you crazy? Cakes don't talk!" In a worst-case scenario, one boy became a target for some older boys at summer camp. One of them told him to go jump in a lake—so he did, fully clothed. The boy jumped into the lake because:

- The other boy was older and perceived as intimidating or in authority, so the boy did as he was told (being a "pleaser").
- There *was* a lake there so it didn't occur to the boy that his tormentor could be referring to anything other than *that lake.*
- He was unaware of the slang expression that means the same as "Buzz off" or "Get lost."

These expressions will need to be taught to the child with Asperger's. As an exercise, you may wish to sit with your child and develop a list of words and phrases that draw inspiration from the previous list of subtleties in language. It will be helpful if you are prepared to give examples for each item on the list. Your child will be greatly amused if you are able to share your own experiences of misunderstanding someone's meaning and intent, and ask your child to provide his thoughts about what you might've done differently, or how you would know better next time. When discussed as a "game" in this manner—and outside of real-life, potentially threatening, or scary situations—your child will likely feel comfortable and at ease deconstructing social idioms. Reinforce that it is always considered acceptable to politely request that someone repeat what they've said, or ask for clarification by simply stating, "I don't know what you mean. Can you please say it another way?" By doing this, you can help your child become adept at cracking the social code.

Additional Social Strategies

It is easy for your child to misunderstand communications and do something other than you intended, or react with frustration when she tries and fails. Your child may be additionally challenged when interacting with peers and others because she:

- Has difficulty understanding the rhythmic flow of conversation (i.e., the reciprocation, or "give and take").
- Talks off topic or interjects information that doesn't fit the moment.
- Is direct and honest and, in so being, is offensive to others.
- Doesn't understand how to maintain personal space.
- Has trouble deciphering people's body language.

There are a number of concrete strategies you may explore to address such issues.

Figuring out the peculiarities of human nature is a lifelong art that comes more naturally to some than others. We are all a work in progress as is your child with Asperger's syndrome. For your child, getting the "hang of" people may just come harder and require more effort to understand. Our goal isn't one of mastery but of knowing just enough to get by and be okay.

Debriefing

Try debriefing social situations that were confusing or upsetting by privately, gently, and respectfully deconstructing them portion by portion. Request your child to model his recall of others' body language and facial expressions, or model them yourself and ask, "Is this what you saw?" Once you identify the breakdown in communication, you can better explain what transpired. You may wish to take the subtle language that was originally confusing and exaggerate it in an obvious way. Once your child "sees" it, talk about the less exaggerated communication originally used.

Carol Gray, a special educator, has developed "Comic Strip Conversations," a wonderful, visual cartooning technique whereby you and your child literally draw—comic-strip style, panel by panel—social conversations using voice balloons to contain dialogue. Gray encourages using a color-coding system to identify emotions for further clarification. Many kids with Asperger's enjoy drawing, and this strategy is a safe and comfortable way to give your child control in deconstructing social misunderstandings or ideas to apply in the future. It is also a *visual* way to show turn taking in conversation, approximate comfort-zone distance from others, and how people's conversations can become jumbled and overlap when someone interrupts too frequently or disrupts the flow by talking off topic.

Making Lists or Videos

Develop a written list of key phrases that your child can use as a socially acceptable entry into conversation. There can be a hierarchy in the sequence of phrases such that they may flow into broader, larger conversations, such as "Hey, what's up?" "How's it going?" "What's new with you?" "What did you do over the weekend?" "What did you watch on TV last night?" Such standard questions also promote turn taking that includes eye contact (where possible). If your child gets stuck, she may also fall back on using typical "scripted" but kid-acceptable responses such as "Cool" or "That's awesome."

You may also wish to consider videotaping. The caution here is that none of us see and hear ourselves as others do, and it can be quite disturbing for any one of us to watch ourselves on video. If you wish to try it, ensure that you have your child's permission. It may also be helpful not to single out your child but to naturally capture him engaged in some activities with others. Be certain that any debriefing you do with your child occurs in a gentle, unconditionally accepting environment. This was the case for one teenage boy videotaped during a discussion group at school. When he privately viewed the video of himself, he was astounded that he came across very differently than his personal perception of himself, and after that he worked to tame and refine his presentation style.

Essential

To support your child using video to deconstruct his social interactions, do it as naturally as possible. If your child knows you are singling him, he may "overact" and play to the camera unnaturally. Try videoing at family gatherings or picnics, at parties, while playing games, or during other activities. Always watch the video with your child in privacy.

Writing

Many people are better at expressing themselves in writing than through verbal communication. Here is where computers are a tremendous benefit to kids with Asperger's. The computer is liberating because your child is free from social pressures with regard to immediacy of response, body language, facial expressions, personal space issues, and eye contact in conversation. Using e-mail to communicate with others *is* social! With e-mail, you can respond in your own time. You may be amazed at the incredible and eloquent global and personal insights your child types out in her own time and in the safety and comfort of her own home.

Many kids with Asperger's feel so socially inept that in-person "talk therapy" or group counseling is oftentimes ineffective. Try reaching your child with pressing questions and concerns by sending her an e-mail; you will get a reply that may surprise and enlighten your own understanding of the situation at hand.

If your child is receiving formal supports from your county's service system or your school district, you may wish to encourage the professionals with whom your child interacts to pursue these and other strategies of effective communication. They should be in a position to do so, or may already be knowledgeable about them. Other helpful ideas will be explored in Chapter 17.

CHAPTER 6

Physical Health

The child with Asperger's syndrome may experience great pain and discomfort that goes unreported, unnoticed by others, and undiagnosed and treated. Enduring pain and allowing it to become chronic is extremely detrimental to your child's ability to function, grow, and learn. Untreated pain and discomfort will also seriously impact your child's behavior and ability to communicate with others. It is crucial that parents foster a child's self-advocacy by emphasizing the importance of one's physical well-being.

Recognizing Pain

Of the three meltdown triggers that drive behaviors, experiencing pain and discomfort is extremely significant. This is because pain affects behavior—in us all. Think of the last time you were sick and feeling significant pain or discomfort. Was the pain a symptom of flu, migraine, menstrual cramps, a pulled muscle, or some other physiological condition? Now, think of how being in such pain manifested in your behavior. Perhaps you:

- Were especially hypersensitive to light or sound.
- Just wanted to crawl under the covers and stay there.
- Lashed out or snapped at loved ones.
- Lashed out or snapped when anyone made a demand of you.

- Just wanted to be left alone.
- Felt especially vulnerable.

Once your brain recognized the signals your body was sending it, you sought relief from the pain because you wanted to feel better. You also knew that relief was available to you. In assuming personal responsibility for your health and well-being, you took medication, pampered yourself, slept, or made a doctor's appointment. You did these things with the expectation that the pain would be alleviated in short order and you would return to feeling "normal" once again.

Fact

At times, some individuals have difficulty verbally communicating their pain or the exact point of its origin. Others may not know how much pain they should endure before telling someone. The opportunity to access visual alternatives to speech such as pictures, written language, and scales of pain levels and intensity may be especially useful in addressing this issue, especially in young children.

But what if the pain was not treated and allowed to persist? Suppose relief was not immediate or an option? Revisit the previous list and consider how your behavior might intensify the longer you had to endure pain. Not only would you feel lousy, you would also feel disoriented and distracted. Your attention focused on trying your best to cope and manage the pain that threatens to overwhelm you at any moment. In short, slowly but surely, your mental health would be impacted, eroded, and, over time, seriously impaired. Your ability to function, care for yourself, or interact with others with a measure of quality would be greatly reduced. Your self-esteem would suffer as well and you might not care about your appearance. The culmination of feeling physical pain would converge with mental anguish, leaving you weak and vulnerable.

Now, reflect on your child's experiences with pain. Take your own experiences and multiply them using this perspective and you may quickly understand how debilitating the experience of enduring pain may be for your child, especially if the pain goes undetected, unreported, and untreated.

Allergies

One of the two most prevalent forms of pain in children with Asperger's syndrome is allergies. The challenge is that many parents do not recognize this and see their child's symptoms in isolation, if at all. For example, the child with Aspeger's may frequently experience ear blockages and ear infections, sometimes from a very young age. Perhaps the child manifested outwardly visual symptoms such as red, sore, pussy ears that drained spontaneously. The child may have been treated with antibiotics or had tubes in her ears to relieve pressure. More often than not, the ear problems were *one symptom* within a cluster of other symptoms, indicative of allergies.

In addition to ear blockages and infections, the child with Asperger's may also manifest symptoms of allergy such as:

- Headaches and migraines
- Red, itchy, or runny eyes
- Sinus pressure over or under eyes
- Congestion and runny nose
- Swollen glands
- Sore throat
- Coughing and sneezing

Upon careful investigation, you may discover that several of these symptoms manifest together at the same times of the year. The culprit allergens could be absolutely anything—from one indicator, such as seasonal pollen, to an entire and exhaustive collection of many known indicators. While you may have been treating one or two symptoms, you may not have been addressing the bigger picture, that is, the chronic allergies.

Essential

Err on the side of caution. Take a moment to reflect upon the last few meltdowns your child endured. It might be that she was experiencing physical pain and discomfort that triggered her behavior or otherwise contributed to her in-the-moment communication of extreme distress. Take note of any physical symptoms apparent at the time.

Treatment is available to relieve many of the physical side effects of severe allergies, like those listed, but testing is necessary to determine the allergen type and degree of severity. This may be problematic for many children with Asperger's, especially if they have had unpleasant experiences with doctors who were not as patient or sensitive as they should have been. Some of the testing and treatment may involve drawing blood or receiving steroid shots, which may be a horrifyingly overwhelming experience and, ultimately, perhaps not worth the potential trauma. Another type of testing is nonintrusive and involves the client holding various physical examples of allergens to ascertain a reaction. It is also possible that standard, over-the-counter medications may work to contain some or all symptoms of the allergies—at least until the individual can determine if she wishes to pursue other forms of obtaining relief.

Gastrointestinal Issues

Another prevalent factor that drives pain and discomfort in children with Asperger's and autism is gastrointestinal issues. That is, severe gas and cramping, bloating, constipation, impaction, and diarrhea. A number of such children have an inability to properly digest dairy and wheat-based food products (among others), such that the enzymes from these foods "leak" through the gut and into the bloodstream, potentially creating an adverse reaction described by some as an "opiate" effect. In clinical trials, the dairy products are referred to as "casein," and the wheat-based foods are referred to as "gluten."

Parents may find themselves frustrated with a child who seems "inappropriately" or embarrassingly gassy or who seems to have bowel complaints. Again, the child is not being deliberately difficult; there is a legitimate issue that is driving pain and discomfort.

As with pursuing the treatment of allergies, there are options that range from restrictive to less intrusive forms of treatment. In some instances, a bacteria of the lower gastrointestinal tract may be responsible for creating these issues. This can be an excruciatingly painful experience that may cause a child to double over in pain. If the child is unaware of the root of the problem or doesn't know how to describe the pain in the moment, his "behavior" may be misinterpreted instead of correctly identified as a communication. Consult with your family doctor to determine the appropriate treatment to eradicate all traces of the bacteria.

Antibiotics used to treat gastrointestinal bacteria can have side effects that are very difficult to physically endure. Be sure to talk these over carefully with your child's doctor.

Treating Problems

The procedures to determine the cause of the gastrointestinal tract maladies may be very physically intrusive. You may wish to explore less invasive methods of intervention as an alternative first if the child has not had a good history with medical practitioners. These may include:

- Pursuing a diet free of dairy and wheat, in partnership with the child and in consultation with a dietician or nutritionist.

- Avoiding foods with dyes or preservatives.
- Cutting back on red meat proteins in favor of chicken, fish, or other food options.
- Considering soy and other substitute foods, perhaps for a select time frame, to note any cause and effect.
- Using any over-the-counter products designed to aid gas relief or alleviate bowel distress, like fiber-based additives.
- Increasing fluid intake, especially water, may prove helpful as well.
- Increasing consumption of natural food fiber found in fruits and vegetables.
- Promoting massage and exercise.

Fears Surrounding Toileting

Some gastrointestinal concerns may be compounded by the child's fears and anxieties around toileting. Children with Asperger's syndrome tend to be careful observers. Most will attempt toileting—especially urinating—in their own way and in their own time, just at a time later than what might be considered developmentally appropriate. Still others may appear to deliberately wet or soil themselves. Please be patient. Recall the positive philosophies and know your child is not deliberately being insubordinate; he really is struggling and feeling just as frustrated as you. Here are some thoughts that may help clarify your understanding of toileting issues in the child with Asperger's syndrome:

- Your child may be frightened by the toilet, believing that he may fall in and get sucked down.
- Your child may be overwhelmed by the loud roar of a flushing toilet.
- If the child is not feeling safe and comfortable and in control, withholding body waste is one way of independently attempting to gain control.
- Your child may panic, believing that in making a bowel movement, she is shedding a vital, living piece of her body.

- Your child may be in a "perfectionism" mode, unwilling to admit his need to use the toilet when asked, or embarrassed to confess the need.
- Your child may not be well-connected enough with her body to consistently receive the physical "signals" or pressure indicating the need to evacuate waste.

To counteract these and other issues, it will be important to deconstruct the whole toileting process for your child using very basic, *visual* information. The *Once Upon a Toilet* books have the right idea in explaining the process of how and why the body rids itself of waste to very young children, but these books may be far too immature for your child. You'll need to adapt this concept, expanding upon it by using your own visuals such as graphics explaining the human digestive system, naming internal parts of the body.

What are the typical environments in which your child may be exposed to potential physical pain triggers?
Allergens or foods that are historically difficult for your child to digest can cause problems in his daily life. Your preventative measures to guard against such unforeseen pain may include gathering information in detail about school parties, assemblies, special gatherings, and field trips. Ultimately, you want your child to speak up for his own needs as a good self-advocate.

Reinforce with your child that the process of eliminating waste from one's body is natural. In partnership with your child, explain that *everyone* with whom your child interacts does this regularly and that it is natural—family, doctors, caregivers, teachers, and others all do this daily. You may be surprised to find this is a significant revelation for your child, especially the child who is struggling to match the perceived perfection of the adults in her life. Just as important, also ensure you reinforce that using the toilet is a *private* matter. It is not to be discussed freely in public; it should only be discussed with close, trusted individuals (list them in writing), usually if there is cause for concern like constipation, impaction, diarrhea, etc.

Some children will also want specific assurances about exactly what happens to their waste once it gets flushed away—where does it go and what becomes of it? You may need to research this yourself, or look it up on the Internet with your child. If you are uncertain if your child experiences the sensations indicating the need to evacuate waste, first ask her about it. Talk about the ways in which you know your body gives you the appropriate signals, and plan daily, gentle exercises designed to better connect your child with her body, such as yoga, breathing, and stretching exercises.

Additionally, there may be adaptations and accommodations you can make in giving your child control in toileting, such as adjusting the water pressure to avoid a rushing roar when the toilet is flushed or partnering with your child to select a new toilet seat that is more comfortable and makes the toilet opening less foreboding. Implementing some or all of these strategies should enable your child to attain greater comfort in his approach to toileting.

Why Does Pain Go Unreported?

As we've discussed, it is absolutely critical that the child with Asperger's grows into an adult able to identify and advocate for her own relief from pain. As with toileting, it will be useful to visually explain how the brain and body usually work together to send signals indicating pain. Sometimes the signals are accompanied by visuals that help reinforce that something is wrong, such as a bleeding cut or blister. Other times, the signals may be exclusively inside the body and unseen, just felt. The Internet or your local library should be a resource in accessing images, books, or videos that describe this physiological process.

Reasons for Not Reporting Pain

Still, there are some children with Asperger's who are inconsistent in reporting pain, if at all. Here are some speculations as to why this may be:

- Your child may not understand that there exists an unwritten social expectation that we all report pain and discomfort in order to gain relief.
- Your child may not realize that what he's feeling in the moment is anything any different from what anyone else feels.
- As with toileting, your child may not have a nervous system she feels fully connected with, such that the pain is delayed or not "registering" properly.
- Being inherently gentle and exquisitely sensitive, your child may have been severely traumatized by experiences with doctors and nurses so that she considers enduring the pain the better option.

One mom shared the following observations about her young son:

> People had told me that Alex had a high tolerance for pain. He broke his arm one day, and the teacher saw it happen, but he just winced and went on. Later, she realized he couldn't use the hand. I started realizing that Alex had experienced pain from an early age. He knocked his four front teeth loose at three years, and then hit them again at four and five. (We now know he has no depth perception and was extremely farsighted.) He probably had experienced pain as a part of daily life without being able to explain it. I went home and asked Alex about his body. He felt sure he wasn't registering pain well, but when he came down to it, he reported what turned out to be plantar warts, which are quite painful.

Another young boy suffered with mild asthma for several years of his young life. Upon gaining diagnosis and treatment, his first exclamation was to say, "Mom, I didn't know it wasn't supposed to hurt when you breathe."

On occasion, medical professionals are not patient, gentle, or sensitive to our needs. Until your child can advocate for her own needs, never hesitate to advocate on her behalf. If necessary, cancel an appointment, switch doctors, call in, or write a letter of (tactful) complaint, or otherwise diplomatically make your child's needs known.

Ascertaining pain in your child may prove especially challenging if she is often expressionless. During an assessment with a teenager with Asperger's, she stunned most everyone in the room. When asked about pain and discomfort, she rattled off a long laundry list of ailments with which she coexists on a daily basis. No one would have ever guessed her struggles simply by looking at her demeanor; her facial expressions revealed nothing. It was a matter of asking the question in order to receive the answer.

One young man in his twenties was grappling with severe, debilitating dental pain. He adamantly refused to seek treatment because of prior traumatic experiences with the dentist. (Who among us *doesn't* feel anxiety about dental appointments?) Not seeking medical treatment for his pain became the path of least resistance for him. However, his pain was chronic. He opted to self-medicate by using nicotine, marijuana, and alcohol.

Teaching Your Child Self-Advocacy

In addition to educating your child about how the body works when communicating pain, it will also be important to partner with your child in gaining self-awareness and control leading to lifelong self-advocacy. This means reinforcing that it is good and desirable to identify and report one's own pain. The message to the young girl who endured a litany of daily pains (and others like her) needs to be loud and clear. It is *not* okay to live with chronic pain. Other thirteen-year-old girls don't live with it, it is not normal or typical, and relief is available once proper diagnosis is made. Imagine how detrimental enduring chronic pain would be for this young girl if she were thirty-three instead of thirteen. How productive would her life be, and how would others characterize her "behaviors"?

Additionally, it will aid tremendously in quelling your child's anxiety if you endeavor to demystify the entire concept of going to the doctor *in advance* of an appointment. You may do this by partnering with your child to consider doing the following:

- With your child, schedule a time to drive to the doctor's office before the appointment day.
- Assign your child the responsibility of reading you driving directions to and from the office location, noting street names and landmarks.
- Once at the office, empower your child by allowing him to take photographs inside and out. Review these later at home (where your child feels most comfortable), eliciting details from him.
- If at all possible, arrange to meet the doctor, the nurse practitioner, and—at the least—the receptionist. Again, provide the opportunity for your child to take pictures.
- Suggest that your child photograph a typical private room, being remindful that, next visit, you may not get that exact room but one very much like it.
- Before making the trip, partner with your child to develop a list of questions to ask the doctor, nurse, or receptionist. If there's the opportunity to do this, allow your child to take the lead in gleaning the information desired.
- Arrange to get as many specifics about the appointment as possible, including approximate wait time and details of any procedures, along with literature and other visuals.

- Discuss flexibility of time frames with your child, and empower him to keep track of the time during the actual appointment.
- Gain clear information about the tentative sequence of events in order to visually list these out with your child (he can bring this list with him on appointment day).
- Because of downtime while waiting, suggest your child bring something to read or work on, possibly to share with the doctor as well.
- Schedule a pleasurable activity for your child to follow the appointment. Ensure that the activity occurs regardless of how well you think your child does or if he "earned" it.

Essential

Doctors' offices can be very busy settings with appointments often backed up and running late. Time permitting, call before leaving to confirm your scheduled time. Don't be surprised, though, if, upon finally meeting with the doctor, your child doesn't give him or her a good dressing down for "being late"!

If this sounds like a lot of prep work and a significant investment of time, it is. But in the long run, this initial investment of time upfront will go a long way in supporting your child to feel safe and comfortable and in control. Empowering him to take the lead during this process promotes his ownership and sense of self-advocacy.

Stories for Reporting Pain

As with the discussion of toileting, it will be helpful to partner with your child to gain an understanding of what and how much pain she experiences as it relates to signals received from the brain to the body. Again, becoming literate and articulate about body parts and how the body functions, paired with gentle exercise, may enhance your child's ability to respond to pain in a timely way.

Entering these discussions using visuals—diagrams, charts, pictures, videos—will aid your child in retaining the information but won't tell him what to *do* about it. This is where instructional stories come into play. What follows are examples that you may use to adapt and make specific in reflection of your child's needs. If you feel there is too much information for your child to take in at one time, break it down into manageable bits. Your child will feel personally invested if you print little portions of the story on separate pages so that he may illustrate it. This has been very successful with a number of children with Asperger's, and you may be surprised at what you learn, such as seeing the imagery your child associates with his pain (for example, a prickly monster).

Feeling Pain

My body is my own. My body is beautiful. I will try to take good care of my body so I can enjoy good health all my life.

My body is made up of many different parts inside and out.
Inside parts are like my heart and stomach.
Outside parts are like my arms and legs.

Sometimes my body is hurt. When my body is hurt, I may be in pain or I may feel discomfort, like an ache or a pinching feeling.

The part of my body that hurts could be an inside or an outside part.

I know when my body is hurt because my body will give me a signal.

A signal is a sign that something is wrong with a part of my body or that a part of my body is hurt.

This is normal.

Another word for signal is symptom.

Recognizing Pain

Everybody's body gives them symptoms or signals when a part of their body is hurt or they are feeling pain or discomfort.

If I don't report the pain, it could get worse.

If I don't report the pain, it is difficult for others to help me feel better.

A symptom or signal that my stomach is hurting may be that I am unable to eat, or I feel a burning in my stomach, or I throw up.

A symptom or signal for my throat hurting may be scratchiness or burning and difficulty swallowing or eating.

A symptom or signal that my head is hurting may be pain in my forehead.

A symptom or signal that my acid reflux is causing me pain or discomfort may be when I have burning in both my throat and stomach.

Reporting Pain

It is important for me to report when my body gives me signals that it hurts or is in pain.

I can report when my body is giving me a signal and I am in pain or have discomfort.

One way I can report this pain or discomfort by pointing to a picture of my body that is hurting me. Another way is to point to the place on my own body where I feel pain or discomfort. Another way is to write on paper where I am feeling pain or discomfort.

When I report this pain, others will know how to help me get relief from the pain. This may be by getting extra rest. It may be by taking a warm bath or shower. It may be by taking medicine to make the pain go away. It may be other ways, too.

Sometimes, I might have to go to the doctor so he can give me a different kind of medicine to help the pain go away. The doctor will know best of all how to help me feel better.

You may also script similar stories to address precisely what your child can do to gain relief from a variety of ailments. Review the stories with your child once or twice a week, allowing him to read to you and explain any pictures he has created to illustrate them. As this is a new process, your child may initially require reminders or your prompting to begin to self-report pain and discomfort. Once your child "gets" the concept, you may phase out use of the stories.

If your child is interested in illustrating his or her own stories about pain and discomfort, it may be revealing to you as well. Some envision little monsters or blobs with pincers or jagged edges that cause internal hurting. This concept is similar to other visualization techniques employed by medical professionals supporting children coping with terminal illness.

One caveat of which to be aware is that your child may seize the opportunity to demonstrate this newly learned concept by reporting every tiny nick, scrape, or minor ache. After all, this is what's been taught although others may perceive it as a nuisance. The challenge here is to coach your child about the *degree and intensity* of pain. This is where another visual will be useful, such as a linear scale of smiley faces with expressions in varying states of deterioration due to pain. Use faces that correlate with numbers of intensity, from one to five. (If smiley faces are not concrete enough, work with your child to take similar photos of his own expressions.) Number one on the scale is no pain and number five on the scale is the most pain. You and your child may then practice communicating the intensity of the pain in the appropriate moment and discuss reporting the pain if it gets above a "two" or a "three" on the intensity scale, meaning it cannot be personally managed.

Err on the side of caution so that your child does not feel inhibited about reporting pain. Living in a way that is virtually pain free can dramatically alter the lives of many children with Asperger's in positive ways (the same as it would for anyone), while concurrently quelling some anxieties and so-called "behaviors."

Chapter 7

Mental Health

As an inherently gentle and exquisitely sensitive being, your child may be particularly vulnerable to mental health problems. Such experiences transpire in people with Asperger's syndrome more often than not. As a parent, your responsibility will be to educate yourself and your child about the most prevalent forms of mental health issues: depression, bipolar disorder, anxiety, and post-traumatic stress disorder. It will also be important that you strive to shatter myths and stereotypes about such experiences being an unavoidable, unchangeable aspect of Asperger's syndrome.

Prevention, Not Intervention

You will recall that mental health is one of the driving factors in "behaviors." It is also the most ambiguous factor. Psychiatry, the practice of ascribing probable mental health diagnoses, is not an exact science. Determining a mental health diagnosis is predicated upon educated attempts to pin down the intangible. There is no single psychiatrist who can unequivocally state the precise mental health experience of any given individual; the experience is unique to each individual, so it may manifest in many nuances. The best a doctor can do is make an educated best guess based upon her professional expertise. She does this in conjunction with observing and interviewing a client and consulting the *Diagnostic and Statistical Manual* (or other clinical documents) to narrow it down to a diagnosis based upon a series of symptoms—what the client reports of his experiences and how he presents during the interview.

There is a long-standing stereotype that perpetuates the belief that "junk behaviors" in people with different ways of being (including Asperger's syndrome) are merely by-products of those experiences. But knowledge is power and, as a parent, your approach should be one of prevention instead of intervention. Remember the self-fulfilling prophecy? Understanding how to successfully avert its vicious cycle will directly impact your child's mental health.

To begin with, it is important to outwardly express your love and caring for your child in ways that she understands, using concrete pictures, words, and actions paired with validating statements. For example, you could set aside times to spend with your child and sing her favorite songs or create an arts and crafts project that builds upon one of your child's most passionate interests, while acknowledging that you love her and love sharing this kind of time with her. Together you are creating life movies for future replay.

Reinforce to your child that your love is unconditional—a tough concept for many kids, let alone the child with Asperger's, to grasp. Explain that, even though your child may make mistakes or do things you disapprove of, your love is constant and will never waver. Be certain to praise your child's accomplishments, gifts, and talents often. Highlight his successes, and tell him how very happy and proud he makes you feel. Tell others about the amazing things he's accomplished as well, and, with his prior okay, make such comments publicly in his presence. Ask him to show you exactly how he did what he did and tell him how much you've enjoyed listening to him (even if it gets long-winded and tedious). Tell your child with Asperger's syndrome that he or she is beautiful—not just physically beautiful, but truly beautiful inside. Tell him that his inner beauty is that of being a good human being who wants to give of his gifts and talents to others. Discuss how this inner beauty is the most valuable of all, far more important than physical attractiveness

Why all the emphasis on glorifying your child? In doing so, you are incrementally fortifying the child with Asperger's syndrome by laying a foundation of strong self-esteem. This will serve as ammunition as your child grows and enters adolescence and beyond. Never underestimate the power and long-lasting effect of your most loving words and actions. Your child will retain and replay the most memorable of such experiences for the rest of her life. They will buoy her when she needs it most.

Depression

The mental health experience of depression is extremely common in people with Asperger's syndrome. Many otherwise brilliant and gifted adults are significantly derailed or devastatingly crippled by its effects. They are stymied and unable to move forward, as their Asperger's experience is compounded by the symptoms of depression.

Your child may already be considered moody or sensitive. Indicators that may be linked to depression would be an *increase* in moodiness, irritability, or sadness. The problem is, this describes many typical kids caught up in classic teenage angst. The differences here must be a significant change from what is usual for your child in order to consider it a depressive episode.

Although the *Diagnostic and Statistical Manual* indicates that depression has a typical onset age in the twenties, parents should be mindful of the potential for depression in children with Asperger's starting earlier, from about age ten on (although, in some instances, environment and genetic predisposition can induce depression earlier). This is the age when, more than ever, typical children are propelled into preadolescence with lightening speed. They may:

- Begin to define their personal individuality based upon older role models.
- Give more attention to personal appearance, style, and taste.
- Take on more mature interests, typical of preteens.
- Pair up and develop cliques or specific circles of friends designated by certain criteria (athletic aptitude, superior physical appearance, or academic achievement).
- Become more aware of differences in others.

For the child with Asperger's who doesn't feel included, this is the time when, more than ever, she may become more aware of her own differences or be made to feel different by others. When this occurs consistently and she is without a solid, loving foundation from which to draw strength, she becomes vulnerable to depression.

What Causes Depression?

Like most mental health problems, depression is linked to a chemical imbalance in the brain. It may develop due to family genetics (a history of mental health issues on either side of one's lineage) or environmental factors, such as the child who falls victim to poor self-esteem (remember the self-fulfilling prophecy) through some form of abuse. It may be triggered by an event (or series of events) that so changes the way one is accustomed to being in the world that recovery and return to normalcy is difficult. And, as discussed in the chapter on pain, depression may be brought on by a chronic, deteriorating physical condition. (In fact, it is wise to start by getting a thorough thyroid check for your child; a thyroid imbalance can mimic symptoms of mood disorders like depression.)

If you sense that depression may be plausible for your child, it will be important to become savvy about its symptoms and how it may manifest through your child's words and actions. It will be equally important, especially at this time, to recall the positive philosophies as they apply to your child. And remember, no matter what it looks like, mental health problems, including depression, are *no one's* fault.

Chronic endurance of physical pain and discomfort without adequate relief can induce depression. Think of those you've known grappling with cancer or some other intense, long-term physical ailment. It is easy for anyone to succumb to depression under such devastating circumstances.

Depression is defined using a list of symptoms. As an aid, those symptoms are indicated here as they may appear in *any child*, but are embellished with specifics to show how depression may appear differently in the child with Asperger's. When examining the signs of depression or other mental health problems, it is very important to bear in mind that the symptoms:

- Must be significant differences from what is typical demeanor for your child
- Must occur in clusters or groups—single symptoms in isolation do not a syndrome make

Additionally, pay attention to the presence of any "cycles," that is, times of year during which your child experiences differences in how he talks and acts. Genetics and family history can also affect your child's experience. This includes not only mental health history but also alcoholism or substance abuse in families. People in denial or who believe that accessing mental health services is stigmatizing will often self-medicate using these substances.

What Are the Symptoms?

The foremost symptom of depression is that of an overall depressed mood. This includes spontaneous crying and weeping (for no reason apparent to you), whining, moaning, or a general sense of sadness and melancholy longer than two weeks in duration. This type of behavior would not be considered a symptom if it followed a death or significant life-changing event (like the family moving and changing schools), after which it would be typical for your child to mourn.

Remember to be sensitive about how your child processes a loss. The child with Asperger's cannot simply "get over it" in reaction to a situation that others may consider insignificant. Be mindful that your child may grieve over losses that are not readily perceptible by you.

Abuse by peers can contribute to depression and even post-traumatic stress disorder. Additionally, if your child is severely depressed, she may feel such worthlessness that she deliberately antagonizes, bullies, or instigates further abuse by "offering" herself up to them, being well aware of the impending harm. This may be incomprehensible, but such behavior may be a symptom of depression.

A depressed child may seem fascinated by morbid thoughts about funerals, disease, and death. The preteen or adolescent may despair, not wanting to be seen as "different." Your child may make remarks that are self-deprecating such as "No one loves me," "I hate myself," "What's the use," or "I'm not wanted here." In extreme instances, your child may try to seriously harm himself by attempting suicide or recklessly placing himself in harm's way.

Another symptom of depression is a decreased interest in pleasurable activities. If your child is depressed, this symptom will likely be quite distinct because she has lost all or most desire for her most passionate area of interest. Your child may pass up opportunities to participate in activities related to her passion or intentionally withdraw from those activities in favor of isolation or seclusion from others. (This includes intentionally setting herself up to be forcibly excluded or grounded via parental discipline.) Your child may also give away or destroy items that you immediately recognize as personally valuable or meaningful to her.

Additional, supporting symptoms of depression may include:

- Increased agitation.
- Psychomotor retardation, which is an overall, noticeable "slowing down."
- Fatigue and difficulty in physical movement (in which the smallest of feats require great effort).
- Clinginess, meaning that your child wants to physically "hang" on you, and needs repeated assurances that everything is okay.
- Requiring too much or too little sleep or being difficult to rouse.
- Loss of appetite or feeling nauseated at the sight of food. (Your child may also try to make himself feel better by eating too much food—especially sugary or fatty snack foods.)
- Seeming confused, listless, or disoriented. (He may urinate in places other than the toilet, such as a corner of his room or in a dresser drawer.)

Again, some or all of these symptoms may manifest in any child but may appear more peculiar or intense in the child with Asperger's.

Bipolar Disorder

You've just reviewed some symptoms that may be indicators of depression. Many people find themselves depressed at various points in their lives; it is a fairly natural thing. Depression is a mental health problem that can "stand alone." This means it can occur without association with another mental health problem.

When someone has a bipolar mental health experience, there are two components to it. Depression is one of those two components.

The other is called mania. While depression can occur without mania, mania never stands alone without depression at some point in time.

Fact

The characters from the classic *Winnie the Pooh* stories make a good bipolar analogy. Think about Tigger the tiger and Eeyore the mule. Tigger demonstrates the intense, "wired" energy and grandiose self-esteem associated with mania. Eeyore is typically self-loathing, lethargic, and full of hopelessness for the future. If they were both one and the same, that character would be the epitome of bipolar disorder.

When you've heard people disrespectfully described using the label "manic-depressive," it refers to someone who experiences bipolar disorder. (Bipolar means two opposite ends of the poles, or two extremes—mania and depression). Bipolar may also referred to as severe "mood swings." When someone has bipolar disorder, there may be periods of time when he is level or even, as is typical of many of us on an average day. The person may experience the onset of a manic experience that may develop gradually or skyrocket rapidly—it all depends on the individual. At some point, the person de-escalates from mania and either returns to feeling level or begins a descent into depression. Many of us feel similar highs and dips but they usually do not impair our daily lives. The difference here is that being bipolar can seriously impact one's life if not properly treated.

You are now familiar with the primary symptoms of depression as it may appear in your child. Now review the symptoms of mania for any child, augmented with details specific to a different way of being.

Mood Swings

The first major symptom is a euphoric or irritable mood. Your child may seem delirious or giddy, with an increased intensity of laughing and grinning. At times she may have a fixed grin while speaking that appears forced or unnatural. Her speech may be pressured, meaning it is bursting forth hard and fast as though her thoughts are speeding. You may notice your child forcing laughter at inappropriate times, like during serious discussions. If your child has always been a "kidder," you may notice him taking things too far, unable to cease the joke telling or pushing physical slapstick that gets out of hand or causes others harm. Your child's tolerance threshold for autistic-like sensory sensitivities may also be vastly diminished, heightening irritability.

Inflated Self-Esteem

The next manic symptom is a sense of inflated self-esteem, known as grandiosity. A child with Asperger's may project a sense of omnipotence and control over persons in authority such as mom, dad, teachers, doctors, or caregivers. He may "hire" or "fire" you, threaten to withhold your salary, or physically direct you and others where to go in a given environment. In one instance, a young boy insisted, "God's not the boss, I am!"

Fact

One boy with Asperger's syndrome and undiagnosed bipolar disorder clearly demonstrated the manic symptom of grandiosity when interacting with his counselor. He told the man that he intended to (creatively) kill his family, marry the counselor, and then kill him to assume his identity. Others might label this psychotic, but this fit within the bipolar framework in consideration with other symptoms.

The child may believe himself to be a childhood "celebrity" such as a popular TV, movie, or cartoon character, or even Santa Claus. The child may try to assume all or part of an authority figure's name. Similarly, the child may believe he possesses superhuman "superhero" strength. He may climb on top of furniture, windowsills, and countertops, out onto rooftops, or into the street. There, he may bodily hurl himself into space with the belief that he will fly, or that no harm will come to him. Grandiosity may also manifest in your child damaging property, like trashing her bedroom or attempting to lift and throw heavy objects such as a television or pieces of furniture. The distinction is that ordinarily you know this would never be a consideration for her.

In extreme instances, your child may smear or throw feces, or urinate in places other than the bathroom. You may notice your child hoarding food or taking someone else's food, even if your child has the same portions in front of him. Finally, and most significantly, your child may physically attack and harm people very dear to her—people she would otherwise never dream of hurting. This may include hitting, punching, pulling hair, biting, scratching, head butting, pinching, or using weapons like knives. Once the manic "high" has blown over, it is *very common* for many children with Asperger's to be extremely remorseful for his or her actions during the times they were not in control. They may sob bitterly, want to be held, or plead for forgiveness.

Obsessions

Another primary symptom of mania is an increased intensity in pleasurable activities. This is when the child's special areas of interest, or passions, may seem like an obsession. The child's focus may be so absorbed that she cannot be dissuaded away from the activity. If you insist, she may lash out verbally or physically. For some children, especially teens, this symptom may come through with a sexual intensity, called hypersexuality. He may make wildly inappropriate remarks to others (including adults), touching others without permission, or masturbating openly or with greater frequency.

Other Symptoms of Mania

Instead of jumping to conclusions about "delinquent behavior," see if other symptoms support a case for mania. Additional symptoms of mania may include:

- Increased agitation, like your child has a "short fuse."
- Being able to describe your child as "wired" with energy. (Perhaps he doesn't sleep, sometimes for days in a row, or naps sporadically.)
- Changes in appetite. (Is your child gorging herself or hoarding food, such as in dresser drawers or under her bed?)
- "Racing" thoughts or ideas. (Does your child rapidly shift topics without any apparent connection between them? Or does he seem physically indecisive, moving from one activity to another without any rationale? Do your child's racing thoughts spill forth in her speech? She may talk at a very fast pace, tripping over words or spitting while talking.)

If your child is bipolar and he experiences periods of mania and depression, it will be important to stay focused on the child, not the behaviors. This will be your single greatest challenge as a parent. Remember, it is not your child's fault or are you to blame. It is no one's fault, but it *is* serious and you must be aggressive in seeking relief for your child through proper treatment.

Anxiety and Post-Traumatic Stress Disorder

Mood disorders (depression or bipolar disorder) are commonplace mental health experiences for the general population and, especially, for people with different ways of being, including Asperger's syndrome. Because of the pervasiveness of mood disorders, the *Diagnostic and Statistical Manual* compels a clinician to rule them out *first*. Afterward, other mental health problems, including those that may occur concurrent with mood disorder, may be considered.

Anxiety

When we think about kids with Asperger's and mental health issues, we often think about anxiety. Anxiety is typical of many children with Asperger's because of their gentle and sensitive nature, and their need to feel safe and comfortable within a range of predictability. We all feel nervous or anxious about lots of things in our lives, but, as a parent, you know that the things you consider minor can snowball into something huge for your child. "Big world" complexities may seem beyond your child's control, and his perceptions can become exaggerated or blown out of proportion. Some kids really torture themselves, agonizing over details, particularly with regard to the future. Events like impending appointments, tests, or social activities—especially in which your child is expected to "perform" or excel—can cause him to be unable to keep things in perspective and keep anxiety in check. Your child's anxiety may also be driven by feelings of distress or guilt due to family disharmony.

Essential

It's important to keep anxieties in check before molehills become mountains. Encourage your child early on to communicate her concerns to you, no matter how minor. Some kids are martyrs, believing they must suffer in silence; so if your child approaches you with a complaint, accept it as legitimate to her. You may also wish to process the day at bedtime and provide soothing assurances or a plan to make things right as part of a nightly ritual.

You may notice your child's anxiety through her inability to remain calm, focus, and rest. She may ruminate on certain topics, or request that you confirm the same information over and over again. We may very well be doing anxious children a disservice by rushing to medicate the anxiety without first understanding its roots, or providing coping strategies to help them independently relieve stress and anxiety. Strategies to quell anxiety while exploring medication will be discussed in Chapter 17.

Post-Traumatic Stress Disorder

In many instances, anxieties can escalate into post-traumatic stress disorder (PTSD) if they are not addressed. This is especially true if your child has participated in or been the target of abuse (in any form), or has witnessed some disturbing or violent event, such as a car accident. After September 11, 2001, many of us mourned and grieved, but it was a particularly difficult time for those of us who are most sensitive.

The symptoms of PTSD may look very similar to depression, but remember, depression must be explored first. Additional symptoms of PTSD may include:

- Nightmares and night sweats.
- Re-enactments of sexual abuse or attempts to impose sexual behavior upon others.
- "Clinginess" or a general sense of fearfulness.
- Increasing withdrawal from social activities.
- "Flashbacks" triggered by people, places, visuals, and smells. (Your child may "replay" mind movies at this time.)
- Acting out past events verbally, physically, or both.
- Bedwetting.
- Feeling unsafe or unprotected in familiar environments, or violently refusing to be in a particular environment.
- Complaints of feeling physically or sexually "dirty," and desiring to bathe frequently.
- Illustrating a traumatic experience through writing, art, or music.
- Being hypervigilant, which means your child may appear to be "on guard" or easily startled.

It is imperative that you support your child to the best of your ability to work toward resolving issues of depression, bipolar disorder, anxiety, and PTSD. The future of his mental health and his capacity to function as an effective contributor to his community depend upon it.

Ways to Approach Mental Health

It is often difficult for parents to see the forest for the trees. That is, people tend to recall major, cataclysmic behavioral "events," as opposed to being objective—stepping back to notice a trend or cycle of symptoms. Some parents may also struggle with issues of guilt or denial. This is where consulting with a professional will be of great value.

There's a phrase used to describe untreated mental health issues: "The longer the needle plays on the record, the deeper the groove becomes." Some parents become oblivious to the obvious because of their guilt or denial. If you believe that your child demonstrates highly unusual or out of control behaviors, please actively seek timely clinical support.

Finding a Psychiatrist

The challenge may be finding a clinician who is abreast of recent "best practice" trends (what is presently acknowledged as the "right," or respectful, approach) and does not buy into stereotypes that your child's behavior results from being a kid with Asperger's. As with seeking the initial diagnosis for Asperger's, you may encounter difficulty in locating a psychiatrist who meets this criterion. This is where networking with other parents or Asperger's/autism organizations in your area may be helpful. As before, be prepared to travel, especially if you live in a rural area and resources are sparse.

Preparing for the First Visit

If you believe your child is experiencing a mental health issue, prepare yourself and your child for the appointment with the psychiatrist just as you would for the appointment to interview for a diagnosis (review these steps in Chapter 3). In addition, it will be of greatest benefit to a psychiatrist if you come prepared to discuss *symptoms* and not *behaviors*. This text has provided you with the language used to describe symptoms—euphoric mood, grandiosity, and the like. This is language a good doctor will recognize and understand.

You know your child best; a psychiatrist is especially vulnerable to whatever you do and say. After all, unless you have a previously established rapport, she's meeting you and your child for the first time. You have an obligation to your child to be direct and concise and to stay focused on discussing symptoms. When you enter a doctor's office venting with lots of storytelling about how difficult it was last weekend when your child trashed the house, punched his sister, and threw a TV out a second-story window, you are discussing behaviors. It may be natural to want to do this, especially with someone whom you hope will understand, validate your experience, and provide you with answers. However, in describing behaviors, you've just significantly broadened the doctor's challenge; the previously listed "behaviors" can crosswalk to dozens of potential diagnoses. When this occurs, you risk your doctor "falling back" on ascribing stereotyped diagnoses like schizophrenia, borderline personality disorder, obsessive-compulsive disorder, oppositional defiant disorder, or intermittent explosive disorder.

These and others are commonplace in people with differences. Yet, we are all more alike than different, and mental illness is an equal opportunity offender. It is not selective, nor does it distinguish between brains. Doesn't it make sense that mood disorders, the most prevalent mental health experience for us all, would also be typical of folks with different ways of being?

You can prepare for an initial appointment with a psychiatrist by doing the following:

- Organize your child's symptoms as best you can by breaking them into categories for depression or bipolar to start.
- After listing out the previous two, list symptoms of anxiety and PTSD.

- Keep everything brief and concise—to one page if possible. Use numbered or bulleted entries so your doctor can easily scan the information.
- Be prepared to discuss your family's mental health history (including alcohol and substance abuse) *and* any cycles you have noted in your child.
- Do not provide the doctor with anything more than what she is requesting, but be prepared to offer it if she does.
- Become educated about medications traditionally used to treat mood disorders, like Lithium, Depakote, and Tegretol, and other newer mood stabilizers such as Lamictal, Zyprexa, Trileptal, Neurontin, and Topomax. (Be wary of antipsychotic medications except for short-term use in extreme, out-of-control instances.)
- Ensure that you have a way that your child will either participate in a gentle, respectful discussion with the doctor, or ensure that there is someone with whom your child can stay in a waiting area while you discuss specifics that may be very upsetting for your child to hear.

Essential

It may be a distinct and profound relief for your child to realize that what has been compelling him to "be bad" isn't his fault. Remember the circular wheel of the self-fulfilling prophecy? Self-loathing, guilt, and remorse can become its lubricant. Wherever possible, partner with your child to educate him while gently encouraging him to exert control over his mental illness to the best of his ability.

Consider Short-Term Hospitalization

If your child's symptoms manifest in extreme, violent behavior that causes him to seriously endanger himself or others, you may also need to carefully weigh the option of a short-term commitment to a psychiatric hospital in order to keep him and your family safe. The goal of a short-term hospitalization is to stabilize the child as soon and as safely as possible prior to discharge back to his family. There, he may receive observation and treatment in a controlled environment. The treatment may include medication to stabilize him and help him to feel level again.

In gaining control over violent behavior, antipsychotic medications will likely be prescribed. Such medications are usually strong sedatives, intended to "slow down" the child so that he will be manageable and less of a threat to himself and others. Such antipsychotic medications may include Thorazine (chlorpromazine), Mellaril (thioridazine), Serentil (mesoridazine), Prolixin (fluphenazine), Stelazine (trifluoperazine), Haldol (haloperidal), and Loxitane (loxapine) among others. It is not usual for such powerful drugs to be used to treat children and their sedative effect in your child may be alarming. Be mindful that such drugs should be temporary until the mood-stabilizing medications take effect. Your role as a strong advocate for your child is to be educated about the names of medications, the reason for their prescription, their duration and desired effects, and any adverse side effects. This is not a time to be shy, self-conscious, or feel inferior—don't be afraid to ask and re-ask important questions or to request a second opinion if you are feeling dissatisfied. If at any time you suspect your child is experiencing mental health issues, it is imperative that you take aggressive, proactive action to address them before the situation escalates into a severe crisis.

Fostering Mental Health Self-Advocacy

Many people with Asperger's—adults and children—grapple with anxiety, depression, and other mental health issues. Psychiatric diagnosis and medication may become a way of life, especially if the individual receives clinical benefit from this approach. The caveat lies in parents believing that this is the sole answer. Remember, the key is prevention, not intervention. It's never too early to shower your child with adoration and accolades that will become a foundation of strength for him. Finding a medication regime that is a good match is a trial and error process that may take time, sometimes months or years. However, medication isn't everything; if your life is still lousy and there is no positive change, medication can only do so much.

Fact

Creating an informal circle of support around your child (that also includes her) will provide her with an unconditional place of communion with those who know and care for her best. The circle should create a positive, personalized plan of support—a map or blueprint—to complement the IEP (Individual Education Plan), psychiatric treatment plan, or other types of written documents designed to assist your child. Assign roles, responsibilities, time frames for implementation, and gather regularly over food and drink.

If you have confirmed that your child is suffering from a mental health problem, empower her to become self-aware in order to grow into a strong self-advocate. Her ability to recognize her own symptoms and know her individual needs is of great importance. What follows are examples to foster mental health self-advocacy in your child. Here is a sample story that your child may read and personalize by illustrating it.

> There are over 100 different chemicals in your body. Each chemical must have balance with the others so you can feel your best. Sometimes, the chemicals are unbalanced. When there is too much or too little of one chemical, it can change the way you think, feel, and behave. When this happens, you may be unable to control your thoughts, feelings, or behavior until the chemicals become balanced again. Your body may need medication to help the chemicals become balanced again.

Everyone has many different feelings. Some feelings may make you very happy. Other feelings may make you sad enough to cry. Feelings like happy and sad can also be called moods. Most people have moods that go from very happy to very sad. But when the chemicals in your body become unbalanced, your mood can become more high or more low than usual. When these changes happen it is called a mood disorder, because the moods are out of the usual order.

The mood disorder has two parts with different names. The highest mood is called mania. The lowest mood is called depression. Because mania and depression are two parts of one mood disorder, it is named bipolar disorder. Bi means two. Polar means poles, like the North Pole or the South Pole of planet Earth. Bipolar means two different poles that are opposite from one another. We think of being happy and sad as opposite from one another.

People who have mania say it feels like their body is racing hard inside. They can be happier than usual. Or they can get so upset that they break things. Or they may hurt themselves or others even if they don't really mean to. They want to keep doing things they like to do without stopping. It may be hard to sleep or eat or think clearly. They may even believe they have superpowers and can do impossible things. This is harmful.

People who have depression feel sadder than usual. They may cry easily. They stop doing things they used to like a lot. They may feel tired all the time, no matter how much they sleep. Some people who have depression may not feel hungry. Others may feel hungry a lot. They may feel so bad inside that their bodies really hurt, and they can't find a way to make it better. It is like having an engine inside you that just won't start no matter what.

Bipolar disorder happens in cycles. This means that at certain times a person can feel either mania or depression. After the mood goes away, they may feel okay again. If someone has bipolar disorder, it is very important that others understand how it feels. It is especially important that a doctor understands how it feels.

Another strategy that has been effective is to partner with the child to draw the mental health problem as he envisions it. What has worked with many children is to imagine a car in which you are competing for control of the driver's seat. In the driver's seat, you're in control of the car, but if your mental health problem takes control, you may be bumped to the passenger seat, with limited control—or worse yet, you're bumped to the backseat or the trunk. One young teen drew his bipolar as a skeleton dressed in leather; because he was into NASCAR, he actually enjoyed drawing the car in great detail. Many such children are able to accurately tell, on any given day, exactly *where* they are positioned in the car. The ability to independently articulate one's own mental health experience will be of lifelong value for your child.

CHAPTER 8

Passions

As a unique individual, your child with Asperger's syndrome is naturally drawn to very select topics or subject areas. As a parent, it will be important for you to recognize your child's areas of specialty and understand how to build upon them. Doing so will make your child feel tremendously valued, because you are communicating that you "get" the importance of the passions. Passions may be used as links to life-defining opportunities in learning, relationships, and employment.

Identifying and Valuing Personal Passions

You will recall that one of the diagnostic criteria for Asperger's syndrome is "unusually intense preoccupation with one or more stereotyped interests." As previously discussed, this sets a negative precedent in how your child's interests are perceived. The use of words like "preoccupation" and "obsession" are not helpful in everyday life. They imply that such passionate interests are socially inappropriate, inappropriate to one's chronological age, or a hindrance with no real value or purpose. But why are neurotypical people allowed to have hobbies while those with differences are deemed "obsessed"?

What we know to be true of most children with Asperger's is that they have an absolute fascination with certain subject or topic areas and have become expert in their knowledge. The world's most advanced thinkers, talented artists, and brilliant inventors propelled whole cultures with their astounding expertise. As an advocate for your child, you will wish to vanquish "obsessive-compulsive" stereotypes and promote acceptance of his passions in just this manner.

Identifying your child's passion or passions shouldn't be difficult. Her passions are those things that—more than anything else—she loves to:

- Read about.
- Talk about.
- Write about.
- Draw meticulously.
- Sing about or create musical interpretations of.
- Create models or other three-dimensional replicas of.
- Take copious notes about.
- Re-enact or personify.
- Watch on television.
- Research at the library or on the Internet.

Your child's passion may correlate directly to an academic area of school in which he excels such as mathematics, physics, or music. He may also indulge his passion through extracurricular classes or clubs, or after-school or weekend activities. He may "set you up" with questions in which he grills you for answers that only he may know, and then feign disbelief that you don't provide the very complex, intricate correct response. (If you've been through this drill before, your child may even become perturbed that, by now, you haven't *memorized* the appropriate answer in order to "play along.") It may be easy to become annoyed or distracted by your child's focus or to fall victim to the idea that it represents "abnormal" behavior. It will be important for you to learn that your child's passions are an amazing strength to be recognized and validated.

The passions of some children with Asperger's have included:

- Wheels or other parts of automobiles, trains, trucks, tractors, and planes.

- Oceanography and specific marine life species.
- Astronomy, planets, and constellations.
- Cartoon animation and comics.
- Music, especially classical music.
- The animal kingdom, including specific creatures such as horses, reptiles, and insects.
- Architecture, including churches and cathedrals.
- The human body and how it works.
- Dinosaurs
- Specific movies such as *Star Wars*, *Star Trek*, or *The Wizard of Oz*.
- Specific famous people such as prominent scientists and researchers, actors and comedians, or religious figures.

Essential

It may be easy for you to become weary or even fed up with listening to your child discuss her passions. If this describes you, try thinking of all that outpouring of "stuff" as communication. One divorced dad keeps current with his son's interest in heavy metal bands so that the time they share together is made that much more memorable for both because of the lengthy, in-depth, and *reciprocal* conversations they share as father and son.

This list is by no means all-inclusive; the variety of potential passions is endless. At every opportunity, you can find your child steeped in her passion—it's what she wants as gifts for birthdays and holidays or what she enjoys talking about with visiting relatives. You may be astounded at the depth of detail with which your child can conjure up information at will and without effort. She could spend hours absorbed in her most passionate interests, to the point where you might have to insist she take periodic breaks.

Above all else, though, you must understand that your child's personality—her entire identity—is defined by her passions; the two are that closely aligned. How you receive and accept your child's passions will directly impact the quality of your parent-child relationship. You may demonstrate that you value your child's passion by:

- Acknowledging it as a good thing.
- Acknowledging that it is a communication.
- Acknowledging its importance to your child.
- Making time, wherever possible, to interact with your child (looking and listening) about his passion.
- Asking probing questions so that you may learn more.
- Asking probing questions designed to get your child thinking and imagining possibilities related to his passion.
- Suggesting ways your child may introduce family and friends to his passion.
- Partnering with your child to research facets of his passion.
- Participating in out-of-house opportunities you or your child arranges that involve his passion.

How Others Perceive Passions

Be mindful that passions are not always what they appear to be on the surface. Some children's passions have created great concern for adults. The passions may be symbolic and require creative interpretation to ascertain the purity of their motive. Just bear in mind the positive philosophies you have been learning; they will keep you grounded in how you approach these situations.

For example, one young man with Asperger's was passionate about firearms and freely discussed his passion with teachers and classmates. Of course, this alarmed his school administrators who immediately contacted his parents to voice their concerns. While they rightfully erred on the side of caution, what they failed to recognize was that this young man was inherently gentle, and his mental health was unaffected and intact. His interest in guns stemmed from a desire to learn all about how they *worked.* That's all. He had absolutely no intention of harming himself or others. Many teenagers are interested in guns because they hunt, but because this boy had Asperger's, everyone thought the worst.

Your child may develop a passion that you may find alarming due to its subject matter. As a parent, you have the right to set limits around what's acceptable in your home. Your challenge is to determine if the passion is legitimately symbolic of something benign, a possible symptom of depression or PTSD, or a "shock and awe" interest designed to rattle you (typical of many preteens and teenagers).

Similarly, another young man created a similar controversy when he stated that his passion was for medieval torture devices. He spent time in the library reading about them, poring over grisly drawings and diagrams. Again, this caused lots of apprehension on the part of adults—especially because of his diagnosis, which put everyone on edge. When he was allowed a gentle, respectful forum to discuss his passion with someone he trusted, it was discovered that the torture devices weren't so much of a passion as they were a component of an even greater passion. After graduation, he wanted to become a Christian missionary in Third-World countries. He was keenly aware of the potential to be persecuted for his teachings and beliefs and was cognizant that, in some areas of the world, such torture devices are still employed. His rationale in reading about them and understanding how they worked was to gain *knowledge.* He was preparing himself for how they might look and feel should he ever find himself poised to endure their horrors. And yet, he was grossly misinterpreted, and he already understood what it was to feel persecuted for his passion.

In yet another example, one boy spent all his free time drawing comic book–style illustrations with elaborate narratives. His father saw no value in his delicate work and publicly denounced and belittled the boy's art. Because he never made the time to delve further into his son's drawings, the father failed see that the boy had made his dad a central, heroic figure in his comics—a clear communication of the boy's desire to establish a bonding relationship.

Passions and Relationship-Building

In addition to strengthening your personal relationship with your child, her passions can be used to develop additional relationships with others. Because your child could discuss her passions endlessly, it will be important to try to connect her with others similarly impassioned. Your child may already understand that she cannot talk about her passions at school during classroom instruction. But there are other outlets that the school day can provide for social opportunities that build upon her passions. Such opportunities will require the cooperation of teachers, teachers' aides, and others to set up a structure within which the social interactions may occur.

Creating a Comfortable Environment

The lunchroom is often challenging and overwhelming for many children with Asperger's syndrome. It is usually a large, open area filled with many, many children all talking at once. Sometimes there is music playing, silverware clanking, and a social protocol involving where and with whom one sits. Creating "lunch bunch" tables may be an appealing alternative for any number of kids. Your child may know of other children with similar passions, or his teachers may be able to help identify them, even if they are in other grades. The concept is to establish a welcoming structure and routine by assigning students to tables and lunchtime discussion topics based upon their mutual (or similar) passions. If possible, the tables could be moved off to one side of the greater cafeteria environment, away from the distracting noise and visuals, to help foster successful conversations.

Never withhold a passion as a reward to be earned or use it as a punishment as part of your discipline regimen. Your child will grow to resent having someone in authority controlling it instead of allowing him to control it. This does not foster a trusting relationship.

To start, an adult moderator may assist in regulating the conversation, helping the conversation through lulls, and modeling acceptable turn taking during the discussion. The concept is *not* to segregate kids with differences to select tables; the concept is to provide a structure during a typically unstructured time (during which some kids with Asperger's socially flounder). It is nonstigmatizing because the opportunity to participate is open to all, and, depending upon assigned topics, may come to be seen as "cool." Other opportunities to connect socially while building upon passions include after-school clubs, the library, camps, scouts, and other extracurricular activities such as art lessons, horseback riding, martial arts, or swimming.

Communicating via the Internet

Too many people believe that in order for an interaction to be "social" it has to take place in person. How many people do you know in your life that you rarely see but talk to by phone or communicate with via e-mail? Interacting with others using the computer *is* social! There are countless opportunities to make social contacts with others through topic-specific Web sites, chat rooms, message boards, e-mail and e-mail groups, and instant messaging. Of course, you will wish to explain to your child visually, in writing, the rules, cautions, and expectations of using the Internet, including a list of topics that are not appropriate for discussion between children or from an adult to a child.

You may be quite surprised by the eloquent and articulate manner in which some people with Asperger's or autism communicate by e-mail—folks who might otherwise present as socially awkward during in-person dialogue. The reasons for their success include:

- No pressure to respond verbally
- No pressure to reply with immediacy, as in real-time conversation
- No pressure to make eye contact
- No external stimuli or visual distraction to detract one's focus
- The luxury of as much process time as one needs
- The opportunity to be particular in composing and editing one's communication prior to sending a message
- No fear of being judged by others based on appearance
- The pleasure of interacting with others with the same passions

If you or your child is computer savvy, you may even create a personal Web page or Web site to connect people through mutual passions. A circle of friends may grow to international proportions. Additionally, if your child is interested, she should be encouraged to exchange e-mail addresses with friendly classmates in order to maintain social connections after school, on weekends, long holidays, and especially summer vacation. Kids who don't do well conversing by phone because they monopolize the conversation—or have very chatty peers who monopolize the conversation—really flourish when using e-mail to discuss common interests and passions. In fact, you may even glean information from your child that she might not offer verbally, in person, by sending her an e-mail.

Challenges

One challenge your child may face in sharing his passion with his same-age peers, particularly as he enters his teen years, is if the passion is considered juvenile or "babyish." For example, consider the teenage boy who loves *The Powerpuff Girls* cartoon series. His passion is genuine and yet he should exercise discretion to avoid being "set up" as a target of ridicule because of the way others may perceive it. This is a common issue for many children with Asperger's who have passions that have been long-standing since childhood. Such passions may remain constant while the interests of his peers mature into more dynamic areas typical of teens.

The strategy here is twofold. First, privately, gently, and respectfully counsel your child about the ways in which his passion may be perceived. It is important to validate that you "get" it and value it, but explain that others may not see it that way. Visually list the people who can be trusted to discuss the passion unconditionally and without judgment. Next, list places in which it is okay to discuss the passion with these people with some modicum of privacy so others will not overhear, such as your own or a friend's house.

Nowadays, many people—children and adults—are avid collectors of memorabilia devoted to their passions. It's becoming easier for the person with Asperger's syndrome to justify indulging in his passions. The challenge is to balance passions with your parental expectations of responsibilities and obligations.

Second, coach your child to practice "upgrading" the manner in which he presents his passion to others. This means putting a sophisticated spin on it, such as emphasizing how *The Powerpuff Girls* animation team creates the cartoons, or discussing a recent Internet auction in which a rare, limited edition, foreign-market "Bubbles" figurine brought an amazing bid. Articulating this knowledge will go over better than discussing the nuances of a particular episode.

Passions as Bridges to Learning

Once there was a little boy with Asperger's who loved *The Wizard of Oz* more than anything. He had other passions, too, like gargoyles on churches and cathedrals, Greek mythology, and the Loch Ness

Monster, but above all else, Oz ruled. At every opportunity, he would read about Oz or spend endless hours drawing his favorite characters, inventing new adventures for them. When he played with other children, he was the director of elaborate Oz productions for which he insisted upon authenticity from his "actors."

The passion the boy felt for Oz was equaled by his inability to understand numbers. In particular, he struggled with counting items in sets. This required looking at objects or images that were already grouped by fives or tens and knowing that each grouping represented precisely that number. He didn't understand that the concept was to add them together quickly by counting them in sets. Instead, he labored over counting each individual item one at a time. When he did this during a particular math test, he tried to use his fingers to keep count but, of course, lost count and had to start over. As time was running out, he went back and marked each item with a sequential number—the way he knew to count—one, two, three, four, and so on. This was, of course, a very tedious process, and before he knew it, time had run out. He was only on the second problem of a twenty-problem test.

Not only did the boy fail the test, but he was overwhelmed and "blocked" the rest of the day as well. He was physically ill, and felt nauseated, dizzy, headachy, and sweaty. He felt defined by his failure in the moment and could not hear or see or focus upon anything else the rest of the day, so numbing was his experience. He also felt completely inadequate, stupid, and incompetent.

Fact

You may wish to try scheduling a pre-IEP (Individual Education Plan) meeting to discuss with your child's educators those areas of school curriculum with which she is struggling. Come prepared to share your child's passions (with her permission or, better yet, her involvement) and brainstorm ways you can all help her to deconstruct areas of learning using her passions as analogies to understanding.

If only the teacher who noticed the boy's struggle with numbers had also understood and valued his passion for Oz. There was an amazing opportunity awaiting them. She could have found a private time to gently explain that she observed his struggles. She may have suggested another way of demystifying the concept of counting by sets. Knowing his passion, she may have suggested that he work with her to count sets of yellow bricks from the yellow brick road in Oz. Not only would the boy have been relieved of tremendous anxiety, but he would have realized that learning can be fun as well! He would give the teacher his full attention, be engaged and interested, and be poised for success. By building on his passion, he could have also learned additional math concepts such as data and statistics about tornadoes, or the number of miles from the school to Kansas, among others. This concept of cross-walking passions is an educational accommodation that may prove very beneficial to your child.

Noel's mother, Bonnie, has taken the principle of building on her son's passions and expanded it to maximize his learning opportunities. As an example, she wrote:

> Noel just came over to me to point out how two characters on his GameCube speak in Japanese. We talked about how the developers are Japanese and it makes the game interesting. He had discovered the translation by going to a Web site (also good skills for him). This was another chance for Mom to reinforce the value of learning other cultures and languages.

Next, Noel saw a chance to go back in time and connect with scientists, philosophers, and artists of whom he is greatly admiring when he began learning about ancient Greece and Rome. This led to Noel's appreciation for the Latin roots of words common in many languages. By learning the names of Greek and Roman gods, Noel connected that most planets are named after Roman gods. With great gusto, he drew the solar system in elaborate detail with all planet names properly identified. Noel imitated the painting techniques of famous artists in drawings of his own after learning about them, spawned by his passion for history. As Noel grows, the potential to translate his passions to other areas of learning is limitless.

Trieste is another mom who understands the value of her son's passion for numbers coupled with putting her son in control of his passion.

> From age one, my son's passions were letters and numbers. He was reading at eighteen months, and he could count to 500—backward and forward, by odds and evens—by age two. We used both these passions as tools to help him learn numerous skills. Since he loved to read, we presented him with as much information as possible in both written and verbal forms. One example: As a preschooler, he had difficulty following verbal directions from his occupational therapist who wanted him to complete an "obstacle course" of various motor tasks. We placed a large chalkboard in the room and on it we wrote and numbered each of the steps of the obstacle course. He was delighted to read each step aloud and followed the directions easily once he saw them in writing.
>
> When it came to numbers, his object of desire was (and still is!) a digital runner's watch. We carried that watch with us everywhere. One experience I vividly recall is teaching my son to tolerate haircuts. I found a shop that specialized in children's haircuts and zeroed in on a stylist who was particularly patient and easygoing. With the stylist's cooperation, my son would set his stopwatch for five seconds while the stylist cut five "snips" of hair. We increased the time to ten seconds and ten snips, twenty seconds and twenty snips, and so on until, after many, many months, my son could tolerate a complete haircut without any breaks. Although getting a haircut was uncomfortable for my son, he loved the fact that the grownups were sharing in his "watch passion." The look of pure joy on his face when adults played "watch games" with him gave me an early lesson in the value of using passions as bridges to learning and to building relationships.

Never underestimate the power of your child's passions. Think about your child's most passionate interests and brainstorm with her, as well as family and friends, to come up with ways to use the passion to deconstruct and make clearer those areas most challenging to learn. Once you get the hang of it, it will be an enjoyable and bonding experience for all. Incidentally, the boy who loved Oz went on to write popular books on the subject. His enjoyment for drawing the characters led to illustrating an Oz board game. And he was often asked to speak publicly about his passion. He also grew up to become the author of this book.

Some adults with Asperger's syndrome make good teachers or college professors because they've combined their life-long passions with the desire to teach others. Being in control and in authority over a group of students with a scripted lecture only adds to the potential for success as a communicator. Aren't the people you know who are happiest in their chosen field of employment doing what they love?

Passions as Bridges to Employment

You are now becoming increasingly aware of the importance of your child's passions. These subject areas directly relate to his way of being in the world and his aptitude for branching out to learn new things, especially curricula that may be challenging to grasp. Doesn't it also make sense to foster your child's areas of specialty to their fullest potential in order to prepare for future employment opportunities? Many adults work at jobs they dislike, but the luckiest among us have jobs that we love because they interest us.

The time to encourage your child to learn and consume all he can about his passions is now! It doesn't matter that he is a child; he still has the opportunity to become the foremost expert in his field and that can lead to satisfying employment opportunities. Seize the moment; too many people fall back on rushing to find the typical job opportunities at the last minute because a child's high school graduation is impending. Foster your child's passions while he is in elementary and middle school and the range of employment will be far greater when his specialty niche has be so clearly defined that his role in life is apparent to all.

Bonnie's son, Noel, is ten at present. He has a passion for the computer game GameCube, which involves learning color, motion, action, and control. His fascination with all the game's characters enables him to understand what they do and how they do it. Learning the details and game-specific terminology is like learning another language. Over time, Bonnie is supporting Noel in developing career goals all based upon his passion. For example, Noel wants to develop GameCube games using 3DS Max and Flash (computer animation software). He also dreams of developing medical applications using robotics. Bonnie adds:

> Noel wants to learn more about space with the idea that he can use knowledge about gravityless environments to do his inventions or to do space travel (he figures he can use his quick eye-hand coordination that he's developed from playing GameCube). The goals may seem far-reaching or unachievable, but it's not our job as parents to judge this. My job is to help him make the connection between his interests and how he can use that.

The positive approach Bonnie is taking with Noel by building on his passions will be invaluable to him as he grows and furthers his education in pursuit of his visions.

When Is a Passion an OCD?

When we think about people with differences, we can be rather casual in using language that broadens the gap between "more alike than different," such as referring to "our" hobbies and "their" obsessions. The term "obsessive-compulsive disorder" (OCD) is a clinical diagnosis that only a doctor can make. It's true that many children with Asperger's also share an OCD diagnosis—but is it fair or accurate? Remember, the *Diagnostic and Statistical Manual* definition for Asperger's calls for very OCD-sounding behavior as one criteria. For the reasons that we've discussed, this may not portray your child in an appropriate light.

Prior to reading this text, there may have been times when you wished your child's most passionate interest would just disappear and go away. Foremost, it is important that you not withhold a passion as a reward to be earned or use it as a punishment as part of discipline. Imagine struggling to achieve success in an academic area that was your worst subject in school. If your success is contingent upon earning your passion, you'll rarely enjoy it; and you'll resent someone in authority controlling it instead of allowing you to explore it. You know now that this strategy can be severely damaging, breaches trust, and can break your child's spirit. But when is a passion simply a passion, and when is it legitimate OCD?

If you are uncertain if your child's passion might be an obsessive-compulsive disorder, try considering what might be going on for him prior to jumping to conclusions. When did his interest become so intense or all-absorbing? Has he recently had to relinquish control and independence such that the passion has become a safety valve? Try this approach to assess the circumstances before further exploring your concerns.

Every parent has the right to have expectations of his or her child. You expect your child to uphold the standards you've set with regard to house rules and moral obligations. (Hopefully, you've made these expectations concrete for your child by putting them in writing using accessible language and giving your child a copy.) In keeping with having expectations of your child's responsibilities about chores, homework, and other obligations (we all have them), it is fair to set parameters around the amount of time your child indulges in her passion, especially if you can readily foresee the potential for your child to get "lost" in it for long periods of time. Set parameters in partnership with your child with the understanding that you will be flexible in making certain allowances, such as staying up past bedtime on a school night to watch a special TV program.

OCD Criteria

If your child's desire for her passion becomes driven with an intensity that has not previously manifested, it may be cause for concern. OCD occurs when your child has thoughts (obsessions) or physical actions (compulsions) that seem out of her control, such that it becomes unpleasant, very stressful, or harmful for her. This may *or may not* involve her passion; it may involve some new, seemingly odd or purposeless focus on a bodily function, for example, or the need to repeatedly check one's hands for cleanliness. Some "red flag" indicators that your child may have OCD could include the following:

- She is quick to lash out and becomes verbally or physically abusive when you try to redirect her away from her activity.
- Her need to indulge in her activity causes her to lose sleep, skip meals, or be late for school.
- She withdraws from family, friends, and pets in favor of spending unusual amounts of time involved in the activity.
- She cannot seem to focus on or discuss anything but the activity.
- She has lost interest in her appearance, dress, and hygiene because the activity has become all-consuming.

Taking Charge

If you note any of these changes—and they must be changes—in your child, it will be important for you to gather as much information about what you are observing in order to prepare for meeting with a psychiatrist. Follow the same protocol of preparation for such an appointment as you would when seeking an initial diagnosis or exploring other mental health issues. Your doctor may recommend antianxiety or antidepressant medications, including Anafranil, Risperdal, Prozac, Paxil, or Zoloft as treatment to reduce the effects of OCD. As before, be assertive in exploring any recommended medication to learn of its clinical trial (time it takes to notice effectiveness), intended effect, and adverse reactions and side effects to determine if it makes sense for your child.

Essential

If your child takes medication, it is important that she is a partner in understanding why and knowing its potential side effects. One young boy with Asperger's quite clearly communicated how his OCD medication made him feel, saying, "It makes me crazy"—and this showed in his behavior. Listen to your child and consult with your doctor to appropriately adjust or discontinue medication that is not a good match for your child.

In the interim, if your child's passions fit the OCD criteria, you may find yourself needing to reinforce parental parameters by being very firm about scheduling activities and responsibilities, and holding your child accountable. Use visual time frames such as calendars, clocks and watches, and personal schedules to set limits for the amount of time your child is permitted to indulge in an activity, if you can abide it as socially acceptable. Educators will also need to be clear and concrete about rules and responsibilities during the school day. Apply proper disciplinary measures, as suggested in Chapter 4, once you ensure all expectations have been made clear to your child. Appropriate medication may be a sound, time-limited resource for your child, but, as noted in the last chapter, medication can only do so much. If your child receives a clinical OCD diagnosis it will be important to reflect upon the whole person—what's going on in her life and what might be driving this experience? As before, remember that this is a mental health experience that is not your child's fault and may well be beyond her immediate control.

CHAPTER 9

Family Dynamics

Family dynamics can be challenging and complex, especially when faced with learning how best to support a child newly diagnosed with Asperger's syndrome. Another layer of complexity may be added when one (or both parents) has Asperger's as well. With the child's diagnosis may also come thoughts about how Asperger's may impact siblings and other family members. Dealing with this information can be a delicate process for the entire family.

Parents with Asperger's

When you received your child's diagnosis, you probably endured a number of thoughts, feelings, and emotions. It may have been difficult to make sense of them at the time until you sorted them out and processed them through. As you learned more about Asperger's syndrome, some of your thoughts might have begun to crystallize more clearly.

Among these thoughts may have been reflections of the diagnosis as it pertained to you and your own childhood, or that of your spouse. Were there times you endured growing up, or while attending school, that now have meaning? You may find that your child's diagnosis puts into perspective your experiences or makes sense of your spouse's quirks and idiosyncrasies. If your child's differences went unnoticed and undiagnosed until he was in his later childhood years, could it be because no one in your immediate family observed anything unusual about him? Was his way of being already firmly entrenched with your family's typical, ordinary, everyday-life way of being?

These are some of the thoughts you may be pondering, and they are not unusual. This chapter is a resource to mothers and fathers who are beginning to understand that their child comes by his Asperger's syndrome honestly; that is, it may be a genetic reflection of his parents.

Could It Be Genetic?

As previously noted, little factual information is known about Asperger's syndrome. For many, it is an invisible disability because it is so subtle it can go undetected. At present, statistics and other data are sparse, and we may speculate that there are any number of adults with Asperger's living and working in our communities that are undiagnosed. One recent theory hypothesizes that certain types of people with "Asperger-like" traits—smart but antisocial—attract one another, leading to such couples bearing children with the same traits, only magnified due to an overload of genes. Dr. Fred Volkmar, a child psychiatrist at Yale University, estimates that Asperger's correlates with a genetic component more apparent than even autism. Dr. Volkmar suggests that about one-third of fathers or brothers of children with Asperger's show signs of Asperger's themselves, and there also appear to be maternal connections as well. This information increases the likelihood that Asperger's may be present in your own family. Think about your child's lineage—are there, or were there, brilliant and creative but blatantly eccentric family members?

Depending upon your personality and the strength of your coping skills, this may be either relieving or disturbing information to consider. If the diagnosis is given and received with a "gloom and doom" mentality, you may lapse into a period of guilt or self-punishment. You may find yourself unjustly bearing the brunt of blame induced by yourself or your spouse. Parents of children with autism do tend to reflect stress tied to anxiety and depression when compared with parents of typical children. But remember, Asperger's is a naturally occurring experience and is no one's fault. Hopefully, this text will empower you to avoid believing negative Asperger's stereotypes in favor of focusing on the positives.

Psychologist Elaine N. Aron has developed a profile for individuals whom she distinguishes as "highly sensitive people." Her criteria are remarkably similar to traits in those with Asperger's syndrome and may provide a gentle, less-threatening basis from which to enter into a discussion about Asperger's in your family. Check out Dr. Aron's Web site and take her highly sensitive person quiz at *www.hsperson.com*.

Confronting the Possibility

For Dr. Liane Holliday Willey, author of the book *Pretending to be Normal: Living with Asperger's Syndrome*, learning of her daughter's diagnosis was personally liberating because it wasn't until then that she realized she, too, had Asperger's. She defined the experience as reaching the end of a race to be normal. At long last, she embraced self-acceptance and was now in a position to articulate her sensitivities using the framework of Asperger's. Dr. Willey's journey was challenging but she was supported by a husband who walked beside her on the path to self-discovery. Regrettably, not all families handle the experience of recognizing Asperger's in themselves as well as this.

The Struggling Mother

Sarah is a support coordinator for a family that is really struggling. The family that she knows and cares for is processing the Asperger's diagnosis for one child and simultaneously grappling with understanding a father and older brother, both of who are self-diagnosed with Asperger's. The mother fears she and her child will never connect and bond with one another. The family lives in a very rural area where the medical profession offers drug trials or hospitalizations as a method to resolve behaviors without taking into consideration the family dynamics. As such, the mother must confront the fear of making the wrong decision that, she believes, will have a devastating impact on her child and family. This is a mother who continues to grow each day in understanding her child's Asperger's experience, but her husband hasn't shown a desire to understand a person who *doesn't* struggle with Asperger's symptoms. Their marriage has become tense and she lives in fear of losing those she loves most and everything around her. She acquiesces, giving into threats to avoid conflict and confusion by "tip-toeing" around, taking care not to be seen or to say something that may trigger more conflict.

Essential

There are those marriages that simply do not sustain well under real or perceived pressures of raising a child with a different way of being. Families of children with Asperger's syndrome are no exception. Educate and inform yourself and your spouse early on. Connecting with other parents in similar situations can dispel stigmatizing myths and stereotypes.

This family is clearly in need of the kind of professional support that can put Asperger's syndrome into positive perspectives. Yet, the steps toward accepting that support must be agreed upon by all, and that may present challenges.

The Struggling Wife

In another instance, one mother was just beginning to learn about Asperger's syndrome by looking up information on the Internet. Her three-year-old daughter didn't have a formal diagnosis but, when it was suggested that her daughter might have Asperger's, mom took the lead in pursuing it. As wise and intelligent as this mother was, she was unable to see the forest for the trees where her own marriage was concerned. After more than fifteen years with her husband, she could no longer tolerate his moodiness and fragile emotions, his need for solitude, and his socially withdrawn behavior.

As she was gaining more information relative to her daughter, her marriage was crumbling before her. She told her husband she wanted a separation, after which she would pursue a divorce.

Once a professional enabled the mother to see that Asperger's syndrome made sense for her daughter *and* her husband, the walls came crashing down and she finally understood where he was coming from. She realized he was coping the best way he knew how and was certainly not trying to be difficult. He loved his family dearly, and she called off the separation and all notions of divorce.

Recognizing Asperger's in You or Your Spouse

If you find yourself suspecting that you or your spouse also has Asperger's syndrome, please consider the following:

- Arm yourself with knowledge and gather as much information as you can from the Internet or the resources listed in this book.
- Broach the subject with your spouse by asking open-ended or leading questions that will provide opportunity for reflection, like, "Do you think our child gets her love of science from your side of the family?"
- Because you are both still assimilating your child's experience, allow yourself and your spouse time to process this new twist on the situation.
- The conversations you have about Asperger's in the family should build slowly and incrementally.

- Avoid guilt, blame, and finger-pointing accusations like, "It's all your fault our child is this way."
- Offer to explore and research Asperger's syndrome with your spouse or to provide your spouse with whatever literature you've already gathered.
- Discuss marriage counseling or other professional supports in partnership with your spouse.

Understanding Asperger's as a probability for you and your spouse will be a learning time for you both. It can create marital stress and turmoil, or it can be an opportunity to strengthen and enhance your marriage.

Is there an online resource for spouses if one or both are suspected to have Asperger's syndrome?

Yes. Asperger's Syndrome Partners and Individuals Resources, Encouragement and Support, or ASPIRES, is a Web site for spouses and supporters of adults diagnosed (or believed to be) on the autism spectrum, with emphasis on problem solving within marriages and relationships. Check it out at: *www.aspires-relationships.com.*

Sibling Relationships

Some families are remarkably resilient. Through unconditional love, they are able to persevere and meet new challenges while remaining whole and intact. Others seriously struggle or fall apart, and still others fall somewhere in between. Just as your family dynamics determine how your marriage will fare as you understand the significance of Asperger's for you and your spouse, so will your family makeup also determine how your child's brothers and sisters receive the same information. In other words, your children will take their cues from you and your spouse; the attitudes and actions you model will be reflected in them. They will not only project the values about their sibling's differences within the family, they will demonstrate these beliefs in school, the community, and the world at large.

Setting a Positive Example

It is crucial that you work toward setting a positive tone when first presenting your child's Asperger's syndrome to his brothers and sisters. It not only impacts the quality of your immediate family relationships, but it also impacts the ways in which *all* your children perceive all people with differences for the rest of their lives.

When you broach the topic of Asperger's syndrome with your child's siblings, consider these points:

- Partner with your child about the issue of disclosure to agree upon how much or how little to reveal.
- Decide if it's best to share the information with each sibling in privacy or if it should be done with the family as a group.
- Begin by highlighting the ways in which we are all more alike than different.
- Discuss the gifts and talents of your other children first and then discuss those of your child with Asperger's.
- Emphasize Asperger's as a natural experience and dispel fears about it being a contagious disease or something that can suddenly happen to just anyone.
- Don't play the pity card—you want your kids to be kids and to maintain their typical relationships as brothers and sisters, not walk on eggshells.
- Don't put unfair or unrealistic expectations on your child's siblings about increased responsibilities or the burden of future care-taking.
- Do discuss the ways in which the entire family is going to strive toward being more sensitive to the needs of your child—needs previously unacknowledged or unrecognized.

- Talk about respecting your child's ownership of confidentiality, discretion, and disclosure.
- Allow for process time and questions.

Finding a balance in how you love all your children is a fine art for any parent. It may be tough for your other children to see the kind of time you may invest with your child with Asperger's and not feel jealous or envious. Wherever possible, try to engage all your children in any activities that can include them all. If your child with Asperger's is receiving special instruction from an educator or therapist, are there games and routines that your entire family can take on? This will work toward family bonding, patience, and tolerance, and it will make learning fun for your child with Asperger's. The more you treat your child's way of being as natural and "no big deal," the more your child's siblings will automatically pitch in, help out, and pick up the slack without thinking or complaining beyond typical sibling bickering. The terrific ripple effect from this will be in how your children will grow to value diversity in all people.

Helping Siblings Cope

Still, there will be occasions when your child's siblings require your solid parental support when they are unable to manage or self-regulate internal or external pressures. Some pitfalls to be mindful of in observing your child's siblings may include coping with:

- Manifestation of mental health issues due to the stress (self-imposed or imposed by you), especially in older daughters who may develop depression or an eating disorder
- Perceived embarrassment caused by their sibling's way of being, especially in public
- Being ostracized by peers who don't want to hang around them or come over to your house because of your child with Asperger's
- Feeling perpetually pressured to "parent" or protect their sibling with Asperger's

- Becoming weary and worn out from constantly defending their sibling
- Feeling guilty when they want to go places and do things alone
- Feeling pressured by peers to reject their sibling

As your child's brothers and sisters grow and mature, their sibling relationships can become strained. They may take on other interests and broaden their circle of friends and as a result, the child with Asperger's (who may remain static despite ongoing change) is left out. Remember that change can be very difficult and saddening for your child and he may require you to facilitate scheduled "family" or "sibling" time to help him cope.

Hopefully, none of these areas will manifest as concerns because you and your family have, from day one of the Asperger's diagnosis, set a positive, inclusive tone in relation to each family member's place in the home, school, and community. But if you should recognize problems in any of these areas, it will be important to have a private "pow-wow" with your child's siblings to offer your love, praise, and reassurances. Are there ways that you can compensate in partnership with your other children, especially if they've been feeling left out? Parenting is never set in stone; it changes from moment to moment. Be willing to admit it's true if you've inadvertently been neglectful. Plan some quality time with your child's siblings apart from the rest of the family. It may be rejuvenating for you all.

Extended Family

Revealing your child's Asperger's syndrome diagnosis to extended family members is an issue of disclosure. Sharing such information should occur in partnership with your child in order to determine how much or how little others need to know.

Do They Need to Know?

In weighing your decision, please consider the following:

- How often do you see these relatives?
- If you only see them once or twice a year, is it necessary to say anything?
- Can you foresee their reactions?
- If there's potential for gross misunderstanding, how will you handle that?
- If they are intrigued and interested, how will you handle that without breaching your child's trust about disclosure (sharing more than what you agreed upon)?
- Can extended family be entrusted to honor disclosure?
- Can they treat the subject with sensitivity and respect?

In the long run, the pros may outweigh the cons, and you and your child may decide it's simply no one's business at present. So many children with Asperger's can artfully "pass" and blend for the duration of a day with family that any differences may go completely unnoticed given all the other distractions. (Is it possible that your child comes across as downright complacent when compared to some of the more flamboyant children and adults at some of those gatherings?)

Prepare for Their Reactions

If you decide it is appropriate to disclose information about your child's diagnosis, you may need to be prepared to deal with the potential for extended family to show their ignorance (not a bad thing if they're open to education), overcompensation, or discomfort. You will need to consider how best to quell any situations that may arise from overreactions should your extended family express their concern about the entire family being stigmatized by the diagnosis.

They may openly express hopelessness for your child's way of being, deluge you with literature that focuses on cures or "quick fixes," or, worse yet, confuse Asperger's syndrome with autism or some other diagnosis. Passive-aggressive behavior may transpire if extended family members become increasingly distant due to their own issues in processing the information, or only want to spend time with your other children. The worst-case scenario may be if they exclude or uninvite you and your child from future family get-togethers. A better scenario might be if they are overly cautious—trying not to do or say the wrong thing. In the latter situation, there is, at least, a way to offer assurances and education.

Hopefully, your wisdom and savvy as a parent who is fast learning to be a strong and knowledgeable advocate will be of good service to you in setting the proper tone of sensitivity, respect, and unconditional love where extended family is concerned. In any case, to aid your child in surviving a day or more with extended family, you will wish to arm her with ammunition in the form of self-advocacy and coping skills prior to attending family gatherings.

Fact

You may be approached by family, friends, and relatives who genuinely desire to learn more about Asperger's syndrome. Hear them out and allow your intuition to guide you in how much you wish to be their single "point of contact" where all things Asperger's are concerned. You may want to let them borrow this book for starters or refer them to specific Web sites that you found of good service.

Agree upon the time duration of being there (and *stick to it!*), and ensure that your child has some materials related to her passion to quietly indulge in if she feels overwhelmed. Also be certain to locate an area where your child can retreat, undisturbed by others, to recuperate during much needed "downtime." Show her where it is and assure her that she may use it at will. Check with your family in advance to find out what materials your child may access with their permission. Then, make sure your child knows where books, TV or videos, crayons, pen or paper, and Internet access can be found for solitary downtime activities. Other strategies that will be of enormous benefit in such situations will be discussed in detail later on in this book.

Your Community

Sharing information about your child with neighbors, acquaintances, or total strangers in your community is no different than the process of determining when, where, and how to share the same information with family. Weigh carefully the drawbacks and positives that may come from sharing this information. It is an issue of disclosure that you should discus in advance with your child in order to be as considerate and respectful of his feelings as possible. As before, ideally, your child should be encouraged to be his own advocate as early as possible in order to decide how much or how little to tell others about his way of being, if it's even necessary at all.

Some parents find themselves exasperated and embarrassed by their child's public meltdowns. They may garner stares, raised eyebrows, whispers, or flat-out denouncements of "Why can't you control your child?!" There are those who decide to forego discretion and bluntly address gawking onlookers by revealing there child's diagnosis right there, on the spot. They may pass out "For Your Information" business-size cards that state, "My child has Asperger's syndrome and this is what you might see," followed by a list of meltdown behaviors or behaviors others may find quite peculiar. The mother of one young girl explained her daughter's prolonged staring at a neighborlady exclusively in terms of her Asperger's syndrome.

You may find yourself in the position of these parents who want to educate others and simply want a little patience and understanding in the moment. But are you best serving your child by revealing such intimate information, or are you fueling misperceptions and stereotypes—especially if you explain "This is Asperger's syndrome"—at the height of your child's public meltdown? Aren't you, in effect, sending a message to the community that "This is what Asperger's syndrome *looks* like"? You know Asperger's syndrome encompasses many things, and your child's inability to endure certain environmental stimuli is but one sliver of who he is as a human being. Think of the impressions people take away with them after being told, "This is Asperger's syndrome." Would you want to be regarded in this way when you know you aren't at your best and you're coping the best way you know how?

Gradually you'll learn (through trial and error) the situations and environments not conducive to your child's sensitivities. Be careful of sharing too much personal information during public meltdowns. Contain meltdowns as quickly and concisely as possible (easier said than done, as this is what you'd wish for any of your children). Remember to ask yourself if you would be willing to offer strangers the same information about yourself.

As one mom asked, "Isn't it okay to express your anger, upset, and disappointment to your child for the way she behaved?" We're all human and as the parent of a child with a different way of being, nerves will fray and are bound to wear thin. In these times, you would vent your frustration to *any* of your children. Bottom line is, parents can "lose" it from time to time, but before expressing your extreme dissatisfaction with your child's conduct, ask yourself:

- Am I being fair?
- Am I making this an issue about Asperger's?
- Am I disclosing information publicly out of anger?
- Have I been clear in giving my child concrete, visual information in advance about my expectations?

If you believe you've been fair, then remember to focus on addressing your child's behavior in the community as inappropriate to the environment, instead of making it about Asperger's syndrome. The mom who "outed" her daughter when she stared at a woman too long had the best solution of all. She decided that, next time, she would simply point out that her daughter appreciated the diversity of people's faces, jewelry, and clothing. She may be surprised at the way her positive "spin" creates an opportunity for relationship building.

CHAPTER 10

Fostering Relationships

Because your child may have difficulty perceiving the ebb and flow of typical social interactions, she may feel uncomfortable or pegged as socially "awkward" when it comes to conversation with her peers. Navigating the ins and outs of everyday communications can be an art for any one of us. With your support, your child can grow to learn ways to improvise and improve the quality of those interactions.

Your Child's Interactions

When you consider your child as an individual with Asperger's syndrome, how does he fare in social conversation? Some children may appear shy and withdrawn, rarely speaking unless spoken to. Others may dominate the conversation with lengthy discussions about their most passionate interests. Your child may reflect these traits at different times, or fall somewhere in between. The social interaction skills you instill in your child now will have long-term benefit as he matures through adolescence and into adulthood. Learning how to develop social circles and relationships that can lead to friendship is important to your child's future successes and mental health stability.

The child who appears shy and withdrawn likely wants to feel welcomed and included by others but doesn't know where to begin. Similarly, the child who releases the equivalent of a verbal dissertation knows how to talk circles around that topic and may think that everyone has the same degree of interest such that they are spellbound. This child also doesn't realize the mechanics of social conversation.

The Dance of Reciprocal Flow

As metaphors and analogies help to enhance our understanding, consider that, in both instances, each child wishes to partake in the "Dance of Reciprocal Flow" (not to be confused with "The Electric Slide"). The first child is partnerless, awaiting an invitation to the dance. When the invitation doesn't come, she may feel hopeless. She may internalize these feelings, frustrated by not understanding others or herself. This may lead to a sense of guilt or blame, which could fuel depression. The second child has leaped into the dance without first having learned the steps. He, too, is partnerless but believes that all those present are his exclusive dance partners, available to him at any given moment. Both children are set up to be singled out for their differences and potentially stigmatized for not knowing the dance that most everyone else was *born* knowing, or absorbed simply by growing up neurotypical.

Developing friendships means either learning the Dance of Reciprocal Flow (and some are more masterful dancers than others), or approximating it well enough such that one blends nearly seamlessly for the time spent on the dance floor. It is a gradual process. Not one of us masters the dance immediately; we improve and gain more confidence as we practice the dance steps. As you've learned, most children with Asperger's syndrome assimilate information in ways that are concrete and visual.

As your child's instructor in the Dance of Reciprocal Flow, you will wish to map this out for her, similar to the way that some people learn to dance by following the black, silhouetted footprints positioned on the floor. As they memorize the dance routine and position of each step, they make fewer and fewer missteps. The dance becomes more fluid, requiring less effort and less thought. Finally, the footprint outlines fade altogether. They are now visible only in one's consciousness, unseen by others. Some will require intermittent, periodic "polishing" to brush up on the dance steps; others will retain it always, permanently etched in their minds. The importance in learning the dance is to know when and where to buoy your partner so that you both work together to create one whole presentation.

How often have you had a friendship damaged, harmed, or extinguished altogether as a result of misunderstandings or misinterpretations of communication? It happens all the time, every day. You may have a natural advantage in knowing how to adeptly discern slang and sarcasm, tempered with understanding body language, facial expressions, eye gaze, and the tone and timbre of one's voice. Remember, for many people with Asperger's, this must all be learned.

A challenge is that, while everyone dances the dance, we've all had different instructors or role models. As such, we approach the dance with our unique, individual style and flair, reflective of our personality. Some of us may even improvise and break the rules, like those with a penchant for interrupting conversation or talking with their mouth full of food or gum. These nuances make discerning appropriate conversational flow difficult, but it really is a matter of etiquette. Your child should never be faulted for being polite during conversation, even if it sounds a bit "stiff" or formal.

Using Music to Teach

To poise your child for developing friends, you will wish to explain the Dance of Reciprocal Flow using a similar analogy—unless your child is passionate about dancing and would relate well. Another analogy that might be helpful in your child's understanding may include deconstructing your child's favorite song. Music can be extremely important to kids with Asperger's, and all music is based upon the principle of call and response. According to the song's composition, there is a time when one sings or plays an instrument; this is the "call." Then there are times to pause and remain silent in order to await the "response." It is similar to the way in which two-way conversation is supposed to work.

To solidify this concept, you will want to draw this with your child while you start and stop the song. Help your child identify one singer or one instrument and represent that on paper. Your child may even wish to use different colors to differentiate the participants in the song. Break the song down into portions and support your child to understand how all the pieces flow through call and response. In the most basic example, think of "Frère Jacques." If sung in "round robin" style, the song begins with the initial call being echoed in a response as additional communication partners are gradually added in.

Using Cartoon Characters to Teach

Your child may respond well to understanding social conversation when her favorite TV cartoon characters are involved. Again, it will be best if you are in a position to start and stop the action in order to highlight good and inappropriate conversation styles.

Fact

Visuals are very useful survival tools in learning for many children with Asperger's syndrome. Your child may already enjoy drawing or creating computer art now. Often, kids fabricate elaborate characters and complex plots and scenarios. It might be good sense to build upon that when mapping or reviewing social interactions between real-life people known by you and your child.

Help your child to reinforce what she's just seen by drawing it out on paper. Suggest that you both modify the conversation a bit. It may be a good, objective opportunity to demystify a real-time social interaction that failed your child. Using cartoon characters to take on a similar situation is a nonthreatening way for your child to deconstruct the issues. When finished, you may ask, "Isn't this like what happened with you and Leslie last Saturday?" Next, discuss ways your child might approach the situation differently if similar circumstances arise.

Other useful analogies to conversation may include observing how animals interact and envisioning their "voices," or using the concept of maps where streets and highways converge and intersect. As always, maximize the benefit by using words and pictures, reviewing the information routinely until it is no longer needed.

Conversational "Bag of Tricks"

Another way to get to know others with the goal of making friends is to have a "bag of tricks," consisting of Conversation Starters and Enders. Developing a repertoire of such tricks or skills will be of lifelong good service. Many children with Asperger's have terrific rote memories if they are able to create images of situations to best "match" the Conversation Starter or Ender. To begin, partner with your child to break down, in writing and pictures, lists for each area. Here are a few sample Conversation Starters:

- Greetings like "What's up?" "How's it going?" or "Hey" are fine for interacting with typical peers.
- More respectful greetings for teachers and other adults may include, "Good morning/afternoon, Mr. Eschelman," or simply, "Hello" or "Hi."
- "What did you do over the weekend?"
- "What did you watch on TV last night?"
- "What are you doing after school?"

Sample Conversation Enders may include:

- "I gotta go now."
- "I'll catch (or see, or talk to) you later."

- "Take it easy."
- "See you tomorrow (or tonight, or Monday)."

With your child, try coming up with additions to the list. What do favorite cartoon or TV characters use as Conversation Starters or Enders that are socially acceptable and fit well on these lists? Talk about how no one "owns" these Conversation Starters or Enders; anyone can use them. Your child will need to be prepared for what comes next should he not initiate a Starter or Ender.

Feedbacks and "Slip-Ins"

Next, discuss and map out lists for Conversation Feedbacks and Conversation "Slip-Ins." Conversation Feedbacks are responses to Conversation Starters or Enders initiated by someone else. Conversation Feedbacks may include responding with a question in order to elicit more information from the other person. Think of it like constructing a building or a model of some structure. Each piece of the conversation can add layers to the foundation either person began. When conversation changes topic, the process should begin anew—even if the building is uncompleted.

Still, there may be times when we don't know how to respond and a simple, affirming interjection will indicate that we're at least listening. Conversation Feedbacks are always useful tools to "fall back on" whenever one is uncertain of what to say and may include phrases such as:

- "I don't know what that is; tell me more."
- "I never heard of that before; can you explain it better to me?"
- "That's really neat!" or "That's interesting!"
- "Cool!" or "Awesome!"
- "I'm sorry about that."

Conversation Slip-Ins are socially acceptable alternatives to interrupting conversation. Your child will need to appreciate, through words and images, that it is considered rude to interrupt in conversation, but there are ways to "slip in" without being rude. You and your child will wish to identify when this works best (usually during a conversation lull or when someone has stopped talking). Conversation Slip-Ins may include:

- "Is it okay if I say something now?"
- "Excuse me, please."
- "May I add to what you're saying?"
- "Pardon me for interrupting." (formal or professional setting)

Essential

Interestingly enough, many adults with Asperger's syndrome concede their struggle to understand the flow of conversation. Some have said it's tough determining where to appropriately pause or interject. One man had no idea he was being rude by constantly interrupting others until a close friend gently brought it to his attention.

Some of these might be too formal for a child and would better suit a young adult. Perhaps you and your child can come up with others to add to this list. Once all the lists are in writing with images (or keyed into the computer), your child will be in a better position to practice these strategies in real-time situations. If you are very familiar with how you have both formatted or coded the information into imagery, you can support your child by discretely coaching her to call up the proper analogy suited to the moment. (For example, "Remember, this is just like when Daphne told Scooby Doo, 'Take it easy.'") Mistakes and unexpected circumstances are bound to arise, and these will require private and respectful debriefing to explain. With time, you and your child can modify and adapt his bag of tricks to become adept in the Dance of Reciprocal Flow.

Opportunities for Bonding

There is no guarantee that understanding how conversation flows will lead to friendships. As previously discussed, building upon your child's most passionate interests and connecting to others with the same, or similar, passions will usually foster a depth to the relationship beyond mere surface conversation. Where your child may need you is in fostering situations in which she can meet others who are as equally impassioned. Once connected with at least one other peer who "gets" her and speaks the same language, your child will feel terrific. Knowing that others value what she has to offer will bolster her self-esteem. There is no better way to feel bonded with others than through mutual love of something or someone.

Finding Opportunities

What opportunities are available in your community by which you can support your child in making contacts to build upon his passion for insects, astronomy, Japanese animation, or other topics? If you are uncertain, start by pursuing the following:

- Programs and special events offered by your local library.
- Community projects or special celebration days.
- Opportunities offered through the newspaper, local circulars, or "merchandiser" type papers.
- Opportunities offered through local television and radio stations.
- Community classes such as arts and crafts, or martial arts.
- After-school activities sponsored by your school district.
- Programs and special events offered by your local historical society or museums.
- Special events sponsored by local athletic leagues.

You may find other venues in your community to add to this list. As noted before, one of the most powerful and advantageous ways to connect with others with similar passions is through the Internet. The possibilities are endless. Your child may learn more about other kids of the same age, beyond just the passion they share, by locating them on a map and learning about the local industry, economy, and more. The child passionate about Japanese animation may even have the chance to communicate with someone of that culture. They can compare notes and exchange ideas about the video games each is developing.

Your child's use of the Internet should be determined by the same rules and cautions you'd set for any of your children, but communication with others by e-mail or instant messaging is social and it should be valued as such.

Social "Practice" Groups

In some communities, parents and professionals have banded together to form meeting groups for kids with Asperger's syndrome. These gatherings provide a forum for unconditional acceptance in a safe and comfortable environment. Such groups do not advocate exclusion from typical children; rather, they are an opportunity for some children to learn social skills in a place where it's perfectly acceptable to mess up as you learn and practice.

One such social group for kids was initiated in Cherry Hill, New Jersey, in the spring of 2003. The Friendship Club was begun by a group of interested parents wanting activities and resources for their children with Asperger's. The program is sponsored through the Jewish Family and Children's Service of Southern New Jersey and staffed by parents, educators, and therapists.

The group meets weekly, teaching socially accepted rules and skills through role-playing games and worksheets. The lessons may involve comprehending that it's okay to make mistakes, dealing with teasing from others, or learning how to take "no" for an answer without melting down. The Friendship Club also emphasizes practicing eye contact and turn taking in conversation. Visibly posted rules and goals aid the children in staying focused when they require visual reminders.

Your local school district or county human service program may be able to tell you if any such meeting group already exists in your town or a neighboring town. If there is no such gathering group in your community, you may wish to consider establishing something similar in your area. Most likely, parents, previously unconnected, will want to meet in person to discuss the similarities of their lives; but the focus in this instance will need to be on supporting the children to meet their individual needs in a comfortable atmosphere.

Finding Allies

When your child becomes an independent adult, you want him to know how to surround himself with good, honest, and trustworthy people who will be kind and understanding of his different way of being. Such folks will be there for your child (and vice versa) unconditionally to aid him in navigating real life when he needs it. Professionals in your child's life may come and go. An ally is someone not paid to be a participant in your child's life and who is there for the long haul. Empowering your child to identify the qualities that make a strong, reliable ally is paramount.

Fact

Your child's closest allies should be immediately apparent to you. They are those persons to whom she naturally gravitates and who welcome her unconditionally. Can you accept that, despite being a parent, you may not be considered by your child to be an ally? Allies should be natural—not forced—relationships in order for them to endure.

Allies may include siblings (without external, parental pressure to be caregivers), extended family, neighbors, friends, members of the clergy, and others. An ally may even be someone in a romantic context; the person in your child's young adult or adult life that becomes his partner or spouse. Of course, there are no guarantees that an ally will remain a permanent fixture—people move, change jobs, divorce, or drift apart. But ally relationships tend to be long-standing personal investments.

Allies can serve as friends, confidantes, and advocates. Sam's next-door neighbor in the movie *I am Sam* is a good example of an ally—someone who takes a strong personal interest in seeing an individual succeed despite his differences. Sam's neighbor is an older woman who is accessible to him when he needs her, especially for tips in raising his baby. The relationship is not one-sided, however, and the woman derives great pleasure from watching Sam grow and learn about life as a parent.

The qualities found in long term-allies may include someone who:

- Accepts your child just as she is.
- Is patient, sensitive, and loving.
- Makes the time to be present with your child.
- Returns phone calls and e-mails promptly and reliably.
- Is interested and intrigued by your child's passions.
- Is willing to apply his or her own life experiences and expertise to the relationship with your child.
- Believes your child is a beautiful, gifted human being with lots to offer the world.

Some kids with Asperger's relate better to adults. Because your child may portray herself as adultlike in her use of conversational language and interests, she may be treated as an equal and indulged by other adults. Your child may already have a strong rapport with one or more of your adult friends. This is okay—relationships are relationships; don't knock it. While you and your child continue to seek opportunities to connect with same-age peers, do not discourage your child from developing relationships with adults (unless you suspect their motives to be impure, which is likely not the case). If you seek to squelch those relationships simply because of age differences, it could be devastating to your child. Weigh your child's relationships with adults with your comfort level and allow your intuitions to guide you.

Is It Okay to Be Alone?

It is a stereotype that people with Asperger's syndrome want to live solitary lives and deliberately isolate themselves from society in hermitlike existence. As more children are recognized to have Asperger's, there is a broadening awareness of the diversity among *all* people.

Essential

Many of us cope with everyday stressors by indulging in our own personal relaxation techniques and routines, free from the demands of others. You may consider it *"my time."* Some people exercise, soak in a hot tub, read, or watch TV. We are all more alike than different, yet oftentimes parents and professionals place demands upon children as soon as they come through the door from school.

Remember the phrase "inherently gentle and exquisitely sensitive"? When one is bombarded daily by sensory stimuli that is irritating or hurtful, or when one is challenged to decipher the logic and rationale of others, it can become physically, mentally, and emotionally exhausting. We all relish our downtime—those fleeting opportunities when we can change into comfortable clothes, relax, and reward ourselves for having made it through another day. The child with Asperger's is no different, but his desire to be alone can be perceived as "abnormal" simply because the clinical diagnosis says so.

As a parent, you will wish to set rules for all your children about free time versus time you expect chores and homework to be accomplished. It is likely that your child with Asperger's loves nothing more than becoming deeply absorbed in his most passionate of interests—reading, drawing, Internet surfing, or watching TV. Ask that he abide by the rules you have agreed on, but don't penalize him for losing track of time unless you have just cause to believe it is deliberate. Be cautious of imposing your own biases about how "long is too long" to spend alone. (If you suspect your child might be experiencing a symptom of depression, then you will notice his need to withdraw becomes more and more pronounced.)

You may also have expectations about what being "social" should look like. But "social" should be defined differently for each individual, depending on that person's needs. You may value many friends as a mark of being socially successful. Some people with Asperger's are content with just a very few, select friends. Many are not social butterflies, don't wish to be, and never will be. Unless they wish to endeavor to become more social, such individuals may simply be the kind of folks who are completely comfortable with a small group of close-knit people. As a parent, you can arrange to expose your child to a variety of people within a range of environments and circumstances. Your child will guide you to those with whom she feels connected and wishes to know better.

CHAPTER 11

Educational Programming

Wherever possible, children with Asperger's syndrome should be fully included with their same-age peers in regular classrooms. In an inclusive environment, your child may enjoy the opportunity to grow socially and academically. But inclusion, in and of itself, is not enough. A range of professionals who support your child's education must have a working understanding of your child's individual needs. Without such collaboration, your child may face social and educational challenges in a typical school environment.

Your Child's School Experience

One distinct advantage to obtaining a formal Asperger's syndrome diagnosis for your child is that she will be eligible to receive certain educational services and supports. (As Asperger's is not an "officially" eligible diagnosis, according to federal law, your child's eligibility may be determined with a diagnosis of autism, other health impairment, or speech and language impairment. This is explained in the next section.) One reason why school districts are sometimes unable to provide such services is because the child has not been identified as needing support services. In some instances, even if educators are aware of your child's diagnosis, some may misinterpret your child's individual attributes. Sometimes, children with Asperger's are accused of being "lazy," inattentive, or simply not applying themselves to the best of

their abilities. This may be true in some children (as it may be for any neurotypical child) but such accusations have become so overused that they are Asperger's stereotypes. In other examples, schools may overlook the child who maintains during the day (by being quiet or compliant) but has legitimate educational needs.

Other children, who are fine academic achievers but experience meltdowns during the day, may be "missed" by school districts for needing a select educational program. Instead, such students may be placed in classrooms for children with emotional disturbances.

Such placements may be truly harmful to the child with Asperger's. In one instance, a child was set up to fail and the self-fulfilling prophecy was perpetuated. This particular fifteen-year-old had Asperger's and was extremely sensitive to touch. One day he was very upset about not receiving his report card when he expected it. When his teacher touched his shoulder, he reacted by striking her. The school resisted the Asperger's syndrome diagnosis in favor of (inappropriately) placing the boy in a classroom for emotionally disturbed students.

Individuals with Disabilities Education Act

A safeguard to ensure that your child's educational needs are met by your school district is the Individuals with Disabilities Education Act, known as IDEA. (In this instance, the word "disabilities" is a necessary evil, and it shouldn't define how you or the world view your son or daughter.) IDEA is the federal law that guarantees your child's entitlement to a Free and Appropriate Public Education (FAPE). The types of disabilities covered by IDEA include the following:

- Autism
- Mental retardation
- Hearing impairment (including deafness)
- Speech or language impairment
- Visual impairment (including blindness)
- Serious emotional disturbance
- Orthopedic impairment

- Traumatic brain injury
- Other health impairment
- Specific learning disability

Fact

Your child's most pressing needs, as you see them, may not be academic at all but social. This subtlety may be challenging for your child's educators to concede, and this may lead to unfair labeling of your child's way of being. Remain confident of the fact that you know your child best, and advocate on her behalf.

As noted, some school districts may oppose the need for an individualized education plan as it applies to the child with Asperger's based upon this list, or based upon the failure to recognize the educational implications of Asperger's. The last bullet, "specific learning disability," may apply to your situation if your child "does not achieve commensurate with his or her age and ability levels," or if your child "has a severe discrepancy between achievement and intellectual ability" in one or more of the following areas:

- Oral expression
- Listening comprehension
- Written comprehension
- Basic reading skills
- Reading comprehension
- Mathematics calculation
- Mathematics reasoning

These are all areas identified by IDEA (specifically in 34 CFR, section 300.341). As you can see, many children with Asperger's may readily qualify for educational support—especially the comprehension portions—based upon the breakdown definition of "specific learning disability." Other school districts may use the designation of "other health impairment" to qualify a child with Asperger's. This is where a comprehensive evaluation by a psychologist, psychiatrist, or other qualified professional experienced in diagnosing Asperger's syndrome will be most helpful. The school district should offer to provide such an evaluation if you do not already have a diagnosis for your child. If not, the process can be initiated at your request. Ensure that you make this request in writing, include language giving your consent to an evaluation, and retain a copy for your records.

The conclusions of the professional conducting the evaluation will likely show discrepancies between your child's intellectual abilities and his ability to achieve in any of the previously listed areas. This is vital in order for your school district to appropriately qualify your child for an educational program designed to meet her needs. (Districts are mandated to have "Child Find" policies in effect to identify, locate, and evaluate children who may be protected under IDEA.) In this way, you can begin to establish a proactive, working partnership with your school district.

A comprehensive evaluation by a professional experienced in identifying Asperger's syndrome should also contain recommendations for how you and your child's educational team might move forward in developing a plan to support your child.

Special Education

The phrase "special education" can be very frightening to some parents. It may conjure images of your own recollections of classes tucked away in far corners or the basement of a school, and peopled exclusively by children with mental retardation. Remember FAPE? Part of the acronym stands for "Appropriate Education." Placing your child with Asperger's syndrome in a stereotypical special education classroom with children not on par with his educational intellect (meaning those with mental retardation) would be inappropriate. (In fact, IDEA provides that, wherever possible, *all* children with disabilities, including mental retardation, should receive their education alongside typical peers such that there is gradual momentum toward phasing out special education classrooms.)

Many children with Asperger's syndrome communicate their desire to just fit in and be like the other kids. And yet, some may have daily needs for which they are unready, unable, or unwilling to articulate. Be prepared to creatively discuss options and opportunities to include your child throughout the school day.

So if someone from your school district happens to slip and use the phrase "special education" in reference to your child, don't freak out immediately; this person has most likely used the term *generically*. But do ask for specific clarification. Nowadays, special education can take many forms of service, and may be as subtle as supporting your child's learning comprehension using a teacher's aide, for example.

Developing a Plan

The evaluation for your child should determine his special education (or related service) needs and will generate an appointment for a team meeting to develop an Individualized Education Plan, or IEP. The IEP is the document that will detail, in writing, an individualized approach to meeting the unique needs of your child. The team should include:

- You and your spouse.
- One regular education teacher.
- One special education teacher.
- A school representative who can make decisions about the delivery of services (usually the building principal).
- Someone who can interpret the evaluation results as they apply to your child's educational instruction.

- Other participants with special expertise or knowledge of your child.

Your child may also participate if he chooses to be present. Participants with special expertise may include a parent advocate knowledgeable about IDEA and the IEP process, a professional consultant who specializes in developing IEPs, or a professional consultant who specializes in Asperger's syndrome. Finding a specialist can be a crucial issue, and it can be frustrating to both parents and school officials when one is not accessible.

At this point in our collective learning curve (and depending upon your geographic location), it may not be realistic to have the expectation that your child will be taught by a teacher experienced in educating students with Asperger's syndrome. Because you know your child best, you may become fiercely protective and defensive of what you believe your child needs. On the other hand, most willing and cooperative school districts may lack such expertise and may be of the position that they are doing all they can. Such disputes are addressed later in this chapter.

The Evaluation Process

If you have requested that your school district evaluate your child, the district must comply, and this process should be completed within sixty days after your first written request. Following this, the district will ask that you sign a "Permission to Evaluate" form. The evaluation should be completed within sixty days after your *original written request* (that contains consent from you to evaluate your child) *not* sixty days after you've signed the permission form. Once the evaluation is completed, a team meeting should be convened to review the evaluation. You should receive your child's evaluation well in advance of the team meeting, but no later than ten days prior to such a meeting. This team meeting may also serve as the first IEP meeting if you wish.

If your child has been deemed eligible for services, IEP team members should be identified, and the first meeting should occur within thirty calendar days of the original determination of eligibility. The completed IEP must then be implemented within ten school days. It must also be reviewed yearly and can be revisited in a team meeting *upon your request* outside of the annual meeting date. The IEP must also be in effect for your child at the beginning of each new school year.

Don't be intimated to request an advance, blank copy of the tool that will be used to evaluate your child. It will help you understand the special education services process and provide indicators of areas in which your child may excel or fail. One excellent Web site with information on special education law is *www.wrightslaw.org.*

Creating the Individual Education Plan

The initial IEP meeting is the time and place to develop the document that will be the blueprint for your child's educators. The draft document should be transcribed into the final document immediately following the meeting. It should include:

- A cover sheet with a sign-in page listing all participants.
- An acknowledgment of your child's eligibility.
- An area for you to sign, acknowledging that the school district has provided you with a copy of your rights during the process, known as "procedural safeguards."
- Basic information such as your contact numbers and address, your child's date of birth, and anticipated year of graduation.
- A list of "special considerations," such as visual or hearing impairment, behaviors that impede your child's ability to learn (or that of classmates), and communication issues.

- A summary of your child's strengths (his passions and interests).
- A summary of your child's needs (those areas in which he requires special support).

A strong IEP team should be able to find a balance between your child's strengths and needs. Too often, such meetings can focus upon issues that others may perceive as "behavioral" or emotional disturbances. When this occurs, teams get sidetracked and lose their focus. Teams may digress and deteriorate. Parents may leave feeling angry or upset, and the self-fulfilling prophecy is perpetuated. For this reason, and particularly in very sensitive situations, it is advisable to have a professional in attendance who fits the bill of "other participants with special expertise or knowledge of your child." In partnership with the team, this person can help keep things focused on your child as a child first and foremost.

Establishing Goals

The next step is to set IEP goals that are specific to your child's strengths and needs in order to track your child's educational progress and ensure that the team is implementing what they committed to doing. The goals should be realistically achievable for your child and written in such a way that they are easy to track or "measure," in order to see your child's growth and keep the team accountable. For example, an appropriate goal for a kid with Asperger's of any age might be in the area of developing computer skills (if she's not already a computer wizard). While this may sound rather generic, the spin here is to make it specific to your child's Asperger's. The purpose of the goal should be clearly stated, such as a goal for accessing the Internet: "The student will develop skills to use a computer to communicate, to gain information, and to increase social relationships independently three out of five times." Next, objectives to meet the goal should be identified in sequence. The sequence for the computer goal might look like this:

- The student will learn the functions of the computer, including turning the computer on, signing on to the Internet, and using the keyboard and other functions while exploring her passions (such as searching for information about insects as they relate to a lesson plan).
- The student will create and access a file and store information she wishes to save in the file.
- The student will learn methods to access social interaction through electronic media (e-mail).

A method and schedule of evaluation for each goal objective should also be included. For example, the method for the last objective listed might read, "During computer learning opportunities, the student will be afforded opportunity to increase social interactions by learning to use e-mail and other communication avenues."

Essential

Consistency in communication of your child's needs from school year to school year is imperative. Don't take for granted that strategies, adaptations, and accommodations discussed but *not* recorded in your child's IEP will be carried over unless they are clearly documented. This assures accountability as well as consistent support.

A goal for enhancing self-advocacy might address your child's ability to identify and communicate her sensory sensitivities in the school environment. A goal or objective might read, "The student will be able to communicate in a socially acceptable manner the specific change she requires in her educational environment four out of five times." The method should include supporting the child to identify environmental stimuli that are irritants and detract from learning.

Modifications of Programs

The IEP should also list "program modifications and specially designed instruction" that may include elements incorporated into goal areas, which team members should bear in mind. Such a useful list may include examples like:

- Limit or eliminate visual and auditory stimulation and distractions in the learning setting.
- Explain directions clearly, in steps and with visual representations.
- Allow extended wait time and processing time.
- Use photo depictions where possible instead of cartoons or drawings.
- Provide advance notice of schedule and special situations.
- Be consistent with the expectations established for the student.
- Provide an individual, weekly schedule to follow.

The IEP document will also indicate the projected date for implementation of services, the anticipated duration of services, and any revision dates. Specifications addressing how the school district intends to report IEP goal progress should be clearly stated. There must also be a statement reflecting why your child's current educational placement represents an inclusive environment as fully as possible (called "least restrictive environment") as opposed to an alternative placement.

Resolving Disagreements

Some parents and school districts are possessed of more experience and greater expertise in educating children with Asperger's than others. There will always be kinks to iron out in the IEP process, and these can usually be addressed at the annual IEP meeting or at a requested reopening of the IEP. When parents encounter resistance from a school district it is usually because the district:

- Doesn't "see" the Asperger's syndrome as a viable diagnosis
- Believes your child's challenges to be exclusively behavioral issues
- Believes they are meeting the goals and objectives of the IEP to their best ability

Where parents resist a school's efforts, it is usually because they are extremely frustrated that the school district doesn't understand Asperger's and, as a result, doesn't "get" how to educate their child. Ignorance can be used as an initial excuse, but it is not an acceptable long-term excuse. School districts have a responsibility to make provisions for the continuing education of teachers and to seek outside technical assistance and expertise as necessary. Parents have a responsibility to serve as a resource concerning their child's strengths and needs, as well as directing the district to viable resources and expertise wherever possible. When the circumstances of educating your child through proper implementation of the IEP goals and objectives become less than satisfactory, you have recourse available to you, provided by the IDEA law.

Fact

Challenging the system, as it were, is pleasant for no one. Defending your child's educational rights may be extremely stressful and exasperating. Your repeated dissatisfaction with your child's education may, however, compel you to take further action. If so, know that passionate parents have initiated significant changes to laws that support those with different ways of being.

You may request an Impartial Due Process Hearing (in writing) at any point in which disagreement arises about the delivery of education to your child. This includes your child's identification, evaluation, placement, or implementation of the IEP.

The Impartial Due Process Hearing takes place with an "impartial hearing officer." The hearing officer is the "fact finder" who hears all the evidence and makes a ruling on the issues presented during the meeting. Such individuals are employed by your state government's education office of dispute resolution, and are of varied background and position, such as former education administrators, attorneys, or psychologists.

If you are in conflict with your child's school district, you need not go it alone. Connecting with other parents who have "been there, done that" should be of enormous benefit in your endeavor. Some such parents, who have become quite savvy to special education law, may be available to support you in meetings as parent advocates.

A hearing is to be held within thirty days of the request. The school district must forward a parent's request to the office of dispute resolution within five days of its receipt by the district office. The hearing officer's decision must be issued within forty-five days of the request for the hearing.

Be advised that there are often delays in scheduling or a hearing officer may not be timely in making his or her final determination to settle a dispute. During the dispute, the child in question is to remain in his current educational placement (unless he is a danger to himself or others). The hearing officer's decision may be appealed and taken to an appeals panel within thirty days. The appeals panel must render a decision within thirty days after the review request.

Hopefully, such measures will be entirely avoidable, but if a parent remains dissatisfied after exhausting local administrative avenues, action may be brought in any state court of competent jurisdiction, or in any district court of the United States, as provided for in IDEA.

There is no statute of limitations for commencing such action in federal court, but it is advisable to file as soon as possible. There may be time frame limitations for filing a case in your state court.

Moving to file a case is stressful, frustrating, and draining for all parties involved. However, court rulings can set precedent for changes in law to the benefit of all. Anytime significant change has occurred in how children with differences are educated, it has been at the instigation of passionate parents simply wanting fair and equal opportunities for their children.

Alternative Education Programs

Hopefully, you will be a persuasive advocate when interacting with your child's school district. You just may be the person to educate and enlighten the professionals in your district if they require a better understanding of Asperger's syndrome. In some extreme instances, families have moved to another school district or another state in order to have their child attend a certain school program. Unfortunately, in addition to the stress on the whole family that this type of upheaval can cause, it also allows school districts to remain uneducated about how best to support students with Asperger's syndrome.

The Delta Program

Some progressive school districts have developed alternative education programs available to those students that want them. One such example is the Delta program in State College Area School District, Pennsylvania. Since its 1974 inception, the Delta program has become a national model for alternative, "nontraditional" educational programming for eligible children from grades seven through twelve. Delta is founded on the belief that students are motivated to do their best when they are responsible for their own learning. Classes are not arranged by grade level, but by learning level, from introductory to midlevel to high level.

Delta is a partnership between the student, parents, and staff through shared decision-making. Enrollment does not exceed 200 students at a time in order for teachers, administrators, and support staff to provide quality, personalized interactions with students. Students are required to complete all state-mandated requirements for education the same as their peers. The program differs in that each student has an advising team (like an IEP team), and an open campus structure allows for flexibility, experiential learning, and community service projects.

Each semester, students in tandem with their advising team members design personal educational schedules by choosing from courses offered in required subject areas. However, as a guide, each course has a difficulty level that ranges from introductory to midlevel to high. When planning student schedules, the set number of credits required in each subject area is taken into account along with the difficulty level. In advance of course enrollment, each Delta student is aware of the course content, learning objectives, and the manner in which their work will be evaluated—all of which serves to promote independence and personal responsibility in learning. As an added incentive, further program flexibility is offered by allowing students to take certain classes in the regular high school or middle school, attend nearby Penn State University, or participate in other opportunities available through local businesses or technical schools designed to suit student-centered needs.

The Susquehanna Waldorf School Model

Another Pennsylvania educational model is the Susquehanna Waldorf School, which serves children in grades one through eight. It is founded upon the holistic philosophy of teaching the whole child, mind and body. The school considers that each phase of childhood requires different perspectives. This translates into seven-year spans, starting at birth through age twenty-one.

Throughout, the emphasis is about sequentially teaching what is good, truthful, and beautiful. By these standards, teachers honor the work of all children. The individual interpretations of each child are valued in balance with the contributions of others. Children are shown with care how to be discriminating, thoughtful, and prudent.

Fact

The Regio Emilia model of education (such as that found in Grand Rapids, Michigan, and elsewhere) allows schoolchildren to guide the curriculum. The inherent sense of wonder and curiosity children have about how things work in nature gives educators a "jumping off" point. The child with Asperger's may fit well with a similar program in which interests and curiosities are valued.

Charter Schools

Most states have an educational option called charter schools, in which the school district has received a "charter" from the state. The charter provides rules, such as where it is located and the maximum number of students permitted to attend. With a charter, the school district receives the funding and allocations based on the number of students. The state Department of Education grants the school district funding to pay for teacher salaries, equipment, and materials to meet the individual needs of each student in a charter school.

Charter schools are considered "public schooling," and must abide by all state regulations. The charter school may have an emphasis on the arts or science with a smaller teacher-student ratio.

Virtual Charter School

Another innovative program, called a virtual charter school, uses the charter school model with a couple of differences. The virtual charter school is like a "public school in a home environment," but it is not the same as home schooling.

Former U.S. secretary of education William Bennett and some others started a company called K12, headquartered in McLean, Virginia. K12 provides the curriculum and management services; the virtual charter school hires the teachers and support staff. The head of the school, the controller, and a few others are employees of K12.

To attend a virtual charter school, the student's parents unenroll him from the local school district and enroll him in the virtual charter school. The school district funding follows the student and encompasses books, materials for art and for science experiments, a computer, and other materials. The student also receives a regular education teacher, a special education teacher, and an IEP, just as in the local school district.

The teachers become the educational supports working in partnership with the parents (who have the lead) to educate the child and ensure he or she takes all the state-mandated standardized tests. The parent must log time daily on a Web site and track the student's progress, such as what lessons he or she has completed; lesson plans are also received via the Web site. Frequent field trips, all of an educational nature, are planned as a way for the children, teachers, and parents to connect with one another.

Home Schooling

Home schooling may be another option to consider, but be cautioned that the parents who undertake it tend to report that it's a lot of work and social opportunities for the child with Asperger's are curtailed. Parents wishing to home school their child select the educational curriculum and design the child's program. An affidavit must be filed with the state Department of Education attesting to the home schooling program, and parents must submit documentation at the end of each school year showing that the student has completed either a set number of hours or days of educational programming per year (it may vary from state to state). Another requirement is that a portfolio containing the child's work must reflect that the she has made the equivalent of one year's educational progress.

Also, private schools or educational institutions affiliated with religious denominations may offer a more individualized curriculum with one-on-one instruction, but the cost of enrolling your child may be prohibitive.

Benefits and Disadvantages

Alternate educational placements may benefit the child with Asperger's syndrome through smaller teacher-child ratios, leading to more individualized attention and quality assurance in your child's learning comprehension. Smaller class size may afford instructors the luxury of time to focus attention on meeting the unique educational needs of each child. Educational curriculum in alternate settings may also have greater flexibility and provide for enhanced opportunities to reinforce educational curriculum in ways that may be tangible and concrete for the child with Asperger's, such as regular field trips to museums, businesses, landmarks, and other community attractions. There may also be opportunity for creative programming in which the child may have myriad choices from which to select when planning class projects, presentations, or reports. Greater individualized attention may also mean that your child's personal passions can be used to underscore his learning in ways that might prove difficult or impossible in larger public school classes.

Be aware that some alternate educational placements that offer your child individualized guidance and one-on-one attention may only extend up until a certain grade level. You may need to determine, in partnership with your child and the alternate school administrators, if the transition to and from such a setting will benefit your child.

A disadvantage to alternative educational programming and placement may be the cost. If a newly designed program is considered, planning, implementation, and start-up time are all factors that may be deterrents for some as well. Social opportunities may be more limited with smaller or one-student classes unless efforts are made to compensate for this. Your local school district or state Department of Education should be able to provide you with details about a range of education program options, as well as funding options and obligations in order for you to make an informed decision about where your child receives her education.

CHAPTER 12

School-Related Issues

During the school year, the majority of your child's time is spent in a school environment. It probably feels like her teachers see her more than you do! As the expert on your child, it is important that you are in a position to suggest that certain adaptations and accommodations be made in your child's school environment. Identifying and addressing your child's needs while she is at school will create an atmosphere conducive to a successful balance between learning and socializing.

The School Day

School presents an environment in which children are expected to be attentive listeners and ready learners. In addition, the school day provides numerous opportunities for students to spend time getting to know one another. It will be important that you, your child, and your child's educators have a clear understanding of the most salient points of communicating with a child with Asperger's syndrome (as discussed in Chapter 5). Specifically, how educators communicate information and the process time they allot for it can make or break your child's ability to assimilate educational curriculum on a day-to-day basis. If your child is very passive or is a "pleaser," he may readily get swallowed up in confusion and misunderstanding—all the while giving the impression that everything's fine, until it's too late.

Question?

How can I help my child handle the demands of school?
Understanding how your child thinks and learns in her own words is a powerful alternative for some professionals who may perceive certain parents as overzealous or overprotective. Encourage your child to privately write or type some of her personal thoughts about coping (without fear of getting in trouble).

How Your Child Learns

It will be crucial to communicate with your child and his educators, preferably prior to the start of the school year, in order to clarify your child's needs. Do his teachers have a clear understanding of what his needs will be (perhaps as dictated by the Individualized Education Plan), and does your child know what to do and say if he gets "stuck"? If you know your child to be a strong visual thinker and learner, ensure that any verbally communicated curriculum is reinforced with visuals. Some children cannot process visual and auditory input simultaneously without distraction; they are "monochannel," meaning they cannot absorb what they are seeing and hearing at the same time and can only attend to one or the other. As many children with Asperger's syndrome are so visual, this means there is potential for them to be distracted by everything in the room, so that they absorb only bits and pieces of the instruction.

In one instance, a young boy's school team was frustrated because they thought they were supporting him fully by assigning him a classroom aide. However, the aide was verbally reiterating the classroom teacher's direction in such a way that their words overlapped one another. The boy was receiving almost exclusively verbal instruction, out of sync, and *in stereo*! Now, consider his predicament in desiring to pay attention to his teacher, but knowing he must also attend to his aide. Layer on top of that the constant motion of a typical elementary school classroom setting and it was a recipe for disaster.

Your Child's Strengths

Many children with Asperger's sydrome generally possess a number of strengths upon which educators may build. These include:

- A strong knowledge base for individual topics of passionate interest.
- The desire to conform to rules and boundaries.
- Retaining information best when it is visual, sequential, and linear.
- Best understanding logical, concrete topics of discussion.
- A willingness to please and to keep trying.

Essential

There are some truly wonderful school administrators and educators who love teaching and enjoy kids. You'll recognize them immediately because *they* will remind *you* of your child's gifts and talents. When this occurs, remember to validate their observations and courtesy.

Your child may well benefit from a classroom aide in order to support her comprehension. It will be best—and nonstigmatizing—if *all* the children in class understand that the aide is accessible to them if they have questions or need guidance to reinforce the teacher's instruction. In this way, the aide's role is discreet.

It will also be important that your child's educators embrace the concept of building upon your child's passions (as discussed in Chapter 8). It is unrealistic to expect a classroom teacher to center educational curriculum around one child's passions; however, wherever possible, it will help engage the child if the teacher can artfully introduce elements of the passion(s) in the instruction. Strategies for linking passions to learning opportunities is best applied by your child's classroom aide or directly by you if no aide is assigned or available. All children are eventually confronted with educational concepts that are vague and indiscernible for them. Connecting passions in the way described in Chapter 8 is intended to occur outside of the classroom setting and, ideally, before and after the confusing assignment. Your job and that of the teacher (and aide) is to "coach" your child on the sidelines before sending him out into the game. That is, deconstruct the concept with which he is struggling by using his passion both before and after he's expected to learn and retain it.

For example, you might suggest that the names given to parts of plants also relate to the hanging vines in a Mario Brothers' computer game. Instead of asking that your child recite the textbook plant parts, request that he link the same information to the Mario Brothers' plants. He will retain this information, and with a gentle reminder, he will "call up" the knowledge when it's required (such as at test time).

Some children take this to extremes and don't realize that they are sidetracking a teacher's instruction with lengthy explanations of their passions (which can fuel educators to stereotype the passions). Children who do this need clear, concise, and *written* rules provided to them about when and where it's okay to expound upon their interests.

Learning by Doing

Your child likely has a strong associative link when learning. That is, she learns on the spot, in the moment while "doing" whatever it is, and will forever retain and "link" that experience with the moment. Many children with Asperger's think and learn this way. It will be important, then, to understand your child's struggles if educators wish to place emphasis on "pull out" programs or classes in which your child works one-on-one with an adult with the expectation that she process, retain, and apply what was just learned to the classroom situation. The two rarely mesh with success because of the strong associative link.

Your child will be poised for greater success if she can learn by doing in the moment and through incorporation of as many visuals as possible to reinforce it. In so doing, a visual "imprint" is recorded in her memory that, with gentle prompting, she can call up and replay. You may then incrementally build upon such pleasing experiences by relating them to something new and different. For example, you might suggest to your child, "Remember when we made homemade peanut butter?" (Give her process time to replay the mind movie.) Then continue, "The way a factory processes sugar cane is similar because . . ." You may be surprised at the quality of detail with which your child is able to relay information. She may become excited about taking a pleasing, fun learning experience and applying it to something novel.

When in doubt about how your child may best think and learn, think back on your own experience with "associations." Recall how certain scents or songs are forever linked in your memory to people, places, and life events and may be inseparable from those recollections.

Environmental Issues

Schools are fraught with environmental stimuli that can conspire to wreak havoc on your child's sensory sensitivities. Many children with Asperger's already torture themselves with anxiety about wanting to follow the rules, live up to teacher expectations, and get through each day without incident. In addition, they must grapple with having their senses assaulted throughout the day. In some instances—if the child is not yet a self-advocate, or if he is unaware of his own sensitivities—he may be unable to pinpoint exactly what triggers him to lose control. This is extremely common.

So many kids with Asperger's syndrome are keenly aware of the social, educational, and environmental expectation that they blend in and "fit in." To compensate, they "hold it together" all day long as best they can. Once they get home, they finally release, lose control, and melt down in the safety of the home environment—where they feel most comfortable to let down their guard. This creates a perplexing situation for teachers who report to parents that their child seems "fine during the day." It also creates a frustrating situation for parents who may internalize their own self-doubts about something they must be doing wrong. It is no one's fault; the child is merely reacting to the relief at dropping the façade he's borne for the past six hours or more.

Here are a number of suggestions that you will wish to share with your child's teachers in order to minimize the potentially hurtful environmental stimuli in typical school settings:

- Hallways can become extremely noisy and "echoey." Wherever possible, keep classroom doors shut.
- The volume of the PA system in the room may be too loud. If it's possible to adjust the volume, this can help. Same for the change-of-class bell.
- Classroom walls can be overstimulating and "busy" with decoration. If visuals cannot be streamlined, at least keep them somewhat static so the child with Asperger's can become accustomed to them.
- Consider felt pads under the feet of all classroom chairs as buffers against the constant scraping noise they make.
- Carrels or partitions around learning stations and computer centers are great for creating visual blocks on either side of a student and can also cut down some noise.
- Classroom announcements or posters like "Ten Great Ways to Treat Others" are most effective if transcribed and distributed to all kids (this makes them easier to retain when outside the room).
- Numbering classroom rules as written reminders for the child with Asperger's is a good idea, but publicly displaying

them on a desktop is stigmatizing. Tape them inside a child's notebook or binder and refer to them discreetly.

- Focus on natural lighting instead of florescent lights when possible, using fewer overhead lights or adding alternate lighting such as floor lamps.
- Give the child with Asperger's advance notice of fire drill times so that she may brace herself for the noise. If she cannot tolerate it, small foam earplugs may help, or wearing Walkman headphones may diffuse the noise.
- Ringing classroom phones can be startling. Switch to a flashing light instead of a ring to indicate a call.
- Ensure that all students have advance knowledge of schedule changes outside of the routine, such as early dismissal or assemblies.

Implementing these measures will significantly help the child with Asperger's to "hold it together" in a more environmentally friendly atmosphere.

Fact

You may be pleasantly surprised to learn that many environmental adaptations and accommodations can be low in cost or cost nothing. In fact, you may wish to apply them, wherever possible, to your own home in addition to those of friends, neighbors, or relatives.

Homework

When you are young and extremely sensitive, school is your life, teachers are omnipotent, and homework is everything. Many children with Asperger's syndrome generate undue stress for themselves by agonizing over homework to the point that they cannot be calm and rest because they feel so overwhelmed. Some may wail, cry, or hyperventilate because they believe homework to be a life or death situation. Parents and teachers may affirm that they *know* the child is capable of the work; however, this is not about incapability. The child with Asperger's syndrome can be overcome with stress and anxiety by a litany of tasks that seem insurmountable. Being simultaneously confronted with homework, impending tests, and assignment due dates may fuel such a tremendous sense of frustration and futility that the child may be totally unable to discern where to even begin.

Problems with Homework

If your child becomes upset and overwhelmed when confronted with multiple homework assignments, he will require your support to break down the tasks (organized *visually* on a timetable that becomes the child's property) so that the assignments are scheduled in manageable portions. Reinforce that the child need only focus on the work scheduled for the allotted time slot. Your child's teacher will be an invaluable resource in helping to "map out" such a timetable into realistically doable bits.

Your child may be stigmatized by peers if they perceive her as the "teacher's pet," having special privileges, or if she is acknowledged as "different" and unable to complete homework assignments. It's important to be discreet in cases where a child's homework assignment is modified in some way from the rest of the class's.

A child's confusion and misunderstanding of directions can lead teachers to inaccurately label that child for his "behaviors." Their observations may focus upon some children's inability to complete homework. The refusal to complete a homework assignment in full may stem from the child feeling personally offended by what is being asked of her. If your child has demonstrated that she can master a concept, she may become offended when asked to demonstrate that capability by essentially "regurgitating" the same concept in various ways (via the homework). A compromise may be to allow the child to do fewer homework problems.

If the homework is going to be publicly reviewed aloud in class, parents and teachers will need to be more creative in conveying *why* completing the entire assignment is necessary. Or teachers could arrange to stagger the order of the assigned homework problems, with both student and teacher being aware of which problems she is most likely to be called upon to report.

Perfectionism and Anxiety

Some children operate in a "perfection mode" because they are "pleasers." They may relate better to adults with more advanced skills or they torture themselves trying to duplicate computer-generated examples in textbooks, like perfect handwriting, for example. Trying to be as perfect as adults appear to be only magnifies the self-imposed pressure to comply with exacting accuracy. Tension and anxiety can balloon out of control for the child who must erase his work over and over again because it doesn't "match" the textbook or teacher's example.

If your child does this, he needs you to express, in writing and pictures, an understanding that *everyone* messes up and does things wrong *every day*. It may come as a groundbreaking revelation for your child to learn that his parents, teachers, relatives, doctors, and others don't do everything exactly right all the time. This is not giving him permission not to strive to do his best; it's a discussion about flexibility within rules and permission for him to go easy on himself. Your child will likely be absolutely tickled to hear your own stories about the times you messed up in school and lived to tell about it!

With patient support and practice, these homework strategies should help your child relax and focus.

Bullying

Like it or not, many kids with Asperger's are perceived as different by their peers despite their efforts to blend and assimilate. Coming across as different can make a child a target in the eyes of those who prey upon the weak and defenseless. Many children with Asperger's become terrified and anxiety-ridden at the prospect of being bullied, especially during the transition to middle school and high school. As freshmen, they are younger than the other students who may traditionally give *all* incoming students a hard time.

When the Bully Is a Student

Many school districts have taken a no-tolerance approach to bullying, especially with the significant increase in school violence nationally in recent years. They have also developed written rules and guidelines about what is unacceptable student behavior and the consequences for not complying with the rules. Your child should receive such a written policy either in advance of the start of school or within the first week of school. If you don't have it, contact the school to request it. Having it may help soothe and appease your child's worries.

Providing your child with your school's written policy on bullying is not enough. She needs to know exactly whom she may trust to approach and confide in (which is hopefully *any* adult in the school). She will, of course, likely single out one or two closest school adult allies whom she knows will take her complaint seriously.

Facilitating partnerships that may lead to friendships (allies) will be critical, starting at an early age. Some schools also have a buddy system, whereby younger students are mentored or assisted by older, supportive students during an orientation period. You may also need to partner with your child to devise a way to hold a frank discussion with her teachers about the need for protection during the school day. Appropriate ways to cope with verbal and physical abuse need to be taught and rehearsed. Give your child a numbered list of actions to discreetly maintain in the event of an incident. The actions may include the exact phrases to use when telling her abuser to stop it, and knowing to whom bullying should be reported. Some children may also require coaching to learn how to recognize some forms of bullying that may be very subtle, such as the student who was coerced by his bullies into swearing at a teacher, and then bore the brunt of the punishment alone.

Luke Jackson, a young man with Asperger's, has commented on bullying in his writings.

> Being different may not be a problem for me, or other kids like me, but it sure seems to cause problems for "normal" (ha!) kids. The result... bullying! I think there is some amount of bullying going on at all times, in schools everywhere. Some have it worse than others, but all have it. I was definitely bullied, and "it" was very painful at times. Always remember that "different is cool!" A lot of teachers and adults think bullying is "part of growing up," but I have written books, talked at conferences, and opened my life up on television just to let everyone know that people with autism in any shape or form are just as entitled to be themselves as anyone else in the world.

When the Bully Is an Adult

In some unfortunate instances, the bully is not another student but an insensitive teacher. One teenage girl with Asperger's honestly did not understand her gym teacher's instructions. After telling her several times (still in ways she did not understand), the exasperated teacher pushed the girl and said, "What are you? A retard?" This is, of course, inexcusable behavior and must be dealt with by counseling the child immediately to prevent the onset of post-traumatic stress disorder. The issue also needs to be addressed with the school administration so that the child is removed from that teacher's class and the teacher's behavior is addressed.

You may also need to counsel your child about reporting extreme cases of bullying; ensure that he is clear about what is good-natured kidding and what is unacceptable to endure. It can be a fine line sometimes, and sorting it through will be an ongoing process.

Unstructured School Environments

Many children with Asperger's thrive during those portions of the school day that are structured by routine. Yet those same students may socially flounder during the many unstructured school events that occur throughout the day. These include:

- Recess
- School assemblies
- Hallway socializing between classes
- Gym class
- Lunchtime
- Riding the bus to and from school

Fact

Nowadays, it is entirely acceptable for *all* kids to spend downtime engaged in inconspicuous, solitary activities like reading, privately listening to CDs using headphones, or playing small, handheld computer games to maintain focus. Determine from your child's school what is acceptable to use on campus, when, and where.

As noted in Chapter 5, your child may also benefit greatly from having a repertoire of Conversation Starters, Enders, and Slip-Ins. Wherever possible, your child will be best poised to weather the awkwardness of unstructured school situations if she can volunteer for, or be assigned, a responsibility or role during the activity. For example, many kids with Asperger's are not as physically graceful as they'd wish to be. Playing on a team in gym class can get confusing and uncomfortable, but this can be tempered if he is also in charge of keeping score.

Likewise, if teachers provide an optional structure for specific playground activities, it may make the duration of time bearable for any number of kids, including those with Asperger's. As discussed, an alternative to being swallowed up by the lunchroom environment would be to establish "lunch bunch" discussion tables in a quieter corner of the cafeteria. Some schools assign seating on the bus, which helps quell anxiety in children with Asperger's, especially if seating is a daily "free for all" and the child must compete for seats with older children. One drawback to the concept of role-assignment is that a child may become so rigid and unyielding that he is inflexible when it comes time to pass on the responsibility to another student. This should take place incrementally to transition the tradeoff of responsibility wherever possible.

CHAPTER 13

Extracurricular Activities

Your school district and your community offer opportunities for your child to develop new skills, enhance existing talents, indulge passions, and foster social interactions. You and your child will need to be selective in planning which activities to sign up for and how involved you want to become. Such experiences will be made more enjoyable if you gather as much information in advance as possible and support your child to identify potential needs and barriers to full participation.

Athletic Options

You may already be well aware that your child is not as physically agile as he may wish to be. It is common for children with Asperger's and autism to experience motor control challenges. It may be very difficult for some to make those brain-body connections necessary to physically produce a movement already envisioned in the mind. This can be very frustrating for all, especially the child who wants to succeed. It can also lead to a child being humiliated and publicly singled out as "uncoordinated." Many school gym classes are shifting away from picking sides for games, which is a blessing for the children who are consistently picked last.

Physically Frustrated?

If your child has experienced public embarrassment due to her inability to physically achieve on par with her same-age peers, it may be tempting for her not to engage in any form of physical activity at all. Instead, she may disengage from any such opportunities in favor of spending more time in isolation. This type of sedentary pattern is not healthy for any child, and can lead to self-image issues, worries about body type, and weight concerns.

Essential

Many typical social interactions among children and teens include physical activities such as sports, dancing, skating, horseback riding, and others. If your child disengages from his peers, he misses out on these and he may be at risk for a sedentary lifestyle that may lead to weight gain.

As a parent you may recognize the benefits that regular physical activity can offer your child, but may feel torn. Some parents go to extremes in attempting to mold their unathletic child into a model of conformity. This kind of pressure to achieve in order to "please" can only widen the distance between child and parent when the child cannot live up to unrealistic expectations. You may have already witnessed, or read about, little league or soccer parents who create such hostility and anxiety for their children that the sport is no longer fun but a fierce, adult-level competition that is unpleasant for all.

In partnership with your child, decide upon some physical recreation activities that may be pleasing for your child to try. The child with Asperger's syndrome will enjoy greatest success with athletic activities that are *self-contained* and *noncompetitive*. Such activities do not necessarily need to occur without partners and in isolation. It simply means that there is no race-to-the-finish time frame within which one must excel to score points. There is no winner or loser, and no undue pressure to perform.

Activities That Work

To start, build upon the movements your child already does well, even if it's simply walking. Being in or near water is extremely important to the vast majority of kids with Asperger's. The buoyancy of the water, the overall pressure it offers, and its solitude is enormously attractive to many. Would your child's health and motor coordination benefit from learning how to swim?

Martial arts also hold a special appeal for many children with Asperger's. Martial arts have a structured regimen with levels of achievement that promote self-discipline. Learning the moves in martial arts involves lots of visual repetition and incremental learning—something your child may already thrive upon. It also promotes making slow, deliberate, and methodical brain-body connections in order to be conscious of how all parts of one's body move and relate to one another. Tai chi is also effective in accomplishing similar goals. Your child can also proceed at her own pace and experience success as she moves up each level.

Fact

More than a few children with Asperger's who have struggled academically or socially have experienced great success and pride through participating in a martial arts program. Moving "up" the tiered level of colored belts is a tangible, *visual* way for them to measure their achievements.

Activities similar to the discipline and coordination offered by martial arts include yoga, gymnastics, ballet, and dance. Other self-contained, noncompetitive physical activities include:

- Walking or running
- Horseback riding
- Bike riding

- Weight training
- Shooting basketball
- Roller skating or in-line skating
- Jumping rope
- Playing hopscotch

Adding your child's favorite music to any of these activities will be a good motivator and make the process that much more attractive. You may wish to participate with your child in some or all the physical activities he selects. Other partners may include siblings, friends, and relatives (cousins, nieces, nephews). These opportunities become ideal times for social interaction and connectedness, free from the pressure to achieve and score points.

Playing on a Team

There will be times in which your child participates in an athletic activity as a member of a team, either by choice or as dictated by the structure of a class, like gym class in school. Being the member of a team can require that your child juggle a lot of things at once. It can quickly get confusing, perhaps for some of the following reasons:

- Although the team sport has rules, the activity is unpredictable.
- In the chaos and excitement, your child may forget the rules.
- Noise from spectators or teammates can make staying focused difficult.
- Your child may forget exactly who her teammates are.
- Your child may get disoriented about the location to score points.

Ways to alleviate some of these issues are to ensure that your child's teammates are distinguished in some way (usually by different-colored jerseys). Take time to go to the playing area prior to a game to familiarize your child with the surroundings, such as where the team will play, where spectators will be seated, and the location of the area where the team scores points. Being able to practice a team sport skill at home with you or siblings or friends can only help her develop confidence in her capabilities. She may simultaneously improve her ability to absorb and assimilate all that the game entails in a comfortable, unconditional environment.

Essential

Encouraging your child to participate in team sports may require "prerequisites" prior to sign-up. Simultaneous with your child's participation in self-contained, noncompetitive physical activities, facilitate opportunities for reciprocal interactions early on, such as sharing and taking turns during computer or board games. This may be useful in aiding your child to better understand the way team sports "work."

Being a Good Sport

Remember the perfectionism mode in which some children find themselves? This can also apply to the concept of winning and losing. Some children (including those without Asperger's) become so intensely hell-bent on winning that losing becomes its own drama, and the defeat represents personal failure.

Your child may have perceived that winning a game is the only option, and that losing is a "bad" thing, or that losing means she did something wrong. Granted, some adult role models are not helpful to this end either. How many of us have watched professional athletes on TV curse, spit, throw things, or start fights? When your child loses, he may internalize a lot of self-deprecating thoughts and feelings. His emotions may reinforce stereotypes he or others may have about him. This is, of course, harmful to his mental health and can deteriorate the quality of his social connections.

You will be wise to communicate early on a balance between

playing a game (especially as a team member) and winning. As always, you will want to communicate this concept *visually* in pictures and words. Be sure to include information similar to that discussed in the last chapter about perfectionism. Team members rely upon one another to cooperate and work together. No one wins all the time; it is impossible because we are all human beings. Two key lessons that your child may wish to remember are:

- You win some, you lose some.
- It doesn't matter whether you win or lose, it's how you play the game.

Not only can these phrases be used as responses to any catcalls of defeat from others, they may be used as effective analogies to "losing" or missing opportunities in any number of real-life circumstances.

Remember that, as a parent, you still have the right to apply fair, appropriate discipline *after* you believe you've communicated your expectations as effectively as possible and they are clearly understood by your child with Asperger's. If, for example, you've discussed, through pictures and words, the concept of behaving like a good sport and your child engages in an irretrievable meltdown after a loss, then it may be the time to consider your parental options.

In dialoguing with your child, be sure to distinguish a bad sport as someone who becomes angry at losing, someone who may yell and swear, cry loudly, or throw equipment. A good sport is still allowed to feel disappointed, but she knows there will be other chances to try again. A good sport is someone who can congratulate the opposing team with sincerity. Some things to say might be, "You played a good game" or "I'm going to try harder next time." A good sport tries his best during every game, whether he wins or loses.

As before, revealing one's Asperger's syndrome and potential needs for accommodation to a coach or teammates is a personal decision of disclosure. Decide with your child if disclosing a diagnosis is helpful or stigmatizing. Perhaps simply being clear and specific when communicating an area of special need is all that is required.

School-Sponsored Activities

In addition to sports-related activities, your school district likely sponsors a variety of in-school and after-school activities that may provide for your child's social interactions with others. These may include:

- Clubs of all kinds
- Organizations designated by academic achievement
- Chorus
- Band
- School plays and musicals
- Dances and other social gatherings

In addition, schools may announce contact information for Cub Scouts, Boy Scouts, Girl Scouts, Brownies, and other community-service type groups. These may also appeal to your child for their discipline, structure, and concrete assignments and tasks within a social gathering.

Many school-sponsored activities are initiated with the transition to middle school and high school, as children begin to mature and take on teenage interests. Prior to the start of the new school year, find out what activities your school will make available to students within the coming year. Get the following specifics about any activity:

- Who is the contact person?
- What are the tentative dates for the activity?
- Where do you go to sign up?

- Where will the activity take place?
- Who will supervise the activity?
- How does one contact this person (or persons) during the activity and after-hours?
- What are the time frames for the duration of each activity?
- Is transportation provided?
- Is there any fee to participate?
- Does your child need to bring money to cover meals or materials?

Discuss with your child any school-sponsored activities that pique his interest. What are natural places to start? Do any of the activities build upon his passions or talents so that he may meet with some success or at least acceptance his first time out? After you've gathered the information listed for each activity (or better yet, ask that your child gather as much of it as he can), talk with your child about the extent of his participation. Can he (and you) envision being able to balance it with school, homework, and responsibilities at home? If it becomes overwhelming, will he know to say so? Once your child signs up for an activity, he may decide it's not to his liking or it wasn't what he expected it to be.

Your child may not realize that he has any other available option. That is, your child may feel compelled to commit to the activity from start to finish without reprieve, even if it becomes distressing or unpleasant.

Providing your child with the option to opt out if he decides he has lost interest or can't keep up is a matter of your personal parenting style. Some families place high value on honoring commitments, even if doing so is dissatisfying. To them, maintaining the commitment builds character. Other parents are more flexible about participating in such activities, and believe that no one should feel obligated to any extra activities if it's uncomfortable. Find a compromise that works for you. If your child is really struggling and has communicated legitimate concerns about continuing to participate, those concerns should be honored.

Question?

In what ways might your child organize and facilitate her own gathering of others interested in similar activities or passions? Many people with Asperger's desire to teach in order to give of themselves and their knowledge. If you and your child can partner with others toward this goal, creating an agenda or outline, or structuring a meeting using Robert's Rules of Order, it might be a successful start for your child.

Above all else, if you've been invited to any events in which your child is participating, ensure that you set aside time to attend, as you would for any of your children. Your being there will be a confidence booster that will greatly enhance your child's (sometimes fragile) self-esteem. You may very well find yourself pleasantly surprised by how well your child maintains—or shines—during an activity that presents a public performance of some kind.

Summer Camp

For many kids with Asperger's Syndrome, time that is unstructured can be problematic. It can lead to overindulgence in solitary passions, or it can lead to boredom from lack of intellectual stimulation. In a child's life, the greatest block of unstructured time is, of course, summer vacation. If your child is geographically isolated from other children or schoolmates during the summer, or community activities are not options (for whatever reason), you may wish to consider summer camp.

For the child with Asperger's who is inherently gentle and exquisitely sensitive, the notion of summer camp can be paralyzing. In her mind, it may involve packing up and leaving home to cohabitate with strangers, without contact with family and everything else that aids her to feel safe and comfortable.

To relieve this kind of exaggerated (but real to her) anxiety, you will wish to partner with your child to research summer camp options in your community or geographic region. Summer camp also doesn't have to be a place where you stay overnight; it can be a place you visit during the day in order to take advantage of an outdoor activity program. If you present summer camp in an exciting, positive way, your child will be poised to receive the concept with enthusiasm.

Perhaps you went away to summer camp every year yourself. Do you have stories to share about what made it so fun and memorable for you? Did you make long-standing friendships or pen pals as a result of meeting someone special at summer camp?

Know, too, that many communities offer "specialty" summer camp experiences that cater to specific areas of interest (i.e., passions) such as acting and theater, music and musical instruments, gymnastics, soccer, and other athletics to name a few. While most only last several weeks instead of an entire summer, such specialty camps are likely to pique your child's interest, value his passion (and talent!), and offer socialization opportunities with like-minded peers.

Fact

Your child's success while away at camp—whether it's a day camp or an overnight, away-from-home variety—will likely hinge upon daily structure. Determine in advance the schedule for each day and ensure it is reviewed with your child the night before. Where there are gaps of time, discuss alternatives for your child with him and his counselors.

Inclusion of children with Asperger's with neurotypical, same-age peers should always be our endeavor. However, in the case of summer camp, you and your child may find relief in an environment in which there are other kids with Asperger's present, and staffed by counselors that are sensitive and respectful of the needs of such kids. This is a personal choice. Finding a camp program near to you that specializes in supporting children with Asperger's may be difficult or even an impossibility. (If you are an impassioned advocate on your child's behalf, you may be the person to collaborate with other parents to officiate the start-up of just such a camp.) Be mindful that it is entirely inappropriate to place your child into an alternate "special-needs" camp because of convenience, staffing ratio, or cost savings. Your child will be miserable in a summer camp for children with mental retardation, for example; and while some camps are strict about entry qualifications, others are not.

Choosing a Camp

Aside from the obvious questions about cost and other logistics like administration of medications, water safety, and environmental allergies, you will want to find out the following about any prospective camp to which you are considering sending your child with Asperger's:

- What is the staff to child ratio?
- Do any of the counselors have special education or teaching backgrounds or credits?
- Will your child be assigned to the same counselor(s) for the duration of the summer?
- How often will your child have the opportunity to contact you?
- What is the camp protocol for managing what may be labeled "behaviors" (not just for your kid, but for others that may aggress against your child)?
- What is the camp's policy on bullying?
- Is the camp prepared to accommodate your child's dietary needs?
- What is the structure and routine of a typical day?
- Are children ever left unattended?
- What are the hours during which parents may visit?

You will also wish to meet with the camp director and staff to share information about what works for your child—that is, what makes for a successful day. This can occur without disclosing an Asperger's diagnosis, if you and your child so desire. Also be certain to discuss what's non-negotiable for your child, meaning those adaptations or accommodations he needs to feel safe and comfortable and in control, like knowing the exact time of activities or having his cabin room arranged a certain way. If the non-negotiables become violated, disregarded, or withheld, inform the staff to expect consequences in the form of your child's meltdown or implosion (shutting down), as the case may be.

Essential

Camp counselors will also need to understand the positive philosophies discussed at the beginning of this book to guard against misperceptions and misunderstandings about your child's "behaviors" versus coping mechanisms and survival tactics. If there's an area that will be problematic for your child while away at summer camp, it will be this communication breakdown.

Preparing for Camp

Obtain a written camp schedule in advance, and give that to your child. Plan to drive with your child to visit the camp in advance of enrollment. Take a camera or camcorder to document the trip. Reviewing the images you've taken of the trip at home will support your child to feel familiar and comfortable with the surroundings. Give him the opportunity to identify what's what to you and others. If siblings, cousins, friends, or others are also going to attend the same camp, find out if they can be paired with your child wherever possible. Arrange for your child to meet the staff and primary counselors, and take their photographs if they'll allow it. Tour the campgrounds and point out the location of various activity sites. If a living quarters assignment has been made, go there as well and give your child the opportunity to acclimate to it. He will likely be strongly attracted to wooded areas and other local flora and fauna, and this will provide him with an incentive to be there.

Going away to summer camp, either during the day or on a twenty-four-hour-a-day basis, can provide your child with structure during the long hours of summer days. In addition, it may be an opportunity to make social connections with counselors and fellow campers that can be maintained by e-mail or letter writing. Your child may also have the opportunity to learn new skills or demonstrate his own. With careful planning, your child's mind-movie memories of summer camp can be pleasing and every bit as enjoyable as your own.

CHAPTER 14

Significant Transitions and Change

As you are probably already aware, change may be extremely difficult for your child. Transitions of any kind, especially those that are unpredictable, can be unnerving and can cause your child to become totally undone. Knowing how to support your child through change in order to make successful transitions is critical. It is especially important in considering major childhood "life event" changes, such as attending a new school, moving, transition to college, divorce, or a death in the family.

Attending a New School

One of the mistakes parents and other adults make in interacting with children with Asperger's is in not preparing kids for what's coming next. Changing jobs, having a new baby, or relocating to a nicer home are all exciting opportunities, but also stressful, overwhelming times. As an adult, you compensate for change by gathering as much information in detail as possible about who, what, when, where, why, and how. When you have incomplete information about future events, it heightens your anxiety in anticipation of the unknown. Too often, parents overlook sharing the same kinds of information with their child—information that would help him feel just as safe, comfortable, and in control of what's coming next.

It is likely that there is little else in your child's perspective of his world as important—or anxiety inducing—as school. If your child is a "pleaser," a perfectionist, socially challenged, or a stalwart rule-follower, school can seem like a life or death situation at times when things don't go as planned. The transition to a new school can include changing from elementary school to middle school or middle school to high school. It can also include moving to a new school district. No matter which, your child will rely upon you to guide her toward making predictable sense of it all. Give it as much attention and importance as it carries for her but balance it with an air of fun and adventure. Remember, your child will reflect back to you what you project upon her. If your stress or anxiety shines through it will directly impact the intensity of her own anxiousness. Wherever possible, partner with your child in information gathering or, at the least, provide daily updates to quell her fears and butterflies. (She's probably already asking you the same questions repeatedly on a daily basis anyway.)

Start by acknowledging that changing schools can be a scary or frustrating time because of so much being unknown. Moving up in grades is also a measure of growth and maturity. Reinforce with your child that he is growing and learning, and that he certainly wouldn't want to stay in his present grade level, even if it meant remaining in the same building. Pledge to support your child in demystifying as many of the unknowns as possible.

The word "change" in and of itself may be disconcerting for some children with Asperger's. Oftentimes, change is associated with loss of security and unpleasant circumstances. Instead, try discussing change from the perspective of opportunities to grow, learn, and mature—with your loving support and guidance.

In addition, a school team meeting should take place to plan for your child's transition, and, to ensure consistency, document the steps agreed upon. If the school does not offer such a meeting, contact your child's school to request that the principal schedule one. If you learn such a meeting cannot be held, request, in writing, to reopen your child's IEP for the purpose of including information in planning the transition. The focus of that portion of the meeting should be exclusively on supporting your child to transition to a new school with as much ease and comfort as possible. What follows are some strategies that should prove useful and might be discussed in detail at such a meeting.

Preparations

If possible, it will be most helpful for your child to meet next year's primary or homeroom teacher *before* the end of his current school year. In fact, in addition to meeting in person, it will probably be beneficial to arrange for that teacher to observe your child in class to glean firsthand information about his learning style, and to demystify Asperger's syndrome in general. (Many teachers may not know much—if anything—about Asperger's syndrome if they haven't had a student with Asperger's previously.)

It will also prove very helpful if your child's new teacher could "make themselves real," so to speak, to your child in advance of meeting face to face. The concept of making oneself real can apply to anyone in your child's life, but in particular adults, especially those in caregiving roles. Adults in your child's life are the keepers of a lot of information about your child. This includes family history, medical history (including allergies and medications), psychological and psychiatric history, dietary background, educational records, and more. The balance of the scales of the relationship is tipped unevenly because your child has nowhere near a similar depth of information about the adults in his life as they do about him.

Many children with differences have a long parade of "cardboard cutouts" (in the outline of caregivers and educators) come in and out of their lives without any personal investment in the relationship on the child's part. By demystifying the adults as human beings, the cardboard facades are shed and there is reason to begin to trust in the relationship. To begin, new teachers can provide your child with a clear, up-to-date photograph of themselves (a photograph in which someone has a different hair color and style or facial hair, where now they have none, will only be confusing and potentially upsetting). Attached to the photograph, teachers may add, in bullet-point sentences, any personal data each feels most comfortable sharing. Some examples include:

- Full name, with an indication that the teacher is *only* to be addressed as Mr., Mrs., or Miss/Ms., unless special circumstances prevail.
- Birthday (note it's birth*day* not birth*date*—no one should feel compelled to reveal their age!) and birthstone.
- Favorite color(s).
- Car make, model, color, and year. (Some kids will *love* knowing how many miles are on your car, too!)
- Favorite music.
- Hobbies and passions.
- Pets and their names.
- Loved ones and children.
- Favorite sports (as a participant or spectator).
- Favorite places to vacation or visit.

Fact

One teacher started off the school year by requesting that *all* students create an "about me" collage of images designed to, at a glance, communicate their personalities, likes, and interests. He also participated and, at the end of the school year, gave his female student with Asperger's a notebook, the cover of which he had decorated with football images—his passion—in remembrance of him.

These are just a few examples to which many more may be added at each individual's discretion. In one instance, a young girl who met her teacher in advance of the new school year was aware that the teacher would have minor surgery before seeing her next fall. Because there was now a personal investment in the relationship (through this process), the first thing the girl did upon seeing the teacher again was to demonstrate her compassion by asking about the surgery and making certain the teacher was okay. The concept of "making yourself real" may also be adapted to aid *all* students in feeling comfortable with their teacher on the first day of school, and can even be used as an ice breaker among the entire class, if a teacher facilitates it. Similarities in likes, dislikes, and passions may emerge that could lend themselves to linking your child socially with others right from the first day of school. Other adults in your child's school career who may wish to consider participating in this process include:

- Principal
- Office secretaries
- Aides, therapists, or instructional assistants
- School bus or van drivers
- Custodians
- Cafeteria staff
- School nurse
- Librarians

Equipped with personal information that deconstructs all these individuals as "real" people, your child may find herself with a greater level of comfort and confidence in approaching each individual as needed.

Adjusting to the School Environment

Your child should also feel a sense of empowerment and ownership if provisions are made to familiarize him with the new school building. If you allow him to take the lead in this, all the better. You can do this by scheduling at least one visit to the new building and arming your child with a camera or camcorder to record the proceedings, allowing him to be in charge of directing the "movie" for the day. In this way, your child can independently quell his anxiety by reviewing the images as often as he wishes at his leisure and at home, where he feels safe and comfortable.

With each viewing, he should feel less anxious and more comfortable about the impending environment (your child will have enough to deal with in getting acclimated as it is). Start by taking pictures or running a video beginning with the point at which your child will be dropped off in front of the building; you'll want to ensure that everything will be replicated as close as possible in "real life" that first school day, but for now, it's a "dress rehearsal." Next, move inside the building and follow the path your child will take according to his schedule (which you and your child should have well in advance of the start of school). Obtaining a map of the property's layout for your child to keep should also prove useful. Specify all the rooms and exits your child may use, identifying each as you go. You know your child best, and, as your child may be preoccupied with picture-taking, be certain to note any sensory sensitivity triggers in the environment—smells, tastes, or visuals. This will help your child to prepare and plan some subtle adaptations or accommodations.

Essential

Many kids with Asperger's have a dramatic flair or are keenly interested in deconstructing live-action and animated films. If your child has videotaped or photographed his new school, try empowering his confidence and further quelling anxieties by creating his initial presentation of the material as a "premiere" (admission by ticket only, naturally), during which he conducts the official debut. A question and answer session may follow at his discretion.

Knowing your child's locker assignment, or the place where his belongings will be stored, should also be captured on film. Additionally, the final product from the visit—pictures or videos—can be viewed with siblings and other family members with your child narrating the highlights (enhancing his personal investment and elevating comfort levels!). The images can also be used to share with your child's same-age friends who haven't had the benefit of the sneak preview of the new school environment.

Finally, be certain that your child has her own way of visually counting down the days until the transition by marking off a calendar or some other time-keeping device. Be prepared for her anxiousness to grow and be ready to offer reassurances, answer questions, or review the materials she already has in her possession (making yourself real pictures and stories, and visual images of the school building). Transitioning to a new school will be taxing and stressful for your child but, with these preparations in place, it should be much more manageable for her.

Concerns about Bullying

If your child has anxiety about being identified as an easy target for abuse, find out about the new school's bullying policy and obtain it in writing to review and share with your child. Follow up with the administration if you have any questions or concerns about incident investigation or accountability. As previously noted, your child should know exactly who she can tell about any incidents in which she has felt verbally or physically bullied.

Does the school provide a peer mentor or some other student who can show your child around in a discreet, nonstigmatizing way with the potential for friendship? How will you receive communication from the school about any issues that arise? Also, it will be helpful to aid your child's transition if she is well aware, in advance, of any responsibilities that can be assigned to her during unstructured activity times. Some schools offer structured indoor activities as alternatives to recess and other unstructured times.

Transition to New Home

If your child's school environment is a social jungle fraught with peril or inconsistency, then home is his fortress of sanctuary. Your child's house—and bedroom in particular—is home base, a safe, impenetrable island in which he can relinquish his masquerade of neurotypical "normalcy" and be himself by himself. You've experienced what can occur if you or anyone else disrupts this sanctuary without adequate notice. Now, imagine what it can mean for your child if the physical structure of his room (and, by extension, his entire home) is threatened or removed because your family is relocating to a new living environment. Your child may experience resistance, denial, and emotional upset when you break the news of the move to another house. Depending upon the reason for the move, it may be easier to accept some than other rationales (divorce versus job transfer). Be wary of your child's potential to dip into a depressed state at this time as well. In any case, it will be important to partner with your child in as many facets of this process as possible.

Once the initial shock and heartbreak of the news subsides (yes, it can be *that* traumatic), share with your child thoughts about all the impending unknowns that face you and your family. If your child is an oldest child, can she assist you in breaking the news to younger siblings, cousins, neighbors, or other family members? This kind of "adult" responsibility can empower your child to shift her perspective of the move to a more selfless position. Think of some of the other responsibilities you can share with your child with Asperger's to make the move more palatable and less threatening. Perhaps your child could:

- Scan the Internet to locate Realtors, new home listings, and other related information.
- Help you to schedule dates and times to meet with Realtors to view prospective homes.
- Help arrange showings of your current home.
- Begin to inventory household and personal belongings.
- Plan a garage sale or designate items for dropoff donation.
- Start to prioritize packing and labeling moving boxes.
- Identify all utility companies that require notification of the move.

- Fill out change of address cards.
- Determine data involving the geographic location of the move, mileage to and from the destination, and other pertinent logistics.

When viewing potential new homes, allow your child to accompany you whenever possible. Encourage her to ask questions of the Realtor related to areas of interest or importance for her. This will help quell her anxieties and you may be surprised to hear her ask questions you hadn't thought to ask yourself. As with transitioning to a new school, once you've narrowed your choices of location to a select few, plan to document the final decision-making visits by taking photos or videos. Not only will this be an aid to your child, it will be as equally helpful to you as well in recalling certain details.

Essential

There are no two ways about it: moving to a new home, especially under duress or unpredictable circumstances (like divorce or a death in the family) will have great impact on your child. Though this is likely a stressful and hectic time for everyone, make yourself available to your child to listen to her (perhaps repeated) concerns. Illustrating or writing about the experience might be a helpful way of venting for her to process the anxiety.

During these walk-throughs, give your child the chance to speculate with you about room designations, potential location of furniture, changes in décor, and so on. If you are building a new home, it will be equally beneficial to you and your child to document the building process (with your child manning the camera). Moving day will still be very emotional for you all, but maintaining a positive attitude about a new beginning and a fresh start will be of immeasurable value.

Transition to College

Another major life change for young people is the prospect of attending college after high school graduation. If your child's diagnosis has been identified and supported in your school district, a transition plan to support your child from graduation to higher education, technical or training school, or employment of some sort should have been implemented by age fourteen with specific resources and contacts identified; a specific vocational plan should be in place by age sixteen. Your child may be eligible to continue attending school until age twenty-one but it is not usual for most students with Asperger's to remain behind their graduating class.

Some high schools may offer a school-to-work transition program or may partner with local colleges to offer higher-education opportunities while your child is still attending high school. Inquire about such opportunities well in advance of your child's senior year of school; there may be a waiting list, limited availability, or sign-up procedures.

The Decision to Attend College

Even if your child's school experience hasn't always been a glowing one, it has offered some measure of life stability. With the advent of graduation, another transition is impending that can, again, create emotional upheaval. Hopefully, at some point in your child's school career, a psychologist or guidance counselor has completed an inventory of your child's aptitudes—strengths, gifts, and talents. While there won't likely be anything there that comes as a surprise to you, the results of such an assessment can provide a valuable starting point in weighing future vocational or educational paths for your child to pursue. Your child's school should also be able to assist you and your child in matching your child's strengths and skills with schools known for their expertise in those select areas, like the college with a strong science program or the university known for its music department. Literature and other resources can be obtained with the support of your child's guidance counselor or other staff. Encourage your child to make appointments to meet with this individual to gather information and tips on filling out applications. (If your child procrastinates for whatever reason, set deadlines by which you expect him to meet your expectations. His internal sense of apprehension may be misinterpreted as laziness or lack of motivation.) Your child's school staff should wish to see your son or daughter be accepted to—and smoothly transition to—college, and should be willing to support this endeavor through to completion. Again, the attitude of everyone around your child will be of immeasurable benefit in framing this time as a maturing "rite of passage" and not something to be filled with dread.

What's Involved?

The word "college" has taken on numerous and varied connotations in recent times. This new flexibility is heartening to those children who have one perception of college as an "all or nothing" scenario; that is, some upset or resistance to college may come from the belief that college means packing up and leaving home, only returning at holidays and semester breaks. In partnership with your child, explore all that "going off to college" can mean, including:

- Attending college in another state (living on campus).
- Attending college in another part of your current state (living on campus).
- Working part-time and attending night classes (on campus or living at home).
- Starting out slowly by taking fewer classes (on campus or living at home).
- Starting out slowly by living at home but commuting to a local college.
- Taking classes online over the Internet.
- Taking correspondence courses.
- Attending a branch campus before relocating to the main campus.
- Considering how to transfer schools (and credits) if things aren't working out, or as part of a plan.

As with transition to a new school building, you and your child will want to feel as fully prepared as possible well in advance of beginning school. This time, there will be far more details to keep track of. Ensure that you are maintaining the literature, directions, contacts and references, and campus maps as organized as possible and keep notes cataloged well and *in writing*. As before, carefully photograph or videotape everything, marked clearly, to review as often as need be in order to make a final decision or just familiarize your child with the surroundings.

Your child's seeming lack of motivation to learn more about or attend college may be due to a combination of several factors. Be cautious of judging him as lazy, and consider that he may be fearful of all the "unknowns," depressed at the prospect, or anxious about on-campus social expectations.

The traditional unknowns include selection of roommates and scheduling classes. Take into account the location of classes and the time allotted between classes, in addition to the distance from your child's residence (or the parking lot, if commuting) to classes. Some kids, not as graceful or agile as they wish to be, may find it physically depleting to spend a lot of time walking long distances, especially in inclement weather. Conversely, if your child has too much time between classes, it can be socially awkward to finds ways to fill such downtime, especially if he is a commuter. Liane Holliday Willey's book *Pretending to be Normal* offers myriad suggestions for new college students for how best to assimilate on campus.

One Program That Works

The Center for Student Progress at Youngstown (Ohio) State University offers a model program of support to students with

Asperger's syndrome. On-site coordinators, who work from the center's office, meet weekly with identified students. Upon admission, any such student meets with a coordinator to whom they are assigned and completes a Participant Agreement that defines the obligation of the center as well as expectations of the student's participation in the program. By signing the Participant Agreement, the student also gives permission for a release of information so that test scores, grades, and other assessments are shared with her coordinator. It is an important function of the contract and allows the coordinator to access student grades and provide feedback early on in each semester so that any action needed to improve grades can be planned well in advance of failing a course.

Other aids provided to students with Asperger's by Youngstown State's Center for Student Progress include a Study Schedule that is filled out with each student and visually maps how to get organized, use time wisely, and plan when and where to devote time to studying. A calendar, again maintained by both parties, records test dates and assignment and project due dates. When a student comes in to meet with her coordinator, the coordinator can, at a glance, get a sense of where the student should be in her class management and can ask how she is progressing. Finally, a Learning Style Inventory is a simple, easy-to-read questionnaire that helps the center's coordinators to determine the type of learning style unique to each student (visual learner, auditory learner, or kinesthetic learner—someone who learns best through moving and doing). Supporting the student to identify her learning style and adapt study habits to some helpful techniques is another of the coordinator's responsibilities. This may, in turn, lead to accommodations necessary to achieve success in certain classes, such as a professor's flexibility in how graded notebooks are submitted if your child reinforces certain concepts with illustrations.

There is also a checklist called Strategies for Reaching Goals that includes not only academic milestones desired but social objectives as well, such as joining a student organization, attending an athletic event, and participating in other on-campus social events. Many other activities may be involved, depending upon the individual needs of each student.

Fact

Your child's selection of higher-education institution may be influenced by the kinds of on-campus supports available to her. Check with each school under consideration to determine the scope and extent of support for students with Asperger's syndrome. This may look very different from services available to students with disabilities that include *physical* adaptations and accommodations.

Determining the type and degree of available support similar to the Youngstown State University program may be a decision-making factor in your child's college selection. At the very least, making that single connection with someone who will function as an ally is crucial to your child's ability to assimilate successfully; that is, your child can likely handle most of the academic requirements, but college is also about broadening one's social contacts as well. An ally may be informal, or it may be prearranged through a student mentorship program on campus. Most forward-thinking, progressive universities have programs established to aid students with disabilities, but finding those that have expertise in the subtleties of Asperger's syndrome may prove challenging.

Handling Divorce

Divorce is rarely an amicable situation. Occasional stress and tension in marriage is inevitable. The outward, vocal expression of arguments between married couples can vary from silent, passive-aggressive behavior to knockdown, drag-out, obscenity-shouting brawls. In any event, your very sensitive child with Asperger's syndrome will probably sense marital discord long before you realize it yourself—even if you believe you've been very cautious. Parents, in the context of a loving and safe home environment, are the very rock of stability for all children, especially the child with Asperger's.

Potential Reactions

No child should have to grow up subjected to a tense, abusive home life in which parents interact in harsh and angry ways. The child with Asperger's syndrome may internalize what is transpiring around her and assume personal responsibility for it—even if none of the marital conflict has any reflection on her. It can be an utterly terrifying time, and the internal personalization of the situation cannot be contained indefinitely. In the child with Asperger's syndrome, this can manifest itself in:

- Depressive symptoms (see Chapter 7)
- Post-traumatic stress disorder (see Chapter 7)
- Heightened anxiety
- Regular symptoms of physical illness
- Rashes and other skin irritations
- An increase in "acting out" or other "attention-seeking" behaviors
- Increased difficulty in school

Resolving the situation, maintaining peace wherever possible, and providing assurances as divorce is impending should aid the situation. Only you can determine if other interventions, such as child protective services or family or psychiatric counseling, would be appropriate to augment your efforts. If so, you will need to ensure that such intervention is tailored to accommodate your child's way of understanding and interpreting information.

Explaining Divorce

Most children are naturally inclined to believe that they are somehow the pivotal catalyst that causes a divorce. This may be intensified in your child with Asperger's and will be reinforced if he or she witnessed or overheard (remember, hearing can be especially sensitive) conflicts in which they *were* at the center of an argument. It is also natural for any child to feel emotional upheaval in wondering who to "side" with, especially if one parent "plays" the child against the other. Even if you are seeking to escape a harmful or abusive situation, your child with Asperger's is likely to feel emotionally torn. In such a situation, all children will require constant assurances during a time in which uncertainty about the future reigns. This will be especially true of the child with Asperger's and, as you've learned, verbal assurances are not enough.

Fact

In certain divorce scenarios, some parents wrongfully manipulate children into "taking sides" with one parent. This can set a regrettable precedent for the child with Asperger's who may maintain a longtime association with the mindset that has been instilled, making reconnecting with the "opposing" parent hurtful or challenging.

Your child will require pictures, words, and stories to help make sense of it all and to foster some measure of safety and comfort. It will be helpful to make private time alone with your child. If you and your spouse are civil with one another, meeting together with your child will be an optimal demonstration of solidarity and good will. Explain the circumstances as you would to any of your children. Don't be surprised if your child with Asperger's punctuates your discussion with her own recollections of marital conflicts that stretch back in time—some of which you may have forgotten or of which you failed to realize the full impact. Encouraging your child to write, draw, cartoon storyboard, or use the computer to communicate her feelings and understanding of the situation should be helpful. Review and fine-tune this information with her regularly and be prepared to follow her lead in opening up discussion at times you hadn't anticipated it. Sights, sounds, and smells can trigger thoughts that will lead to your child's need to verbalize her feelings.

Your child may well have to decide where and with whom she'd like to live. This can snowball and lead to other social upheavals concerning a new home, new neighborhood, new family members, and a new school. It may also mean leaving behind friends, family, pets, and very familiar environments.

It is important to stress and review all the things that *will stay the same* during this transition in addition to walking through the future changes, and to do so often throughout the process (foremost of which should be your unconditional love). Be clear in communicating that the divorce is not your child's fault and demystify any new environmental changes in ways similar to those described in transitioning to a new school.

Loss of Loved Ones

The loss of a loved one can never fully be anticipated. Consider the range of emotions you may experience, such as grief, guilt, shock, loneliness, compassion, and humor, and think of how that might reflect in your child with Asperger's syndrome. The difference may be that while you and others close to you may outwardly show such emotions, you may not readily detect such feelings in your child. Just like you, comprehending the loss of a loved one (even a beloved pet) may take time for your child to completely process. Because your child isn't grieving in "typical" ways, such as openly sobbing or wanting to be with and talk to close family or friends, it doesn't mean he isn't experiencing everything you are. The opposite could, in fact, be true.

Explaining Death

Remember that honesty is the best policy. You may be pressured by well-meaning friends or relatives to offer some alternate explanation for the loss of a loved one, such as "Uncle Rich has gone away and won't be back," "Daddy's just sleeping," "Your baby sister won't be coming home from the hospital," or "Grandma's resting in the ground now." At some point in time your white "fib" will be exposed and the cover-up—despite your original best intentions—could upset the trust between you and your child.

Essential

Remember that it is typical of us all to mourn the loss of a loved one and to become depressed with grief. This, in and of itself, is natural and expected, and does not make for clinical depression unless it becomes prolonged and stymies the person's daily life. Monitor your child's grieving process and be aware of the symptoms of depression as they might apply to her experience.

In explaining death, you will wish to call upon your own religious and spiritual beliefs as the foundation from which to begin such a discussion with your child. Analogies, such as referring to other people who have passed or transition metaphors like the butterfly, may be helpful—as will drawing and writing out what you intend to communicate and reviewing it regularly. Here is a story that was written for a young child with Asperger's and his brother to explain their father's sudden death from a drug overdose. Use it as a guide in adapting it to meet your own circumstances.

> Daddy was a good man. Daddy loved us very much. When Daddy died, he was very sick. When Daddy was sick, it could be scary. He said things or did things that were scary. He did these things because he was very sick. He didn't feel well. But he never wanted to make us feel scared. He loved us very much.
>
> The day Daddy died was scary. He was very sick and fell down. Mommy called an ambulance. People who drive an ambulance are good people. They only want to help other people and do good things. They wanted to help Daddy and take him to the hospital. They wanted him to feel better and not be sick anymore. But then Daddy died.

It was not our fault. It was not Daddy's fault. It was not Mommy's fault. It was not the fault of the ambulance people.

Now Daddy is in Heaven with God and the angels. This is where he lives now. It is beautiful in Heaven. Daddy is not sick anymore in Heaven.

We may not be able to see Daddy every day like we used to. We may cry or feel upset because we miss him and want him to come home. When we miss Daddy, all we need to do is think about him. We will try to think about how much he loves us. We will try to think about the fun things we did with Daddy, like going to Disney World. Even though he lives in Heaven, he will always be our Daddy, and we will love him forever.

Follow-up Support

Follow your child's lead. It is not helpful to exclude your child from participating in any of the subsequent formalities attendant to funerals or other rituals if he expresses his desire to partake (although an open-casket situation can be visually confusing and distressing for many). In fact, if you can in some small way assign your child a responsibility at this time, it may help him to maintain focus amidst what may be a chaotic and upsetting time. This may be especially helpful for the preadolescent or teen.

Don't become angered if your child catches you off-guard with seemingly insensitive questions about the mechanics of embalming, cremation, burial, and the like. These are honest inquiries designed to contribute to your child's understanding and comfort level; answer them just as honestly, or explain your discomfort with discussing those subjects at present but refer your child to others who might, or perhaps look up similar, generic information on the Internet. Also at this time don't be quick to scold if your child's emotions aren't considered appropriate to the moment, such as laughing during a solemn discussion—he may be on emotional burnout and is distracting himself by playing a mind movie. Finally, don't be surprised, dismiss it as imagination, or blatantly disregard it if your child reports that she has seen, talked with, smelled, or otherwise interacted with the loved one who has recently passed. Remember that your child may be very sensitive to many things, seen and unseen. Instead, validate what your child tells you by listening carefully, requesting further information, asking clarifying questions, providing assurances, and reinforcing her communication wherever possible. (See Chapter 17 for more on the subject of spirituality.)

CHAPTER 15

Traveling and Vacations

The key to successfully vacationing with the child with Asperger's syndrome is in advance preparation. Knowing what comes next is of crucial importance to your child. Feeling safe and comfortable in planning for a trip will greatly add to your child's level of enjoyment during the event. Your child's ability to enjoy a vacation will directly impact the enjoyment your entire family experiences. A successful vacation will further your child's desire to travel again.

Fun Vacations

Some families value travel and vacation more than others do. Those that travel often may do so because:

- They are distanced from family or relatives.
- It is family tradition to travel at certain times of the year, or to certain places.
- They enjoy the rewarding benefits of rest and relaxation.
- They are interested in the culture and history of other countries.
- They can afford to vacation as they please.

Other families prefer to stay close to home in order to make day trips, or to gather for picnics, fairs, and sports events. No matter how your family prioritizes travel and vacation, you will greatly enhance your child's ability to enjoy being away from home (no matter the duration) through careful planning.

Essential

If you are the kind of family that vacations with extended family or friends, it will be helpful to provide your child with some self-advocating strategies on the trip. Determine when and where solitary downtime may occur, script in advance some ideas for discussion topics, and review options for pacing oneself such as listening to music or audio tapes or playing hand-held computer games.

As before, whenever possible, partner with your child in planning a vacation trip. Your child may be a person who dreads the thought of leaving home to stay anywhere other than surroundings that are comfortable and familiar. (If your child is in her late teens or of a responsible age and is interested in other things, is her staying home, separate from any travel plans, an option in your family if she voices this desire?) Her anticipation of a trip away will be heightened if there is a way to tie the trip to her most passionate interests. For example, if she is fascinated by cartoon animation, ensure that a trip to a Disney theme park includes an opportunity to observe animators at work. If she is absorbed in learning about the mechanics of railway transportation, can you take a train to your destination instead of flying or traveling by car? If the folklore of a certain foreign culture is of interest, it stands to follow that a trip abroad would be desirable. Explore the available entertainment options in the home state of her favorite actress, inventor, or president. If your child is passionate about certain architecture, determine your flexibility in making a modification in your travel plans to set aside a day for such sightseeing. Building upon passions in this way will turn a potentially anxious situation into something to look forward to.

A Role in Planning

If you are able to link your family's travel plans to your child's passions, then he will be automatically engaged to further pursue the vacation. To ride the wave of this comfort level, consider other ways in which your child can become increasingly invested in the process. What are the roles and responsibilities you can appoint to him in order to plan in partnership? Such responsibilities may include asking your child to research the trip on the Internet in order to gather information important to your preparation, such as:

- Comparing costs of lodging local to the vacation point.
- Identifying local eating establishments and comparing costs. (Some places list online menus so that you can decide in advance if your child's dietary needs will match the available foods.)
- Determining the most cost-efficient way to travel (and then deciding the best match for your entire family).
- Identifying other forms of entertainment (other than what initially prompted you to select the destination).
- Determining the usual climate or allergens of the area to plan for a comfortable stay and seasonally adequate wardrobe.
- Comparing "package plans" against one another in terms of content and economy.
- Learning if any special equipment or other accoutrements are necessary or are the responsibility of the traveler.
- Determining if it's possible to modify or combine travel plans in order to vacation with others or stop en route to or from home to visit friends, family, or another vacation spot.
- Looking up the most efficient route there in terms of mileage and travel (highways versus back roads), and printing out directions using an Internet map locator.
- Requesting to receive any pertinent literature offered online at no cost.

Once your child has completed his "assignment" to glean useful vacation information, ask him to share it with you and others taking the trip. This is another opportunity to highlight the good efforts of your child and aid him in taking a personal investment in the entire process. With the information in hand, your family can decide additional planning from there.

Remember that your child may be especially vulnerable to allergies of all kinds. The environmental allergens in your vacation spot of choice may make or break your child's enjoyment and will require some investigating prior to committing to your final selection.

Your child may relish planning an itinerary for your family. However, communicate to your child that, while it all sounds terrific, it should be understood by all that the itinerary is *flexible*, subject to change depending upon any unforeseen obstacles, delays, or unanticipated but appealing alternative activities available upon your arrival. Brainstorm in advance those things that are out of your control but which might hinder your plans, such as cancellation due to illness, safety alerts, or unsafe weather conditions. In this manner, your child should be less likely to stress about abiding by a rigid schedule. Reinforce that the itinerary must be a group consensus and ask your child to poll members of the traveling party.

Vacation Anxieties

In order to soothe any additional anxieties your child may experience about vacationing, it will be important to make yourself available to any questions she may have about the process. To avoid repeating yourself, request that your child write or type the questions in advance so that you may respond to them in writing. That way, the questions and answers can become the property of your child. If she repeats a question you know you've answered, simply refer her to the original paper if the answer hasn't changed. Your child will feel most at ease if there is a timetable or schedule of activities while away. As a family, you may wish to plan a schedule together based upon the information at hand, with the stipulation that flexibility may be called for; upon your arrival, you may learn of changes, additions, or other adjustments that will modify any schedule. Your child may also wonder if Internet access will be available where you'll be, or if she may bring something to help her feel comfortable and that she associates with home, such as a favorite book, music CD, or object related to her passion. (Agreeing to the latter will go a long way, as will be further explained in Chapter 17.)

Flying

As with the initial steps in vacation planning, your child can also be helpful in locating and pricing air travel to and from your destination, including connecting flights and layovers. If your child has never flown before, he will take his cues from you. If you make it sound exciting, adventurous, and interesting, your child will likely reflect your attitude. If you have a fear of flying but acquiesce out of cost efficiency or convenience, your child will quickly tap into your anxieties and internalize them as his own.

Essential

As a diversion, your child may feel tempted to press the flight attendant call button more often than what is considered appropriate. Even though he may believe he has legitimate needs (or is perhaps just being a typical rascally kid), discuss this nuance of air travel with your child in advance of your travel arrangements, and set reasonable limits as you would for any child.

If your child has enjoyed (or successfully tolerated) flying in the past, he may even be a support to you in providing assurances that everything will be just fine. One young man with Asperger's went so far as to devise a full-color, hand-illustrated booklet of all the airlines that come and go from his local airport. This included detailed statistics and drawings of the various makes and models of aircraft and the special features of each. It was a beautiful, amazing collection of information that enabled him to demystify air travel in order to quell anxieties of his own and others, including his siblings.

The Waiting Game

Waiting in line is an exercise in patience for many people, including children with Asperger's. Recent trends in heightened airport security have made such lengthy delays standard. Request that your child learn about airport safety procedures in order to feel prepared in advance of flying. As before, ask that he develop a list of questions about flying for you to answer. If you are unable to respond to all the questions, find out who can (even if it must wait until you arrive at the airport). He may be able to address them—and feel satisfied in an adultlike manner—by directing his inquiries to a ticket agent, security personnel, or flight crew member. Take advantage of shortcuts to waiting in line at ticket counters, including curbside checking of luggage and free-standing e-ticket kiosks that automatically issue boarding passes with proper photo ID.

Handling the Airport Environment

Large airports can be overwhelming with their bombardment of sensory stimuli. Your child may enjoy taking in all the sights, sounds, and smells, or he may be unable to tolerate the combined convergence of the environment with its crowds of rushing people, perpetual PA system announcements, and other disorienting noises and visuals. Wearing a Walkman may be necessary during this time, or asking your child to check the monitors to confirm arrival or departure information could prove helpful for him. While waiting to depart at your gate, suggest that your child engage in a favored activity or you can play a word or memory game based upon the surroundings. As with all kids, this may also be a good time to get a snack from the airport McDonald's or pizza stand.

If you are not traveling first class, when the call for boarding is made, it may be a good idea to take advantage of preboarding opportunities that usually include people traveling with children or those needing extra time or assistance. This will give your child the chance to take a few minutes to acclimate to the look, feel, and sound of the aircraft before it fills with people. This may also be a time when your child can speak directly to a flight crew member about any last-minute questions (be prepared for your child to wow 'em with some very technical inquiries).

During the flight, your child may become bored, impatient, or stressed. As discussed, ensure that she has plenty to keep her occupied, including favorite books, drawing paper, interactive games, or conversations that you've reserved for the trip. (These strategies apply to long car rides as well.) If traveling abroad, you can also use this time to discuss and review the language and culture differences of the area to be visited. Are there guessing games to be played in which you and your child quiz one another about customs, geography, foods, or words indigenous to the country to which you are traveling?

Fact

If your child is traveling without you, make a cassette tape of your voice for her Walkman that offers a positive, upbeat message and gives gentle reminders of travel etiquette, things to do and say, and expectations you have of regular contact by phone or e-mail to keep you updated until you can hear all about it first-hand.

Having headphones along in order to listen to pleasing music will also greatly help to block out external noise that can consume your child and heighten her nervousness. If she does not articulate the need for such, suggest it yourself if you are attuned to her body language, or model it by putting on your own Walkman (at times designated as appropriate by the pilot of course).

In the Air . . .

All major airlines offer complemintary in-flight magazines providing detailed layouts that map the air terminals of major travel hubs. During the flight, "assign" your child to look up this information and share it with you. This is another helpful and useful responsibility that will occupy your child's purpose, especially during long flights. This is an opportunity to support your child to feel safe and comfortable in knowing what's coming next and what that will look like (that is, knowing which is your connecting gate and whether you walk there or take transportation). Don't forget that being up so high in the air may be a very novel experience for your child. Make use of this unusual perspective to talk about what you both see when looking out the windows, including cloud formations (and shapes in clouds), the minuscule appearance of cars and people on the ground, the winding course of rivers and streams, or the checkered patterns of farmer's fields.

Amusement Parks

Popular destinations of many vacationers include any number of amusement and recreation theme parks geared specifically to family fun and entertainment. They are appealing for all the variety of rides and activities, or for the tie-in with popular cartoon characters or other mascots.

They can also quickly propel the child with Asperger's syndrome into total overload without careful planning. Remember, your child wants to please and wants to blend (and may have enthusiastically anticipated the trip), but no child deliberately seeks the public embarrassment and humiliation of a meltdown in the middle of Frontier Land because of improper planning or pacing. This "behavioral" communication is a last resort when all else has failed. Weigh whether you think an amusement park vacation is appropriate for your child in the context of your family makeup.

As mentioned before, engage your child in assisting you to prepare for attending a theme park by researching all the details: how far, mode of travel, where to stay, how much, etc. Again, if there is a way to link any of the theme park activities to one of your child's passions, this is best. If your child is interested in oceanography, Sea World might be a better option over some other attraction. If the theme park is located in an area with other "spinoff" type activities and amusements on a smaller scale, can your child attend one of those with a designated adult instead of the park? Interactive science or natural history museums, zoos, or a curiosity like a Ripley's Believe It or Not! Museum may provide a calmer, slower-paced atmosphere that your child may find conducive to becoming absorbed in the subject matter.

Essential

When assigning your child the responsibility of looking up useful information about theme parks, recommend she start with *www.themeparks.com*. This Web site contains detailed information about a broad range of the most popular and frequently visited parks, including Disney, Universal, Sea World, Busch parks, and regional parks like Cedar Points and Six Flags.

At the Park

Once you decide upon a place to visit, contrive a schedule in partnership with your child. Theme parks are notorious for large crowds and long lines. You know your child best and have a sense of his endurance and tolerance thresholds. Build in breaks and downtime throughout the day. A quiet lunch may work for some kids, while others may need the total solitude offered by a nap or reading time in the hotel room. Stick to the schedule to the very best of your ability and pay attention to your child for any signs that the vacation is wearing thin on him, which he may not be communicating.

If your child becomes easily distracted by noise—especially unpredictable noises like train whistles, buzzers and bells, or other loud sounds emanating from rides—wearing a Walkman and listening to favorite music will be a survival tool. Another coping strategy is to appoint your child the responsibility of taking photographs to share with family and friends. Disposable cameras make this easy and inexpensive, even if you are also using a camera of your own. You may also allow your child to record the highlights of your activities with a camcorder, with your child directing the "movie" and providing the narration, of course.

Fact

The Walt Disney theme parks (Disneyland and Disney World) offer a free handbook titled *Guidebook for Guests with Disabilities*. It is available by calling ✆(407) W-DISNEY. Most often, businesses consider wheelchair accessibility, blindness, and deafness primary among disability services, so not all the information may apply to your child but it may prove useful in providing ideas and hints for a successful time.

Waiting in line can be a frustrating exercise in patience for many kids. The child with Asperger's may not immediately understand why it's necessary to wait in line. It may be helpful to prepare a written story, in advance of the trip, to review with your child before and during long waits in line. The story should include details about what to do and how to conduct oneself while waiting. It may also be a good time to play visual memory games about the surroundings, review the day's written agenda (maintained by your child), or discuss what you anticipate may be experienced on the ride.

Many theme parks offer a faster, alternate line for people with disabilities to quickly board rides and other amusements. Selecting this alternative may be publicly stigmatizing for your child with Asperger's syndrome, although many parents of children with autism swear by this convenience. Also be advised that, because your child doesn't present with obvious outward differences, you may receive the evil eye from those you are passing ahead of on your way to board a ride. An option may be to purchase an "easy pass" or "fast pass" usually offered for some attractions. Learn about the rules and premium costs involved to access such a system. It may be that the passes are only available at certain times for certain rides, which may cause you and your child to rearrange your schedule. Find out as many details in advance to aid in your planning.

As with any of your children, you will want to be certain that your child with Asperger's is hydrated with cooling liquids throughout the day, wears sunblock (and a hat, if tolerated), and stays as comfortable as possible while waiting in very warm conditions. He may not know to express his growing discomfort or may be oblivious to it entirely.

Check Out the Rides

Riding certain rides can look tempting and exciting—until you're a passenger. Take the time to carefully observe any ride you are considering with your child *prior to* boarding. The thrill of most amusement rides is based on surprise, fear, and strong centrifugal force. The extreme emotional and physical stimulation may be too much for your child to endure. If you feel anxious about how you would feel riding a certain attraction, it's probably a good measuring tool to deny your child admittance. As a guide, many amusement parks and carnivals offer brochures that are coded to indicate appropriate age levels. Usually, there is a size standard against which your child may be measured prior to getting in line. (Visibly posted height-requirement signs may indicate something to the effect of "You must be this tall to ride this ride.") Combine this with your intuition as a parent to make a final decision.

In fact, it will likely be best if you agree to start slowly with gentle rides, paying careful attention for signs of overstimulation (obviously if your child is dizzy beyond ambulation or vomits after disembarking the Tilt-a-Whirl, it's a clear indication that a repeat ride is not a good idea). When boarding a ride, make sure your child is seated properly with the restraint system fully latched before the ride begins. Ask the ride operator for assistance in manipulating the restraint system if you need it. Most restraint systems are not designed to prevent a large child who is absolutely determined to exit the ride from doing so. Of course, this can endanger the child and other passengers, resulting in injury or death. Ensure that your child is clear in understanding the *written* rules about the ride, such as keeping arms and hands inside it and not trying to unlatch and disembark while the ride is in motion. Once a ride starts, it can rarely be stopped except in the most extreme circumstances and only if an attendant can be notified.

Some particular rides may create sensory or cognitive feedback that can be numbing, endocrine releasing, or exalting in the overall physical thrill of the experience. As such, your child may become focused on riding one ride exclusively. As always, use your parental judgment—your child's desire may be Asperger's-driven, but your limits regarding when enough is enough is pure parenting.

Evaluate the Experience

After each ride, process the experience with your child to gather her impressions and tolerance level. You may be surprised—some kids absolutely relish the sensory feedback they derive from seemingly violent, whirling, spinning, upside-down-turning rides. She may beg you to ride "one more time" after the fourth time! As with any of your children, your acquiescence is entirely at your discretion. Be aware that many amusement rides feature flashing and spinning lights that may vary in intensity or kick up in intensity once the ride starts. The concern here is that this constant "strobe light" flickering may induce seizure activity in one already prone to such. In addition to scheduling downtime, it may be best to pace the sequence of activities, like riding a roller coaster followed by attending the dolphin show, then on to an exhibit display before tackling another fast-paced ride.

Chapter 16

Sexuality

Many of us are uncomfortable discussing issues of sexuality. Supporting your child as a person with Asperger's syndrome means supporting the *whole* person, including his sexuality. Some parents prefer not to "go there" in their thinking and struggle with perceiving their child as a budding adult. However, if you stay attuned to your child's growing needs as he ages and matures, you will be a resource to him concerning issues of sexuality.

The Birds and the Bees

As with any of your children, you will want to discuss with your spouse, in advance, how best to explain issues of a sexual nature to your child with Asperger's. Many children broach the topic first—a cue for parents to guide them into such discussions. For example, your child may enjoy watching animal or nature-related programs on TV, or you may own pets that deliver litters of puppies, kittens, or hamsters. Inevitably, your child will be exposed to the facts of life via images of animals mating with one another, and this may prompt questions about reproduction or sexual attraction. Your child may have also intruded upon your own lovemaking unexpectedly; this requires prompt explanation as well for purposes of damage control.

Understand that for all children, observation of sexual acts can be grossly misinterpreted. Facial expressions, vocalizations, and body position can make the scenario appear violent and hurtful, and anything but passionate. The child with Asperger's—witnessing such activity without explanation—may burn this image into her brain and associate it exclusively with sexual activity, setting an unpleasant precedent. Shouting angrily at your child upon discovery will only reinforce such negative thoughts and feelings.

Your child may be especially astute about how animals reproduce from his readings or watching educational programming. When you broach the "facts of life" discussion, you may be greeted with rolled eyes or groans of "I already know all about that!" Still, proceed as intended; there's an emotional bond between humans that adds a nuance to lovemaking between people that you may wish to communicate.

Many people with differences have been taught that it is inappropriate to have sexual thoughts, feelings, or indulgences at all. One young adult with Asperger's has been so brainwashed that he harms himself whenever he has sexual thoughts in order to exact punishment for thinking "dirty" things. As a parent, you may see your son or daughter as a perpetual child because of a childlike naiveté about so many aspects of life and socialization. The truth is, we are *all* sexual beings, even children. Attempting to control or suppress someone's sexuality is akin to assuming authority over that person's humanity. No one has the right to assume such an audacious position over another person, whether that person experiences a different way of being or not.

The best way to enter into what will be a series of ongoing discussions with your child about sex is to be open and honest, using clear language paired with visuals. There are a number of well-illustrated books available that explain animal and human reproduction, including pop-up books, which might be helpful. Videos may also be available at your library or video store (some video stores rent such tapes free of charge).

Approaching the Subject

Your comfort level with your own sexuality will determine how effective you are. Presenting material in a "hit or miss" manner (i.e., you're out of the room while your child absorbs the information alone) may create more confusion and send a message that you are unapproachable. Be available to your child during and after such dialogues so that you can quickly clarify anything that might be upsetting or cause for concern. Quickly dispel any rumors or myths your child may bring home. Your child may hear wildly imaginative and completely false stories about what happens during the act of sex, which is scary stuff that can fuel anxieties about an already confusing process. When discussing sexual organs, avoid using cutesy or slang terms—there is great potential for your child to associate those words with certain body parts exclusively for some time to come, making the introduction of the proper words confusing.

Human sexuality can be a complex matter. Just like everyone else, people with Asperger's syndrome have identified their sexuality as heterosexual, homosexual, or bisexual. Still others communicate a disinterest or lack of desire to engage in a romantic or sexual relationship with *any* partner. Please be prepared to be sensitive and respectful of your child's individual sexuality.

Again, follow your child's lead about the type and degree of information to share, paired with visuals. To alleviate any misunderstanding that sex is a physical act for the sake of sex alone, ensure that the discussion occurs within the context of love—a concept that may be challenging for some children who, at a tender age, associate love exclusively with parents, friends, and family. This will help quell any fears about sexual acts being hurtful or repressive. Explain that, because of feeling euphoric in the moment, sex may look and sound like something it's not. It is important to emphasize that while you are always willing and accessible to discuss sexual matters, it is a *private* matter that should not be discussed publicly, especially within earshot of others. List, in writing, the places and times that sex is okay to discuss, like when you are alone with your child in the car or at home watching something on TV that provokes his curiosity.

Growing Up

You will wish to periodically revisit these conversations as your child matures, if he doesn't broach the subject first. Most significantly, be prepared to discuss sexuality at the onset of your child's adolescence. A changing, maturing body, complete with growing pains, sprouting body hair, or menstruation, can be another very frightening time if not handled tastefully well in advance and framed in a very positive light.

As your child grows, you may discover her sexuality begin to flourish. Be certain to counsel her privately to quickly curb any overtly sexual remarks or similar, flirtatious self-expressions to support her in avoiding social embarrassment. Others may completely misinterpret her communications and label them in stigmatizing ways. If necessary, dig out your old list of when, where, and with whom it is okay to talk about sex. Or compose a new list. At a certain age, it may not be "cool" to continue having these discussion with one's parent, so, while you will always wish to be accessible, the list may be expanded to include a circle of safe and trusted friends who can be relied upon to keep your child's confidence and give accurate feedback.

Masturbation

Remember that many individuals with Asperger's have a strong associative connection when learning new concepts or social "rules." If you send your child the message that masturbation is unequivocally wrong or perpetuate antiquated myths about going blind or growing hairy hands, he will believe it, and such notions will imprint upon your child a disturbing, harmful view of acting upon one's sexual thoughts through masturbation.

For many, masturbation is one of the few forms of pleasurable release that can be individually controlled. The essential concept to communicate here is one of public versus private masturbation. If you are unsure or uncomfortable about broaching the subject of masturbation, here is a sample story used to introduce the basics to a preadolescent boy. The strategy is that he read it with a trusted ally (you, if that applies) and, afterward, has a forum in which to ask questions. The story should become his personal property and he may review the "rules" about masturbation at his leisure. You can adapt the same story to meet the needs of your daughter.

> My body is my own. My body is beautiful. My body is made up of many different parts, inside and out. Inside parts are like my heart and stomach. Outside parts are like my arms and legs. The outside parts that are between my legs and covered by my underwear are called my sexual organs. My sexual organs are my penis and my testicles. Many boys and men touch, rub, or gently pull their penis. When this happens, their penis usually gets bigger and harder. The same thing may happen to me. This is normal and okay. If I touch, rub, or gently pull my penis, this is called masturbation. Many boys and men masturbate. Masturbation is a choice that is my own to make.
>
> If I choose to masturbate it may be because I am thinking about sex. It may be because I am thinking about another person. It may be because I want to feel good. It may be because I want some time alone with my body. It may be for other reasons.
>
> When I masturbate, I may feel excited inside. I may breathe harder. I may breathe faster. This is normal and okay. When I masturbate, I may get so excited that my penis ejaculates. This means that something white and wet comes out of the opening in the tip of my penis. It is called semen or sperm. I may not ejaculate semen or sperm every time I masturbate. But if I do, this is normal and okay.

If I choose to masturbate, I will try to remember to masturbate in a private place. This means I will go to a place where there are no other people around. This means I will go to a place where I can be alone with my body. A private place may be my bedroom or a bathroom.

People masturbate in a private place because sexual organs are private. People wear underwear and clothes to keep their sexual organs private. People expect one another to masturbate in a private place. People will also expect me to masturbate in a private place. It is like a rule. A place that is not private is a place with other people around me. If I touch my sexual organs when I'm in a place that is not private—even if I'm wearing pants—people may be upset. They may laugh at me. They may be angry. They may report me to the police. They may not think I am smart. They may think these things because people expect one another to masturbate in a private place. If I masturbate in a place that is not private, I am breaking a rule that people expect me to know.

I will try not to touch my sexual organs, or put my hands in my pants, or masturbate in a place that is not private. I will try to remember to masturbate only in a private place. Masturbation is a choice that is my own to make. It is normal and okay.

Infatuation

As your child with Asperger's blossoms into a teenager, he is also developing as a sexual young adult. He may be finding himself sexually attracted to others more and more, and perhaps is finding a social niche by imitating the way he sees others interacting. He may develop crushes typical of any young person feeling a strong connection with another because of mutual interests, compatible personalities, or similar skills and talents.

Is It Love?

Like anyone, some young people with Asperger's can grossly misjudge the depth or reciprocation of potentially romantic relationships with others. This may be an extremely confusing time for your child.

Much of what is considered sexual chemistry between two people is unspoken, subtle, or steeped in innuendo—including all facial expression and body language cues your child may have difficulty tapping into. Because many people with Asperger's think of social behavior in clear-cut terms, your child may overestimate the intent of the other party in the relationship. (In the cruelest of circumstances, the other person may be "playing" your child, setting him up to fall for their own amusement; or the person may have been put up to it by others with similarly disingenuous motives.) It may also be that the other person only perceives your child as "just a friend."

Essential

Some high-profile celebrity stalkers may also fit an Asperger's syndrome profile, in addition to being deemed mentally ill. Their personal, unconventional logic, intrinsic backgrounds, and antisocial activities have been cited as contributors to their obsessive drive. Your challenge is to keep communication channels open with your child in navigating and balancing teen and young adult romance to avoid unfair mislabeling.

Unrequited Crush

The challenge is that some kids with Asperger's don't recognize the nuances of what's friendship and what's puppy love (or full-blown, young adult romance). In some instances, this misinterpretation can lead the individual with Asperger's, perhaps driven by genuine affection, to become intensely infatuated. This may demonstrate itself through symptoms similar to those of obsessive-compulsive disorder—not eating or sleeping regularly, inability to focus and concentrate, thinking about nothing but the other person. Be especially watchful for symptoms of depression at this time as well.

If your child is misinterpreting social cues, is in denial or disbelieving of another's communications, or won't take "no" for an answer, there is potential for him to be accused of stalking or harassment, especially if this is the first time he's experienced such intense feelings of affection. On occasion, a person may go to extremes to make his plea known, such as harming himself or threatening to kill the person, taking radical measures in a public environment such as school, or other similar threats. Usually, these are nothing more than cries for attention (you know your child to be a gentle, quiet individual), but, in this day and age, severe communications of this nature are not tolerated and schools are quick to enforce serious consequences in reaction to such threats. Any pronouncement of the intent to harm oneself or attempts to do so must be treated very seriously with swift intervention.

Fact

Having balance in one's life can be of immeasurable aid in how we approach our challenges. If your child's has meaningful responsibilities, unconditional allies, and opportunities to explore passions, coping with relationship obstacles may be less likely to become an all-consuming focus (sometimes easier said than done for us all).

At this time, it will be wise to gauge, day by day, your child's activities; most of his time (and the interactions he enjoys) will occur away from home, during the day, and in school. Ensure that you are regularly asking specific, detailed questions about his day, particularly if you suspect something is wrong.

There is also the flip side to consider. In one instance, a boy with Asperger's misinterpreted the romantic advances of a girl, thinking they were just friends. Apparently she became so impatient and frustrated at his lack of sexual savvy that she stood him up at a school dance. When she finally arrived, she acted cold and indifferent toward him, propelling him further into confusion. Hopefully, with your awareness and early guidance, your child will experience both success and bittersweet (but manageable) romantic interactions.

Dating

When any two people meet and develop a gratifying romantic and sexual relationship, it often stems from a mutual vocation, avocation, or educational pursuit. Remember, passions are icebreakers in conversation and are relationship-builders as well. Building upon one's most passionate of interests can lead directly to interacting with others similarly impassioned. Still, some people are drawn to each other because they compensate for each other's differences, strengths, and deficits. However two people are drawn together, new relationships of this nature can be difficult for anyone to navigate, and this is no different for your child with Asperger's.

Balancing this newfound "like" with advancing the relationship can be an art form for us all. Explain to your child that it's never wrong to simply ask the other person to be honest about what they are thinking and feeling. This is the only way many people with Asperger's will know definitively how to pursue the relationship. Any discussion about dating should also include an explanation of the potential for rejection by the other person. It is a trial and error, touch and go process for anyone. Be prepared to counsel your child in ways that are private and gentle; he has the potential to take rejection hard.

Barney, an adult with Asperger's, shares an anecdote from his adolescence with amusement for the purpose of illuminating others about misunderstanding social customs. When he was in high school, "cruising" in cars up and down a main strip was popular. Boys in cars would shout out introductions to carfuls of girls. Barney, however, felt this was an inefficient way of communicating, since it required shouting over other cruisers. He constructed a small transmitter that allowed him to pick up on the radio signals that girls in a particular car were listening to. He would tune the transmitter to the radio of a carful of girls he was interested in, then pick up his microphone and speak to them "privately" through their radio. He would tune his transmitter, then, interrupting the music playing in their cars, he would describe the car they were driving and the clothes they were wearing. The girls would shriek and change radio stations, which Barney took to be part of a game of "playing hard to get." But soon he realized this wasn't the case, as they screamed at him to get out of their radios, and he received similar reactions from other carfuls of girls.

Fact

There are a growing number of books about Asperger's syndrome and relationships. Many of these volumes are personal accounts written by individuals with Asperger's themselves ("Aspies," as some affectionately call themselves). See Appendix A for a list of books on this subject.

Mark Sachnik, a man with Asperger's syndrome who is a strong self-advocate, shares some closing thoughts about dating and evolving sexual relationships.

> Unfortunately, the "dating game" is probably one of the biggest challenges teenagers or young adults face in the process of growing up. Add autism (or any disability) into the mix and you could have a recipe for disaster because these individuals will feel less and less comfortable with themselves. This is where it is extremely important for those around them to help them become more comfortable with themselves and to emphasize the importance of "being yourself." Accepting who you are and being yourself greatly increases your chances for a successful relationship, while nonacceptance and trying to "reinvent" yourself only increases your chances of failure.
>
> Now for the really hard part. The individual with autism has met an "ideal mate," a common bond is established, and a really good friendship is "in the works." The individual is starting to develop feelings for the person. Again, there is absolutely nothing wrong with that. The problem individuals with autism run into is they will often have "no clue" on how to read "hints," tones of voice, or subtle "body language." It is very hard for them to decipher between romantic overtures and acts of friendship. This is when "social stories," complete with pictures (not the "graphic" kind) would really help.

A close relationship with a member of the opposite sex is usually the time when people contemplate entering into a sexual relationship with their significant other. Re-emphasize the facts of life and also reinforce the concept that a sexual relationship carries a lot of responsibility. This is also the time to discuss the possible consequences of entering into an irresponsible sexual relationship (a commitment before you are ready, unwanted pregnancy, sexually transmitted disease, etc.).

Same-Sex Attraction

Just as the causes of Asperger's are unknown, so are the causes of homosexuality—both are naturally occurring, and neither may be blamed as anyone's "fault." Our society is making slow but positive strides in its growing acceptance of people with same-sex orientation, but there remain those who vehemently oppose and condemn any expression of homosexuality.

As a person identified with Asperger's syndrome, your child is not the child you envisioned when she was first born. Having a same-sex orientation adds another layer to the circumstances that may be challenging for you to absorb as a parent. But as challenging as it may be for you, imagine how homosexuality may further complicate your child's life. Your child's self-image and self-esteem starts with the feedback you provide as a parent. Your child is a person first and foremost—a magnificent, gorgeous, talented human being with so much to offer the world just by being in it. Just as she is not defined exclusively by Asperger's syndrome, she (or you) should not accept being defined exclusively by a label of same-sex orientation.

As your child matures through adolescence, be mindful that a same-sex attraction may be a possibility and, like it or not, be prepared to embrace your child regardless. If your child's knowledge of his same-sex orientation is emerging at this time, he will be more vulnerable than ever before and needs your unconditional love and acceptance to weather any storms ahead. (An exception is the young boy who, seeing something on television, became very concerned that he was gay even when, deep down, he knew it didn't apply to him. This is a different situation than same-sex attraction.)

Fact

At least one Internet group has been established for people with Asperger's syndrome who are "gay, lesbian, bisexual, transgendered or questioning." Parents, supportive partners, and family and friends are welcome to participate as well. You can access the group at the following Web address: *http://groups.yahoo.com/group/ac-glbt/*.

If you are unknowledgeable or uncertain about how to handle your child's same-sex orientation, find out what local resources are available—who to call, what to research on the Internet, or what literature to obtain. Your positive, proactive support of your child will be helpful to him, tempered with a dialogue about privacy and discretion about one's sexual orientation—not out of shame but out of respect for others and oneself.

If you are a reasonably sophisticated, mature human being, you probably know, love, and accept any number of friends, family, and coworkers with a same-sex orientation. One mother acknowledged that her son with Asperger's was enduring tough times socially and emotionally but that his crowd of gay friends provided him a source of invaluable support. Another young man wants nothing more than to find a loving partner but slips further and further into a severely depressed state. Which scenario would you wish for your child? Dating is confusing and awkward for anyone of any age, so remember that your child with Asperger's needs as much support as you can give him during these years.

Chapter 17

Strategies of Lifelong Value

The greatest gift you can give your child with Asperger's syndrome is a full awareness of self—her needs as well as her strengths—in order for her to become a self-advocate. It is important that your child have a "bag of tricks," an arsenal of strategies to employ that will be universally received as socially acceptable as she moves into adulthood.

Personal Schedules

One of the single greatest causes of heightened anxiety in children with Asperger's syndrome is worries and concerns about the future, that is, not knowing what's coming next. Maintaining control is crucial to kids with Asperger's, and they may become quickly and easily unhinged when routines change without warning or others are privy to information that isn't shared with them or isn't communicated until the last minute. As a result, too many kids with Asperger's are medicated with anxiety-reducing drugs. This is intervention, not prevention; and before such medicine is prescribed, consider implementing any number of the recommendations in this chapter, foremost being the personal schedule.

None of us is without some sort of long-term timekeeping device, be it a Palm Pilot, a calendar (perhaps it's even on your computer desktop), or a hard-copy date book in which you can manually plan for a day, week, or month at a time. Have you ever misplaced your date-keeping device? If so, perhaps you can begin to appreciate the kind of nervous anxiety experienced by those who are at the mercy of others to stay informed of what's upcoming. The longer you go without having your schedule—and knowing you are still responsible for keeping to it—the more upset and distressed you're likely to become. Many people joke that they couldn't function without their schedule and are totally at a loss without it. Why should your child be without a similar way of tracking time and independently assessing impending events and activities? It makes more sense to quell anxiety and foster independent resilience in your child by helping her create a personal schedule.

Fact

The advantages to supporting your child in initiating a personal schedule are as varied as they are for us all. Our visual daily schedules keep us focused and oriented with respect to time, sequence of events, priorities, and knowledge of what's coming next. Without this structured information we become lost.

How to Schedule

Here's how it works: If your child enjoys computers and other electronic equipment, go with him to select a Palm Pilot to suit his needs and interest. If your child handwrites legibly enough for him to read his own writing—and he doesn't mind handwriting—then he may choose to use a hard-copy date book, like a daily, weekly, or monthly planner (and an inexpensive alternative to a Palm Pilot that is available at any office supply store). In any event, your child should select what appeals to him most, within your budget.

Wherever possible, in partnership with your child, set up the schedule for the next day (at first) the night before. Some parents already spend time tucking their child into bed and, at this time, verbally review the next day; this concept simply builds upon all that good and thoughtful stuff by making it tangible and concrete. Knowing what tomorrow is supposed to "look like" the night before, and having it all recorded so there's no forgetting or mistaking it enables many kids with Asperger's to relax and sleep through the night (when, previously, sleeping well was problematic).

If you choose a hard copy book, do not emblazon the outside of it with your child's name and an indication that this is his schedule; that's potentially stigmatizing because it draws unnecessary attention to him.

What to Schedule

The times when the schedule will come in most handy are during those large, unscheduled, unstructured blocks of time like evenings, weekends, holidays, and summer vacation. It will be best to arrange the schedule in a specific sequence if possible. Try setting it up like a "To Do" list that you may use yourself to visually identify what needs to get done and what you've accomplished. Start by scheduling one or two "preferred" activities (these may derive from your child's passions or interests) before scheduling a "nonpreferred" activity, like a household chore or homework. Continue in this sequence—preferred/nonpreferred/preferred—as much as possible. In this way, there is an incentive to use the schedule; there is a sense of accomplishment in visually observing one's achievements; and the schedule isn't perceived as a punitive device used by you to control or manipulate. Fade out your involvement as soon as possible in favor of your child having authority over making the schedule, within parental parameters of course. The schedule may also be used to indicate birthdays, anniversaries, special events, and appointments of all kinds.

When your child begins to "bug" you with repeated questions, or if she protests or procrastinates about a nonpreferred activity, simply refer back to the schedule—it's all there in black and white. You may suggest, "Well, what does your schedule say is next?" Many such confrontations between parent and child can be nipped in the bud because the child will realize that you can't argue with what's concrete (this doesn't negate occasional parental leniency, as you'd grant any child).

It's probably best not to schedule activities by specific times, unless your child wishes to do so, or you've agreed that Saturday night he can stay up an hour later, for example. Your child may be the type to become exasperated if the schedule isn't maintained to the minute. However, most children with Asperger's find it to be a very useful tool for feeling safe and comfortable and in control of knowing what's coming next.

The Touchstone

Many people with Asperger's (and autism) soothe themselves by repeatedly manipulating an object such as a straw, a piece of string, or some beads. They find comfort in the sameness of repeating the motion over and over, relishing the calm that the texture of the object in their hand brings. Self-soothing is a strength that should not be misinterpreted or mislabeled. It is used to maintain control, and you'll likely see it intensify when your child is on the verge of *losing* control, like when she's very happy or excited or angry and upset. It may also kick into high gear if your child is in an environment that is assaulting her senses. You do this too—it just looks a little different, like nervously shaking your leg while seated or persistently chewing on a pen or the inside of your cheek when stressed.

Because we are all more alike than different, most of us carry with us a small object that soothes and quells us if we stop to focus on it. Such personal "touchstones" may include a wedding band or favored piece of jewelry, rosary beads or a cross, good luck charms, or photos of loved ones. We carry these objects with us for sentimental reasons or because they hold some significance for us. You may wish to consider offering your child a similar touchstone that will be of lifelong value. The difference here is that of *discretion*, meaning use of the object is secret and private, not public (which may be stigmatizing). The goal here is that the touchstone should remain unseen, such as in a pocket or worn around the neck, under clothing.

Essential

The next time you're feeling especially anxious or distressed, try stopping in the moment to assess your outward expression of those feelings. Many people discover themselves unconsciously toying with a ring, a necklace, their hair, or some other device that provides a comforting diversion. This is not unlike the touchstone concept.

Choosing an Object

To begin, ask your child to select a viable touchstone. It will probably be something related to his passion(s), or it might be an object associated with someone with whom he shares a strong, loving bond, such as a grandparent. Advise your child, using words and visuals, that when he is feeling an extreme emotion—but is still in control—he need only touch the object through his clothing, or reach inside a pocket to hold it, and conjure up all that it means to him in the moment. You may use the following story to introduce the concept and modify it to suit your needs:

> People like objects that make them feel comfortable and happy. My (mom/dad/caregiver) uses a ________________ in this way. People like to be reminded of other people or things that make them feel happy. Sometimes, I like to think about ________ (the reason for the touchstone). It reminds me of how happy I feel when I ______________ (engage in the passion).

> I can't always ______________ (do one's passion), especially when I'm away from home. I can carry ______________ (the touchstone) in my pocket to remind me of good times. When I feel anxious or upset, I can touch or hold ______________ (the touchstone) to help me think about ______________ (the passion) and how happy it makes me feel. It's okay to feel anxious or upset. Everybody feels this way sometimes. By holding ______________ (the touchstone), I may not feel as anxious or upset.

One young man chose to wear a mood ring as his touchstone. While wearing it was not exactly discreet, it was still inconspicuous because it was a piece of jewelry typical of other kids his age *and* no one else knew that he was using it to regulate his own emotions in the moment, according to the ring's color. It became a powerful tool for him to maintain control throughout the day.

Fact

One young teenager with Asperger's beautifully demonstrated his understanding that the touchstone is discreet. During a counseling session, he showed his support team the orange odometer needle he had selected. But afterward, he privately approached his counselor to share his *other* touchstone: a figurine from *The Powerpuff Girls* cartoon. He recognized the need to keep the figurine out of sight and to be selective in showing it to others.

The Social Out

Too many children with Asperger's are able to keep composure all day long at school but then come home and release their pent-up frustration and anxiety in ways that stun parents and perplex educators who don't notice any difficulties at all during the school day. We all regulate our time by interspersing it with breaks, little rewards and other forms of downtime. These include chatting on the phone, surfing the Internet, using the bathroom, getting a drink or snack, breaking to listen to the radio or watch TV, and other mini-indulgences. Because your child is extremely sensitive, she needs to learn how to pace herself during the day in similar ways in order to avoid becoming so saturated and overwhelmed that she melts down completely upon returning home.

There are very few social situations and environments that you can't extricate yourself from if you so choose. You can even decide to discontinue a dental exam and walk out if you wish. The child with Asperger's syndrome may not recognize that any other option is available *other than* to remain in the situation—even if it is a situation that is making him feel anxious, upset, and distressed. When it escalates to the point of no return, the child may have a meltdown, shut down, and become unresponsive. Your child *does* have an option to avert public embarrassment and stigmatization through using the "social out."

Empower Your Child

Any of us can go anywhere in the United States and in virtually any situation use the words "Please excuse me," get up, and walk out and have that communication received in a socially acceptable manner. Your child has the right to be empowered with the same understanding, especially in school where the setting is "governed" by adults adhering to a rigid schedule. Many kids with Asperger's independently figure out how to get their needs met in a similar way; they just do it by going to the water fountain or taking frequent trips to the bathroom. The child who often disappears into the bathroom doesn't have an overactive bladder—he's intelligent enough to have surmised that it's one of the limited opportunities he has to find a relatively calm and quiet place where he can quell anxieties and regroup before going back out into battle.

In collaboration with your child's educational team, teach him to use the words "Please excuse me" or "Excuse me, I need a break." (This will require practice and reminders at first until he gets the hang of it.) It also needs to be understood that his communication will be honored with *immediacy* (this includes you, the parent, while in environments outside the home). If your child's communication of the social out is not honored with immediacy but instead with vague statements like, "Hang in there a little bit longer," or "We'll go soon," you've disempowered him and taught him that he really has no control, that, ultimately, adults retain all the control and don't listen.

Using the Social Out

Interpret your child's social out as a strength. What he is really communicating is, "I've held it together for as long as I can, and if we don't get out of here *now*, it's going to get ugly." It is a mark of self-awareness of one's own experience in the moment. It is not about escaping responsibility; don't see it as manipulation.

Essential

There are very few situations in which we are compelled to remain from start to finish. Reflect on the number of times throughout a typical day that you routinely excuse yourself from social settings in order to address your personal needs. You may be surprised by the frequency.

Once they catch their breath and can process what was happening, most kids will be okay to return to the environment (unless it was overly stimulating). It may *appear* that your child is abusing the social out at first; he's not—your trust is being tested to see if you really will honor it every time. This should fade away as a mutual trust is recognized, but, if not, you might wish to assess your child's environment or the expectations placed upon him in the environment so that adaptations and accommodations may be made.

Acting and Music

Many young people with Asperger's absolutely flourish when given the opportunity to become involved in theater and acting. Many children with Asperger's are naturally brilliant actors and adept mimics, known to entertain others with their dead-on impersonations of TV and cartoon characters. Why not build upon this talent? There is so much to acting that holds special appeal for certain kids:

- You get to become someone other than who you are, which is attractive particularly if you have damaged self-esteem.
- You never say the wrong thing because everything you need to say is already scripted for you.
- If you are challenged in deciphering facial expressions and body language, you get a perfectly acceptable chance to practice understanding such nuances over and over again—it's called rehearsal.
- You are collaborating with others to produce a work of quality.
- There are social connections to be had with others who may be intrigued with or more accepting of others' differences.
- If you're good at what you do, you get positive feedback from your peers or an audience (through applause).

A lot of young people with Asperger's already act every day through using "movie talk." Movie talk (or TV talk) is a skill by which the person has artfully "lifted" lines of dialogue, facial expressions, and even body language from characters in favorite movies, television programs, or cartoon shows and "put it back out" with uncanny accuracy and with all the proper inflections. Many adults with Asperger's have "passed" in life by using movie talk to blend in fairly seamlessly. It is not something to discourage in your child but should be used to facilitate social interactions. The key is not to *become* the fictional character but to assume that character's most socially acceptable traits and make them your own until you feel more comfortable in your own skin. Some folks use movie talk to break the ice in conversation or to initiate an interaction using humor.

You probably recognized early on in your child's development how listening to her music—favored songs and melodies—was extremely important. (Notice it is *her* music, not the music others choose, which may be violently disconcerting especially if played at uncomfortable decibel levels!) Like acting, all of music is scripted as well. Music therapists know the terms "call" and "response" as they apply to the flow of music. In reading, singing, or playing music, there is a time when one is an active participant in the "conversation." At this time, according to the script, you make your contribution to the song, whether it is through singing or playing an instrument. That's the call. The response comes when, according to the script, you are expected to remain silent and await the reply from one's communication partner(s). Your child may be absolutely passionate about music and performing music. You can use the concept of how music "works" as an analogy for how social conversation is supposed to flow.

Essential

Do you have a budding actor or actress in your midst? You may notice it early on if you recognize certain movie, cartoon, or TV character dialogue being repeated by your child. Still, one mom needed to counsel her son after he publicly yelled, "Get the hell outta there!" even though its origin was based in movie talk.

Written Narratives

The concept of writing stories to aid students to understand social situations and peer conversation was pioneered by a woman named Carol Gray, who is a special education instructor working with kids with different ways of being. She discovered that her students who were especially visual learners had difficulty retaining verbal information *and* applying it in the context of social settings that would be obvious to most others. For example, one young man didn't understand the concept of raising his hand and waiting to be called upon in class, especially when an instructor stood before the class and asked an open question. The boy didn't realize that the question was not directed to him personally but was being asked of the entire class with the expectation that hands be raised in response. He instead blurted out his responses in ways that were considered socially inept. As you can imagine, this was stigmatizing for him, and his misunderstanding of the situations was interpreted as being deliberately disruptive, which was not the case. Carol Gray resolved this by providing the boy with a brief, bullet-point sequence of sentences that created a story to convey the proper protocol for raising one's hand. (For further information about Ms. Gray's specific Social Story formula, refer to her books listed in Appendix A).

The concept is not unlike the crib notes or "cheat sheets" that many of us have used in school in order to jog our memories in retaining pertinent information. It's the same thing here, and once the boy memorized the story, he was able to automatically remember the proper thing to do and say. Stories such as these are a tangible, concrete way of demystifying the particulars of social situations or environments that may cause apprehension, anxiety, or distress. This strategy has been tremendously successful with children with Asperger's and autism, and you have already seen some similar stories interspersed throughout this book. When you create these stories, it is important to keep in mind the following:

- Keep the stories simple, with a clear beginning and end.
- Follow a clear-cut, logical sequence.
- Try to keep the story to one page in length.
- Don't state anything definitively without allowance for mistakes (we're all human, after all). For example, "I will *try* to remember to ask to use the CD player." Instead of "I will *always* remember . . ."
- Allow the story to become your child's personal property to review at her leisure.

- Review it with her regularly *outside* of the situation that the story was written to explain.
- Fade or discard the story once it's no longer needed.
- The story may be portable but keep it discreetly in a pocket or inside a notebook (or day planner).
- Your child may personalize the story and take a greater interest in "owning" it if she is given the opportunity to illustrate it.

Spirituality

As a person who may be naturally, inherently gentle and sensitive, your child also may possess an innate sense of spirituality. This doesn't necessarily refer to being religious, but rather *spiritual* in having a deep appreciation for the beauty in everything and everyone around him. These are the children who are drawn to the tiny details in nature.

Fact

A 2003 research project conducted by Tanisha Rose, a psychology student at Lincoln University in Philadelphia, examined the stress levels among parents of children with autism. One of Rose's four hypotheses was that as the importance of religion increased, the level of stress experienced by parents would decrease—a factor largely neglected in past stress studies. Rose's study indicated that parents with elevated stress shared a lack of positive religious practices.

Your child's heightened sensitivity may also predispose him to being finely attuned to his environment. He may sense things that others do not—or cannot—readily perceive. If you see this in your child, you've likely seen it from a very early age. Your child may have had powerful dreams, intuitions, or premonitions that proved accurate, or other experiences of a spiritual nature that some would call uncanny coincidences. There are simply some aspects of the human experience that traditional science cannot measure and quantify, like love or faith.

It is important to assume several responsibilities if your child has such heightened sensitivities:

- Accept it as a natural extension of who he is.
- Do not arbitrarily dismiss it or make your child feel in any way unfit or afraid to discuss his sensitivities.
- Do not sensationalize it by exaggerating it, blowing it out of proportion, or openly sharing it with others without your child's knowledge (remember disclosure?).
- Keep it confidential except to reveal information to those who can be trusted to understand unconditionally.
- Remember that intermittent experiences do not a mental illness make. Review the mental health chapter again if you have concerns; common mental health diagnoses are determined by *groupings* of symptoms, not by sporadic, unexplainable instances.
- Accept what your child tells you to be the truth as he knows it.

As your child enters adolescence and adulthood, his sense of spirituality and commitment of faith to a higher authority may be the very thing that pulls him through rough times. Having these values instilled in him early on in life could prove to be his single most important resource.

CHAPTER 18

Employment

You and your child both wish for him to grow up to become a productive, contributing member of the community. As is true of any significant change in your child's life, the transition from school to work can be a very challenging time. Your child's talents should be encouraged early on so that they may be developed into potential vocations. We all feel valued when we are fairly compensated for what we know and do best.

Identifying Job Interests

In Chapter 8, the importance of valuing passions was explored. Too often, the child with Asperger's syndrome has passions that others disdain or squelch as insignificant, unworthy, or "obsessions." However, building upon passions is a viable bridge to future employment opportunities. After all, aren't the luckiest among us those who get paid for doing what we love most? This is the place to begin. Start by fostering (and valuing) your child's passions *early*. As Temple Grandin, a prominent self-advocate and author, has stated, "People respect talent." Implicit in this statement is the idea that if your child misses the mark socially, an outstanding talent will likely compensate for such shortcomings.

While your child is in middle school, start to have the typical discussions you'd have with any of your children about what she might consider doing "when she grows up." If your child hasn't already been vocal about what she envisions herself doing in the future, you might suggest it based upon your own observations of her strengths, gifts, talents, and passions. Through these dialogues with your child, you may draw out even greater detail from her; remember that some passions may be deceptive at face value and require some deciphering to tease out the true interest they represent.

If your child enjoys configuring numbers and playing number games, those abilities might translate into accounting or data analysis. If your child spends endless hours drawing favorite cartoon characters, creating comic books, and the like, might a job as an illustrator, animator, or computer graphic artist be in his future? If your child devours books and is knowledgeable about various authors or a variety of subjects, a library science career might be a possibility. In which directions does your child naturally lean by virtue of his unique abilities and unusual problem-solving perspectives?

Essential

As is true of us all, our individual likes and interests guide our vocational pursuits. The advantage many people with Asperger's have is that they are already experts in their respective fields at very young ages! Foster passions early with an eye toward future employment possibilities.

Your child's school psychologist or guidance counselor should be a resource to you in narrowing the possibilities in order to explore them with your child (not that he needs to feel "locked" into anything years in advance). Together you may wish to gather additional information by looking up the possible vocations on the Internet or at the local library. Request your school district to complete a vocational assessment of your child's academic abilities. If your child has an individualized transition plan as part of his educational supports, this information should be woven into such a plan to ensure consistency in future planning. Some schools are open to looking at creative strategies such as hiring a job coach or mentor during the time your child is in school—if it is written into her Individualized Education Plan.

Part-Time and After-School Work

As your child gets older, she may notice that her same-age peers are taking on part-time jobs. This may or may not be appealing for her personally. Like many people with Asperger's syndrome, your child may have grand aspirations about what she wants. But getting from here to there can be confusing and intimidating. Your child's reticence about getting a job may be predicated upon:

- Feeling scared about too many "unknowns."
- Not wanting to disrupt personal routines.
- Being uncertain if others on the job will be understanding and supportive.
- Discomfort with work schedules that are unpredictable.
- Worries about transportation.
- Anxiety about disclosure.
- Anxiety about customer interactions.
- Disinterest in typical "teen" jobs because they aren't prestigious.

You will wish to support your child in quelling these concerns as you move forward. Does an older sibling, cousin, or neighbor have an "in" with an employer? If so, that person could serve as a natural, protective ally on the job as your child becomes acclimated to new people, surroundings, and routines. If this isn't possible, is there someone who could serve as a mentor or temporary coach as your child adjusts to the new work environment? Is there an employer who is willing to invest the time and energy in fostering the development of your child's on-the-job skills? Or are there local employers that are well known for hiring students (including your child's friends and relations) for part-time or summer work? If your child receives formal supports, such as a case manager or social worker, that person should be in a position to make vocational connections or referrals to those who can. If your child has an Individualized Education Plan, insist that a transition to vocational opportunities be incorporated into it. Many schools have such work incentive programs set up to accommodate all students, both on and off campus.

Fact

The Tech-Link Program of Pittsburgh (Pennsylvania) is a unique and innovative nonprofit organization designed to help middle school and high school students with disabilities find careers in math, science, and technology. Learn more about Tech-Link at *www.tech-link.org*. There may be other similar high school/high-tech programs in the country. Also, the AAPD (American Association of People with Disabilities) supports summer internships in Washington, D.C.

In considering potential employment opportunities, weigh your child's strengths and weaknesses. Your child may truly love interacting with others, but perhaps he doesn't quite understand when he's giving too much information—like a computer store salesman that, in response to a simple customer inquiry, gives the person the verbal equivalent of a chapter from a computer manual. This may take private practice and coaching through role-playing activities to simulate a variety of such customer interactions. If your child is more solitary in nature, an independent job might be best, such as entering data in a computer program. Once your child obtains a position, you will want to consult with him regularly to find out how things are going. As he may not tell you unless you ask, closely monitor how well he's juggling the new job with his other responsibilities—especially if he's also going to school at the same time.

No job has to be forever, and your child will require your gentle support to find a part-time position that is a good match for him, his skills, and personality. Some parents can be quite firm in insisting that their child work, and you may need to select a job to assign your child if she is overly resistant. The important thing is to encourage a gradual transition to work while your child is still in high school or college, even if it's only over summer vacation or semester breaks. This may be an anxious time, but it's preparation and rehearsal for assimilating with the work force of the larger world.

Applying for the Job

Like it or not, most people place a lot of emphasis on first impressions when initially meeting someone, especially in a job interview. You or a close ally will wish to be a resource to your child in preparing for such first impressions. First, there's the job application. If your child doesn't have a friend or ally who plans to apply for a job with her, it's probably best if you encourage your child to obtain an employment application and bring it home so you can review it together. Do not fill it out for her, but do discuss how to fill it out properly.

It is a stereotype that people with Asperger's syndrome are so absorbed in their "obsessions" that they have no concern for grooming (think Albert Einstein). Still, you will wish to do a quick, at-a-glance check before your child heads to a job interview, especially if she isn't typically conscious of such things.

As with any job, it never hurts to follow up with an in-person inquiry or a phone call to reinforce one's interest and ensure that the application was received. It will help to partner with your child to script the words to say when making this contact, such as, "I'm calling to follow up on the job application I submitted last week. I'm really interested in the position and I am wondering if interviews are being scheduled yet." Most likely, your child will be told his application is on file and that someone will contact him if he's selected for an interview. If your child hasn't heard from anyone in a reasonable amount of time, rather than ruminate about it, encourage him to contact the employer again—and emphasize that this is all perfectly acceptable (remember, this is practice for the big world). It may be that they are simply delayed in the process.

The Job Interview

Being called for a job interview can be an anxious time for anyone, especially the person with Asperger's syndrome. Explain that typical job interviews begin with an introduction, a handshake, and a private interview during which the individuals are seated across from one another. (This first meeting will be the time when making direct eye contact and giving a solid handshake will be most significant—help your child practice this!)

Preparing for the Questions

The prospective employer usually takes the lead by starting the interview with questions. Help your child by strategizing, in advance, the answers to the questions a prospective employer might ask. The questions will most likely center upon why your child applied for the position, what skills she can bring to the job, and how flexible she can be in scheduling. (If a friend or ally already works for the employer, he or she can be of immeasurable support in narrowing the questions most likely to be asked based upon past experience.)

After discussing some hypothetical interview questions, ask your child how she would best respond to them. Reinforce that you cannot predict with certainty the exact questions that will be asked of your child (unless you already have a partnership with a very cooperative employer willing to mentor your child). You won't wish for your child to embarrass herself at the conclusion of the interview by stating, "Aren't you going to ask me about this, this, and this?" Inform your child that the person conducting the interview may well come up with questions you hadn't thought of, which she should answer honestly and concisely (meaning one or two sentences as a limit—she can always add more information if the employer requests it). The flip side is that, if your child was expecting certain questions to be asked and they weren't, she may also volunteer the information at the conclusion of the interview or if the interviewer provides the opportunity.

The Questions Your Child Should Ask

It's also important to support your child in scripting some questions to ask of the prospective employer. Asking questions during a job interview usually communicates the applicant's sincere interest in the job. Work with your child to develop a list of questions to ask. They will most likely focus upon the work schedule, employee responsibilities and job description, and supervision.

One of the great challenges to your child in coming across well in a job interview will likely be maintaining an appropriate level of eye contact (not too much, not too little). Visual distractions of the interview environment may also pose a problem: personal mementoes on a desk, the motion of the interviewer's computer screensaver, and the like. Positively commenting on these items at the beginning or conclusion of the interview, however, might personalize the conversation a bit and set both parties at ease.

If she doesn't memorize the questions to ask, it's perfectly acceptable to write them down. If she's going to pull out the list during the interview, it might be a good idea to say, "Would you mind if I read a few questions I'd like to ask of you? I wrote them down so I wouldn't forget them." This type of honest, tactful approach should smooth over any awkwardness she feels about referring to her list. Discuss disclosure with your child—sharing the information about her Asperger's during the initial interview will be a matter of personal choice, if it is necessary at all. If your child decides to reveal this, she should be prepared to discuss her skills (positive attributes, good at following rules, loyalty) as well as areas needing support due to certain sensitivities.

Coach your child to understand that the interviewer will generally conclude the interview by saying something like, "Thanks for coming in." At this time, it is appropriate for your child to thank the person for her time and ask when she might hear about the job (if the person hasn't already offered that information). As with submitting a job application, it's acceptable to follow up with a phone call to inquire about the job selection process.

The Interview Outfit

You will also wish to discuss appropriate grooming and dress for an interview. Wearing a business suit for a fast-food job interview might be a bit overdressed, but a shirt and tie or a freshly pressed skirt is never out of place. Wearing neat and clean clothing and presenting oneself with immaculate hygiene (deodorant, clean teeth and fingernails, fresh breath and combed hair) counts for a lot in a day and age when it's fashionable for some young people to dress very casually in clothing that looks intentionally worn or overly loose-fitting. Preparing one's personal appearance for a job interview is good practice for interviews as an adult.

If Your Child Doesn't Get the Job

Help prepare your child for rejection. Employers of typical teen jobs rarely, if ever, call those applicants not selected for employment. (This lack of etiquette has become acceptable in the adult corporate world as well.) Your child may have thought the interview went wonderfully but might learn that he wasn't chosen for the job. Your child may internalize this kind of rejection as an offense or attack on him personally.

It could temporarily impact his mental health if he spends a lot of time replaying it and agonizing over the details. He may feel like a failure at this time—even if we're talking about a job at McDonald's.

How can my child find a job?

Scanning your local newspapers or advertising circulars for prospective employment opportunities is one way of scoping out jobs for any young adult. Your child may also wish to devise a brief starter resume or explore online possibilities, such as an Internet job search. If your child is a computer whiz, there may be work-at-home situations available as well.

Your role as a parent will be to listen to his concerns and offer your gentle support. His feelings are very real to him but may be more intense than what is typical for others. This will be a time when friends and allies can share personal tales of jobs they didn't get in order to reinforce that no one is perfect and we're all more alike than different. A job interview is not a guarantee of anything; it's simply a time for both parties to gather information. The adage learned in childhood, "You win some, you lose some," applies here as well. Unfortunately, the reality is that, more often than not, the individual with Asperger's loses more than he wins. Be prepared to help cope with these losses and celebrate the successes.

On-the-Job Issues

If your child is hired for the job, he should be encouraged to bring home as much material attendant to the position as possible. Such literature is usually given out the first day of job orientation and may include rules and regulations, employer expectations, and standard procedural forms to be completed. Review with your child the information in detail and allow her to follow up with questions after she also reviews it privately. Also determine the chain of command to be followed should your child need to voice an opinion or concern.

Employee Interaction

Your child will likely be able to follow rules about appropriate employee conduct but, like many aspects of human behavior, not everyone will follow on-the-job rules to the letter as well as your child. Because of this, social misunderstandings may crop up. Stress that your child is not there to police others (unless she's in a supervisory position and is responsible for monitoring the work performance of others). There will always be those individuals, including supervisors, who break the rules and do things they shouldn't.

Your child will need coaching to recognize when it's imperative to report a situation of concern and when it's a matter for a supervisor to monitor. A perennial "squealer" or "whistleblower" may follow the rules perfectly but will quickly prove very unpopular with fellow employees. Be available for your child to discuss such situations and weigh whether it's something to report (especially if there's an imminent threat of danger to others), or if it is minor enough to overlook (in other words, MYOB, "mind your own business"). A supportive supervisor should be able to counsel your child through such issues.

Temple Grandin learned about such diplomacy the hard way while working for a meat-packing plant. She noticed a serious flaw in operations and, jumping the chain of command, wrote a letter to the company president, who was not pleased that a new employee would bring such a thing to his immediate attention, even though it was a situation that demanded correcting. Temple was stunned that the president was not grateful for the information.

Clear, open lines of communication with coworkers and supervisors can be crucial. In one instance, a young man with Asperger's was suspended from his job when he threatened to kill a coworker. He had absolutely no intention of doing anyone any harm, but in his desperation to be heard, he thought that making such a drastic, attention-getting statement would finally make others listen to his concerns. Another young man, working in a butcher shop, threw a large knife at the wall out of exasperation. He, too, intended no harm to anyone, but such acts have tremendous potential to be misinterpreted and result in serious consequences.

Your child's blatant honesty and high moral expectations of others may create an uncomfortable work environment for coworkers. While your child may never surrender her black-and-white perspective, she will need support to understand the natural consequences—that holding others so closely accountable may foster social alienation, distrust, or backlash. Weighing such options is indeed a fine line for us all.

What's Best for Your Child?

Though no job need be forever, some people may see it that way. They may want more in life and may have dreams of doing great things to benefit others, and yet they are stuck in menial jobs for which they are intellectually overqualified. They may be socially stymied and misunderstood by coworkers and supervisors, which can perpetuate the self-fulfilling prophecy of worthlessness. This in turn leads to damaged self-esteem and depression. This is the rut in which too many adults with Asperger's find themselves.

Regrettably, there are no easy solutions at present. Equal opportunities for those with Asperger's can only come from parents, caregivers, educators, and self-advocates working together to foster global awareness and change. Finding viable employment opportunities—not stereotyped jobs—for people with Asperger's syndrome in our communities is a very real issue. It is important to become active and involved (while your child is still a child) by networking with other parents, local Asperger's and autism organizations, and politically pressing for the creation of more employment opportunities that reflect individuals' true gifts and talents.

CHAPTER 19

Transitioning to Adulthood

The greatest challenge you will face as a parent of a child with Asperger's syndrome is supporting him through the transition to adulthood. As protective as you may be with all your children, at some point you will be ready for your child with Asperger's to leave home to venture out on his own into the adult world. Of course your relationship is not severed, and your loving support can ease your child into the often intimidating arena of adult responsibilities.

Planning for the Future

In addition to your child's transitional Individualized Education Plan, you may wish to consider initiating person-centered planning meetings as your child prepares to graduate high school. If your school district is open to it, and if stipulated in the IEP, the person-centered planning process can dovetail nicely with a transition plan, or the two can be folded together. In fact, the person-centered plan may be more comprehensive in terms of a vision for your child's future.

In the person-centered planning process, the individual remains the focus, but meeting participants include family, friends, relatives, and any others who know the person well and with whom the individual has a personal history. There are a wide variety of person-centered plan formats that may be referred to by different names such as self-determination, personal futures planning, person-centered development, or lifestyle blueprint. The components of each are essentially the same; they are just packaged a bit differently.

The focus of person-centered planning is on the individual's talents, gifts, and skills instead of on identifying all that they *can't* do and then plugging that into traditional or stereotyped opportunities. Common aspects of person-centered planning include:

- The person as the primary focus.
- Involvement of participants who know the person and care about him or her.
- Exploring individual capacity, hopes, reservations, dreams, and preferences.
- Helping the person to attain a desirable future.
- Ensuring the safety and well being of the person's emotional, mental, and physical health.
- Creating systems change wherever possible with creative thinking and innovative strategies—thinking "outside the box."

Fact

Training Resource Network Inc. (*www.trninc.com*) offers a wide variety of person-centered planning books and videos, including an inexpensive pamphlet titled *It's My Meeting: A Family/Consumer Pocket Guide to Participating in Person-Centered Planning.* TRN is also a resource for learning more about employment and community possibilities for people with differences after high school. Contact them toll-free at 1-866-823-9800.

It is a plan created by a network of people who are committed to supporting an individual to envision a desirable future, but it is that person's vision and not what others wish for him or her. While the planning process is one that evolves and changes as it continues over time (this means more than one meeting is involved), it is a process that is outcome based. The intended outcomes include:

- The person will have an enhanced life.
- Relationships or friendships will grow.
- The person will contribute in ways that are meaningful or functional.
- Expression of individual choices, wants, dreams, and desires is valued.
- The person will feel more a part of the community.

The Person-Centered Planning Process

In order to plan for a smooth person-centered planning process, in partnership with your child first identify those individuals she'd like present. Perhaps she'd like to send out invitations and make menu selections for refreshments as well. The meeting will benefit from having a facilitator who is neutral (perhaps unrelated to the situation entirely) and who can:

- Keep the focus on your child.
- Manage and be remindful of time.
- Record and disperse meeting minutes.
- Follow up with participants, including keeping track of the status of commitments and scheduling future meetings.

The facilitator will gently guide the meeting, not control it. Ideally, this person will also help your child and her team visually map the flow of the discussion on an overhead projector, a flip chart, blackboard, or large pieces of paper tacked to the wall. The simplest format of a person-centered plan might ask your child and her team questions about what she wishes to accomplish in areas of education and training, employment, recreation, and community living. The focus should be positive and proactive; worry about deconstructing obstacles later. When this doesn't occur, the meeting can quickly digress into a lot of statements like, "We can't do that because . . ."

The facilitator should also ensure that everyone uses respectful language; this is definitely not a time to rehash unflattering incidents that will cause your child public embarrassment. If concerns arise, frame them in the context of your child's personal and *informed* choice (with full disclosure of the consequences). Tempered with personal and informed choice are health, safety, and personal welfare and compromise.

Essential

When preparing for a person-centered plan meeting, be sure to hold it in an environment that's as comfortable and informal as possible in a neutral setting (somewhere other than a professional office or conference room). Snacks and refreshments are always helpful to increase the comfort level of all participants, especially if formal relationships have previously been strained. Remember, in this meeting no one has any authority to *make* anyone do anything; it's about agreements, promises, and commitments.

The duration of the meeting depends upon the stamina of the team but it is advisable not to go on longer than a couple of hours. Remember, a person-centered plan is a dynamic process that plays out over time. There will be future opportunities to continue dialogues begun at the first meeting. Depending upon the areas identified for each section of the person-centered plan format (regardless of which format is used), there will be assignments made for roles, responsibilities, and time frames for implementation of the plan. Participants, including you and your child, should commit to their responsibilities, be in contact with other team members between meetings (mass e-mailings accomplish this well), and be able to update the team on progress made at each meeting.

Barriers to the person-centered plan process may include:

- Uncertainty about what your child wants (Perhaps he hasn't learned to dream or is afraid to!).

- Breakdowns or stalemates in communication.
- Family expectations versus your child's dreams and wishes.
- Conflicting values among team members.
- Funding and other system limitations.
- The time commitment and responsibilities may be too labor intensive for some team members to be effective.

Remember that a person-centered plan is an actual document, a tool that becomes your child's property. It should be revisited and revised as often as necessary. Those involved in the process need to honor their commitments and be willing to "shift gears" as needs arise that alter the plan's course.

The outcome of the initial person-centered plan meeting should be a document that details how best to support your child's future. If you can gather together a strong, supportive team of people committed to helping your child transition to adulthood, a person-centered plan can be a useful tool in devising a visual blueprint for moving forward.

Independent Living

Moving out of your home will be a major life step for your child. Assisting him in finding a living place in the community may depend upon several things:

- Affordable, acceptable housing.
- Geographic proximity to you and areas of the community accessed by your child.
- Your child's ability to support himself.

- Funds you are able and willing to contribute to supporting your child.
- Outside resources for funding or housing.

Regrettably, there are far more resources available for community living for people with mental retardation or mental health issues than for folks with Asperger's syndrome. The person with Asperger's may present as able-bodied, intelligent, and perfectly capable of caring for himself. When families wish to access services and supports, it may prompt accusations from others that they are attempting to unnecessarily "play" the system, because the subtleties of Asperger's make the need for services less apparent. As you well know, however, the needs are real, and identifying and selecting a living arrangement away from your home can be a time of apprehension and uncertainty for all.

It may behoove you and your child to explore all options, both informal and formal. Informal options may include trying to match your child with an appropriate roommate or roommates, or a live-in ally or mentor (perhaps someone paid through creative funding, such as a local college student or neighbor). In some instances, parents of children with Asperger's have bonded together to fund housing in which several of their children live together.

Fact

On My Own of Michigan is a nonprofit agency that provides services for adults with differences (Asperger's is among them) that includes community housing. But, like so many other human service agencies, there is a waiting list and, if feasible, you may wish to sign up for the waiting list years ahead of time. Through On My Own, individuals with Asperger's syndrome learn life skills, like cooking and paying bills as well as social skills like public speaking and vacationing with others.

Formal options may include exploring ways to access your local human service community providers. You may learn more about them, their credentials, and their qualifications for participation by contacting your county developmental disabilities unit, your child's case manager or social worker, your child's educators, or by consulting your phone book.

Learning New Responsibilities

Issues that may arise during the transition to independent living will likely be followed by lots of anxiety for you and, especially, for your child. If your child has had no previous experience with balancing a budget, maintaining a checkbook, paying bills, grocery shopping, and interacting with a landlord, you both could be in for a rude awakening as your child acclimates herself to life away from home. If your child is renting an apartment, ensure that she has a clear understanding of the landlord's rules and expectations (in writing).

In one instance, a young man with Asperger's came home to his apartment to find a note from the landlord informing him that new carpet was going to be installed on a certain date and that the young man would have to move many of his personal possessions. Never before having been in such a situation, the young man believed that paying for the carpet was his responsibility. He panicked, realizing that he didn't have enough money to cover such an expense (and knowing no ally was immediately available to him). He was also upset that his things had to be moved.

Partner with your child to set up her living space in a way that is comfortable for her, complies with any formal terms of agreement (such as a lease), and meets your satisfaction about safety issues. Consider the following adaptations to your child's independent living space:

- Ensure that all smoke detectors are functional and that your child knows the fire escape route (stress that this is a precaution for *everyone* otherwise you may incite undue anxiety about the likelihood of a fire).

- Purchase a fire extinguisher and practice using it.
- Get a phone with automatic dial or push-button photos of familiar people whose numbers are called often or who should be called in an emergency (especially if your child becomes easily flustered or forgetful when upset).
- Purchase a monthly bill organizer with slots that correspond to specific dates to indicate what gets paid when to help your child stay focused and up to date when keeping track of bills.
- A large wall calendar with large blocks for each day on which to make notes may be a useful visual.
- If your child is not well organized or is forgetful, you may ask her to post a simple checklist by the door that indicates things like checking to make sure lights are off, no faucets are running, appliances are turned off, etc., each time she leaves home.

You will wish to add to this list as the need arises, but ensure that you are not overbearing and overly protective. Living independently may well be a step that your child has wanted to take for some time. Enter into this step of the journey in partnership, and listen to what your child is saying she wants.

Fact

Many mail order companies offer diverse and eclectic novelty-type devices that may be of good use to the child transitioning to his or her own living space in the community. One such business, Sky Mall (*www.skymall.com* or 1-800-SKYMALL), offers many state-of-the-art items designed for adaptability and security purposes, including monthly bill organizers and other organizing devices, photo-button phones, soothing alarm clocks, and sound-muffling appliances.

Don't Get Taken

Unless you've taught your child to crack the code of social slang and innuendo as it applies to various circumstances, he may take what others say at face value and do what they ask of him without question. He may do this because he's a pleaser and wants to be accepted, especially in his new community residence or apartment. However, unless he knows to report an unethical situation, your child may become an easy mark for others to deliberately abuse and take advantage of. Once again, this is where having a close ally, or allies, is significant in the life of your child. Case managers and social workers are required to touch base with individuals on their caseload, but oftentimes that happens infrequently, especially for people under their supervision who are considered "high functioning" and largely independent. Your child needs someone he can contact daily if needed.

Some of the ways your child may be taken advantage of include:

- Others extorting money from him, even under the guise of giving to a charity or worthy cause
- Being deceived into doing something illegal, such as delivering drugs to another individual
- Being verbally, physically, or sexually abused, or deceived into doing these things to others
- Being pressured or deceived into giving away, or selling at a nominal fee, personal possessions, appliances, jewelry, etc.
- Being made to feel accepted by becoming an accomplice to a crime, such as shoplifting
- Succumbing to every telemarketer who calls, or otherwise freely giving out confidential information such as a Social Security number or loaning credit cards or an ATM card to others
- Giving out copies of one's residence key or allowing others to freely use his home and personal property
- Regularly loaning his car to others

In raising your child, you have done your parental best to teach him right from wrong. Now more than ever you will want to ensure that your child is clear that anything that doesn't look, sound, or feel "right" or seems too good to be true is cause for extreme caution. Manipulative people can be masterful in deceiving others who are perceived as naive and gullible. One young man was coerced into having sex with another man in his neighborhood and kept silent about it for some time. It wasn't comfortable or natural for him, but he thought the sex was consensual because he became aroused and even climaxed during it. Another man ran up huge credit card bills because he felt compelled to buy a lot of the merchandise advertised on TV in "act now, supplies limited" offers. He needed extra assistance in budgeting his money and recognizing his financial limitations. These examples are not arguments intended to dissuade you from pursuing independent living for your child; they are merely cautionary tales from which to learn as you and your child move forward.

You can educate your child never to feel ashamed, embarrassed, or pressured into making an on-the-spot decision when solicited in person or by phone. When in doubt, your child should be empowered to contact an ally to ask about decision-making. Even if your child feels uncertain or uncomfortable in the moment, some people can possess very persuasive sales tactics.

Because some people are expert at being sly, many of us have been deceived or scammed at one time or another. From an early age, teach your child to be wary of being taken advantage of. One good rule of thumb to teach your child is the concept of reciprocation. That is, did the person that borrowed something from your child (money, an appliance, a book) return it before asking to borrow again? Or, does the person who asked a favor of your child do the same thing for him or her within a reasonable time frame or upon your child making the request (with notice)?

You may have cause to believe that someone close to your child has impure motives. Explaining to your child that you suspect he is being taken advantage of by someone in his neighborhood, apartment building, or workplace may be difficult, especially if he has come to look upon that person as a friend or feels "accepted" by spending time with this person. Unless your child is in imminent harm or is involved (willingly or unknowingly) in an illegal activity that requires your immediate intervention, you may wish to weigh your options in dealing with the situation. Can you allow your adult child the opportunity to make adult mistakes and support him through dealing with the natural consequences? Sometimes the best education any of us receive comes courtesy of the school of hard knocks.

Mark's Strategies

Mark is a forty-seven-year-old man with a bachelor's degree in business administration from the University of Texas at Dallas, where he is currently employed as a technology buyer. As an adult with Asperger's syndrome, Mark's journey to adult independence has been aided by a wide circle of supporters. He has the good fortune to come from a loving family of six sisters and two brothers. Mark enjoys bicycling, photography, traveling to small towns, and reading books on political and military history and the natural sciences. He is active in his parish's chapter of the Knights of Columbus and acts as the first vice president of the Autism Society of Collin County. However, Mark himself notes, "I continue to face numerous challenges living in the community." To better meet these challenges, Mark has developed some strategies for staying sane while coping with independent living.

Foremost is self-acceptance—understanding one's way of being as a natural experience and not "craziness." Individuals should focus on self-actualization and goal setting (as per a person-centered plan).

Mark next advises adults with Asperger's to recognize that they are most likely not going to have a wide circle of friends. It is best to develop long-term friendships with people who understand that you think differently from the "norm." Mark continues, "By the same token, be wary of those who will try to exploit you. This is where relying on family members and trusted friends for advice will really save you. They will help you 'fill in the blanks,' so to speak."

Essential

We should pause to consider how people with different ways of being are perceived and treated. How many of them are seen as outcasts or charity recipients? Or how many have been belittled, pigeonholed by a stereotype, or made to feel less than equal? If only we invested more time in listening and learning from what our friends have to offer.

Mark cautions young adults with Asperger's syndrome when seeking support of a neurologist or psychiatrist, indicating that, even today, most doctors don't have experience working with individuals with Asperger's. As such, they will often assume the patient has some mental health disorder, and may prescribe inappropriate medication or treatment that will often cause symptoms to worsen. Mark stresses the importance of bringing a written medical history to any psychiatric appointment and advises others to seek a second opinion when in doubt.

Mark believes that joining and actively participating in a local autism society will benefit not only the person with Asperger's but parents, professionals, and other individuals with autism. The camaraderie can foster greater social connections. Of course, other community activities, clubs, and church are additional options.

Mark holds dear the concept of building on one's passions. He promotes taking up hobbies and pursuing them with vengeance. "Take up a sport or fitness activity, especially one that emphasizes development of coordination. Cycling, running, swimming, weight training, or some forms of martial arts are all good options. In some instances, a trainer or coach is appropriate." He adds, "If you believe in God, realize that you, like everyone else, are created in His image and blessed with unique talents. Develop your talents and focus on using them wisely. When choosing a job or career, carefully evaluate how well you can fit in to a given work environment."

Mark believes that these strategies have helped him meet some of the challenges of being an adult with Asperger's syndrome and living independently. When Mark makes presentations to groups interested in learning about him and his life, his main focus is on fostering success. The effectiveness of these strategies as well as other interventions depends on the individual and his team of supporters.

CHAPTER 20

Law Enforcement

As your child grows and matures, he will encounter more and more people at home, school, college, and in the community at large. He may also observe others who do not follow rules—both written and unwritten. He may, in fact, misinterpret "rules" or laws as they apply to his life or the lives of others. Understanding the role of law enforcement in the community and its limitations should provide a useful framework for you and your child.

Understanding Justice

Many people with Asperger's syndrome, children in particular, understand written rules. Once learned, the child with Asperger's may abide by rules with perfection, and she may become quickly critical when others break rules or ignore them altogether. It may be charming when a very young child matter-of-factly corrects an adult with rebukes such as, "That's your salad fork, not your dinner fork!" or "There's no smoking allowed here!" But this trend can create conflicts and misunderstandings as your child grows. One mom recalled, "I tried to explain to my Michael that he really does not need to tell on his friends when they jump off the swings at school. Even though it is against the rules, they are very unlikely to get hurt. He said adamantly, 'It is my civic duty to tell.'"

Rigid Adherence to Rules

Determining whether or not to report rule-breaking can be a very gray area for many of us. The child who "tattles" on classmates every time one of them jumps off a swing may believe he's doing exactly what he should in abiding by the rules. In actuality, though, it is a minor offense, and his constant "policing" of them is likely to make him very unpopular with the other children. Explaining all of this may be challenging, especially if the "rules" have been established by an adult, or if they appear in writing.

Before entering an environment that may be new and different for your child, it will be best to review the "rules" of being there. For example, the etiquette of being in a movie theater means talking in a quiet voice, staying seated with few exceptions, not littering, and respecting those around you (like not kicking the seat in front of you). These rules apply to *everyone*, including your child.

Children with Asperger's can have a very rigid sense of justice and injustice. That is, black is black and white is white with no gray in between. The gray, of course, does exist in life, but learning this may well be a confusing process for your child. This is why driving a car can be problematic for some people; careful adherence to the rules of the road doesn't mean that everyone else is following the same rules as correctly as you are. In fact, when driving, everyone regularly "fudges" and, technically speaking, breaks minor rules or laws all the time to suit their own personal convenience.

Explaining the Concept of Justice

Communicating the concept of justice versus injustice to your child can be difficult, especially in relation to her own behavior and actions. Wherever possible, use anecdotes from your child's past without sounding punitive or accusatory. Though your child may become highly defensive of her motives for doing something, remind her that, as a parent, you made the judgment that she was in error, if that is the case. There may also have been times when a sibling, neighbor, or cousin reported to you that your child did something that you considered minor enough not to act upon. You may wish to reveal those instances to your child as well. Revisiting this topic over time, or as the need arises, will be a "safe" way for your child to practice developing the skill to make judgment calls about those gray areas.

Fact

Like many abused children, the child with Asperger's, in particular, may believe that the abuse is normal or expected, or that he is responsible. It is important to help your child understand what constitutes abuse, and that being abused or abusing others is never okay.

It can be just as difficult for your child to determine when the actions of another are cause for concern. One way to help your child understand this is to discuss it in the context of whether or not the act is harmful to others. Some people with Asperger's who live in the community become nuisances because they repeatedly dial 911 to report a wide variety of infractions that they perceive as legitimate but that are not appropriate to report as emergencies. Coach your child on weighing the potential ramifications of reporting something that either doesn't directly impact her or doesn't cause harm to others or their property—what would any good citizen do? You may even wish to create a visual guessing game using words, pictures, or videos and pausing to brainstorm with your child about each specific scenario. Are there real-life scenarios either of you can recall that mirror your discussion (and reinforce the concept in a concrete manner)? If you use the shows or characters that most impassion your child, this learning time will be especially pleasing and memorable.

The Role of the Police

Police academies across the country are slowly becoming more aware of the responsibility law enforcement officials have to broaden their knowledge about people with different ways of being. California and Pennsylvania are among the leaders in this initiative. You may wish to contact your local police headquarters or state police academy to learn about the status of police training on people with special needs. If you are affiliated with any autism or Asperger's groups in your area, you may wish to volunteer your time and services to support your local police in this endeavor.

Police Purview

While an effort is underway to educate police officers to enhance their understanding and sensitivity toward people with disabilities, law enforcement officials have a difficult job that often requires them to make on-the-spot assessments to ensure public safety. If a police officer has cause to believe that an individual is behaving in a way that may jeopardize his or her safety or that of others, that officer has an obligation to quickly size up the situation. Depending upon the situation and the extent of his or her training, the officer may not have the time or ability to "match" an individual's behavior with a specific disability. A police officer may misinterpret certain actions or behaviors, such as the following:

- Tics, or unusual, repetitive fine or gross motor activity.
- Loud, boisterous, or unusual tone of voice.
- Loitering or lurking around certain people or places.

Check out the Web site titled "Police and Autism: Avoiding Unfortunate Circumstances" at *http://policeandautism.cjb.net.* While the Web site pertains to autism and law enforcement, there may be selective information that will prove helpful to you and your child. Tips include how both parties should interact with one another, how a person with autism can protect himself, and what to do if a person with autism is questioned or arrested.

The officer makes an assessment of the behavior based upon what he or she is most likely to encounter. It is more commonplace for an officer to encounter someone behaving in unusual ways due to a drug or mental health problem, so it is likely that the officer will respond accordingly.

If a police officer suspects that some type of criminal activity is about to happen, he or she can intervene in a variety of ways, depending upon the seriousness of the situation. Regardless of whether your child has Asperger's syndrome, the officer still has an official duty to stop the threat of danger.

Essential

Strides are being made to enhance police sensitivity in dealing with persons with different ways of being. Still, be mindful that many officers are expected to make split-second judgments and not clinical diagnoses. Protect yourself and your child by reviewing ways in which police have indicated it is most helpful to support them in the community during an encounter.

What to Do When Stopped

Police may be familiar only with autism stereotypes, meaning those individuals who outwardly present as severely limited and engage in activities and actions traditionally associated with autism. The subtleties of Asperger's syndrome can be something altogether different. If stopped and questioned by a police officer, your child can protect herself by quietly listening to and complying with the officer's directions, such as a request to put down what's in one's hand (if a weapon is suspected). As always, disclosing one's diagnosis in the moment is a personal choice, and stating, "I have Asperger's syndrome" may or may not have relevance for a police officer at the time. Anyone of us can become quickly flustered or rattled if stopped by a police officer. We may forget information that we should be able to readily provide, or we may feel justified in blurting out our side of the story. If your child chooses *not* to disclose his diagnosis, as is his right, he may have to communicate his confusion in order to understand and cooperate with the police officer. An example may be to say, "You're talking too fast, please slow down." Or "I don't understand what you're asking, please say it another way." Your child may also want to ask that the officer call you or an ally to be present with you.

Misunderstandings

Because people with Asperger's can be pleasers, or perhaps very frightened in the moment, some folks have confessed to crimes they didn't commit in order to end the interrogation or satisfy the inquiring officer. In one instance, a twenty-year-old young man with Asperger's entered into a sexual relationship with a neighbor. Later, when the relationship soured, the woman formally accused the young man of sexual assault. Because of his diagnosis, his confusion about details, and his misunderstanding of the legal system, his side of the story was not believed and he found himself incarcerated, serving a sentence for what his family believes was an entirely consensual relationship.

Stalking is defined differently by each state. The Stalking Resource Center of the National Center for Victims of Crime is a clearinghouse for stalking-related information. The Stalking Resource Center Web site is *www.ncvc.org/src/index.html.* It provides state-by-state and federal statutes, help for victims, stalking profiles, statistics, and other resources.

A Stalking Charge

If your child is involved in a romantic relationship that is not being reciprocated, monitor the situation as cautiously as you can to guard against your child's actions and activities being construed as stalking. When some individuals with Asperger's fall in love, it can appear to be an obsession or infatuation. While the individual's feelings are genuine and sincere, their expression of those feelings, through words and actions, can seem exaggerated. Their desire to express their love can come across as desperate and even urgent, the intensity of which may be quite frightening for the person on the receiving end—especially if he or she no longer wishes to participate in the relationship.

Harassment or Assault

Your child may be genuinely surprised to learn that something she has done is criminal or constitutes unacceptable behavior. Sometimes this occurs because of how films and TV portray relationships between people. So much of what we consider to be entertainment is over-the-top, exaggerated human behavior. We'd never dream of engaging in some of the activities we see, or saying the things movie characters say, because we'd get arrested, fired from our jobs, or damage relationships. Part of the entertainment comes from the comfort and safety of watching what happens to someone who so blatantly breaks the social code of acceptable conduct.

So, for example, in a movie, the leading man can say to a woman, "Hey babe, nice rack! Let's go get it on!" and it works. If your child used this line in real life, he would probably be slapped across the face (in the best-case scenario) or have sexual harassment charges filed against him (in the worst-case scenario). Many instances of alleged sexual harassment by young men with Asperger's is later determined to be a misinterpretation along these lines.

Calling the Police

If your child is living independently in the community, it will be important to discuss emergency situations and when it is advisable to call 911 or the local police. Your child has certain sensitivities and ways of doing things that may not mesh well with what others consider "typical." This has the potential to create conflict for your child. Your child may find himself in altercations with neighbors, other tenants, or people in the community.

If your child is without an ally to help sort things through, he may be prone to blow situations out of proportion. Your child may exaggerate things that other, less-sensitive people may consider simply ignorant or mildly offensive. When this happens, your child may believe he is justified in calling the police. It is important to help your child understand what types of situations warrant police intervention, as well as the priority level of those that do.

Your child should be well educated in determining emergencies that require contacting 911 immediately. However, you do not wish for your child (especially a young adult living on her own) to develop a reputation as a community nuisance because of repeated, inappropriate police calls. You may wish to develop and visually review a list of potential, appropriate 911 emergencies.

When a police call comes in, time and effort is required to ascertain its priority. Calls, such as a loud music complaint, may well be considered "low priority," depending upon call volume and the flexibility of the police force on duty. That a call is low priority may or may not be communicated to the caller. It can be problematic for the person with Asperger's, whose acute hearing is deafened by a neighbor's music, to be told "it will be awhile" or "an officer will be out in about an hour" when calling to complain. This vague response may cause the person to repeatedly call back to follow up, thus increasing everyone's frustration and anxiety.

Remember, police have authority over crime and criminal behavior, not civil issues. It may be a shock for your child (and perhaps you) to learn that there are certain civil issues over which police have limited influence or control, or are considered "iffy" in terms of interpretation. These may include:

- Most circumstances involving landlords—a huge issue for lots of adults with Asperger's who feel mistreated or ignored.
- Verbal agreements with others, such as loaning someone a cell phone and he never gives it back or doesn't give it back by an agreed-upon date.
- Children under ten (who cannot be arrested) running in and out of a yard, or whose ball, for example, keeps bouncing into your yard.
- Certain types of speech, like someone saying mean things.

Unless there's reason to believe there is criminal intent against your child, like plotting harm, these areas are largely beyond police purview. If there are valid concerns that *are* police responsibility but are also considered low priority, it will behoove your child to track the concerns through written documentation that includes dates, times, and succinct descriptions of the offending activity. Acts of criminal mischief, trespassing, or disturbance of the peace, like dogs barking or loud music, are offenses for which the perpetrator may receive a warning or a citation. Depending upon the severity of the situation, it may be that your child can attempt to resolve the situation in a neighborly and civil manner.

CHAPTER 21

The Rewards of Being an Asperger's Parent

Parents of children with different ways of being can lead lives that are often complex, complicated by their child's difference. Oftentimes such complications are imposed by others who do not understand or appreciate your child's way of being in the world. If you have been able to see the glass half full, instead of half empty, then you have recognized the profound journey upon which you've embarked as a parent. It all began with those two words: Asperger's syndrome.

What Have You Learned?

Think back to the moment you first received your child's diagnosis of Asperger's syndrome. What were you feeling in that moment? Confusion? Upset? Despair? Hopelessness? Next, think about how you're feeling now, today, especially after having read this book. How much differently do you feel now compared to then?

You and your child have been on quite a journey together. He or she has worked to adapt to people, places, and things that are often very difficult to discern without your gentle support and guidance. Your child has come a long way toward becoming more self-sufficient and independent. But what about you? What have you learned as an Asperger's parent? One mom, Gina, eloquently summarizes her thoughts and feelings in a way that many parents will relate to best.

I've always thought of having a child with Asperger's syndrome as a journey. It begins with the never-to-be-forgotten moment the words tumble out of a physician's mouth. Little do any of us realize it at the time, but the whole world is about to change forever. Sometimes there is grief, sometimes despair. Yet there are also times of such profound revelation, such profound love, that you find yourself thanking God that He gave you this incredible being who inevitable expanded you and taught you so much.

In the early days, I remember thinking, "Why me? Why Jon?" One day the answer came to me. "Why *not* me? Why not my son?" If there was to be a child with Asperger's, perhaps I was the perfect person to be that child's parent. And perhaps I needed that child just as much as he needed me. I am forever changed because of it. And I cannot imagine being anyone but the person I am today. If Jon is a special-needs kid, then maybe *I'm* a special-needs parent.

Essential

Are you someone who believes that everything happens for a reason, or that our destinies are predetermined? If so, the quote from Gina about her son should have special resonance. Has your role as a parent been reversed, and were *you* the person with the special need prior to your child being in your life? Food for thought.

Another equally wise mother shared her observations as well:

Your job, like Edison's mother, is to develop the child's potential, which may be greater (or not) than your own. You are helping him to unlock his world. You deepen your relationship with the child. He may share some insights only with you, about himself or about what he is learning or creating. What a privilege!

Bonnie believes in using her son Noel's passions in order to gain access to his way of thinking. Not only has this made the teaching and learning process easier and more effective, she has had the pleasure of seeing her son learn and achieve. In so doing, Bonnie has found that she's learned a lot about herself, and calls the special bond with Noel "an amazing experience."

Without your child in your life, you would be a different person, wouldn't you? As the parent of a child with Asperger's syndrome, how has your life been "forever changed"? Perhaps you have become stronger, more vocal, or more defensive in protection of your child and her rights. (By extension, are you more tolerant and compassionate of differences in people of all kinds?) Perhaps your example of total, loving acceptance has been the model others follow, including your other children. Remember that your child will reflect back to you what you project upon her. Armed with your loving support, your trust and your confidence, your child will be poised for great things. And you have every reason to expect them.

The Desire to Give Back

Like all human beings, you have likely done or said hurtful things to your child out of frustration or exasperation. This is typical of any parent, not just the parent of a child with Asperger's. But have you found yourself in a rut? Do you still see the glass as half empty? You may find yourself asking, "Why me?" Your frustration may stem from your child's limitations or your own challenge to cope day to day. You may wish your child would "snap out of it" and get with the "program." Shouldn't your child figure out how to fit in and make a go of it, just like anyone else who's ever had any kind of challenge in life? This question may be answered with another question that will prompt some self-reflection: What do you think your child *has* been doing all this time?

Your child has a great desire to give back to you and others. If you are a parent who has been blocked by myths and stereotypes, you may well have missed the times your child has reached out to you. It can be very subtle and may come when you least expect it, like the child who made his dad a leading character in his hand-drawn comic strips.

Most parents simply want their child to be happy. Your child has a lot to offer you as well as the rest of the world; and he has every reason to assume his rightful place in the world and be recognized for his contributions. The two most important things you can do for your child with Asperger's are to value, encourage, and indulge his most passionate interests (with an eye toward a future vocation), and foster the development of a relationship with at least one ally. In so doing, your child will be better poised to prosper in life.

Essential

As a simple exercise, develop a written list of all the things you've learned from your child with Asperger's syndrome. The list may include items that are academic in nature, inspired by her most passionate of interests, or lessons about sensitivity toward others, or patience. It may be a powerful thing to lovingly share your list with your child, perhaps at a special event like a sixteenth or twenty-first birthday or a graduation.

Asperger's and the World

As we learn more about autism and Asperger's syndrome, a burgeoning community of support has developed. Parents are no longer content to accept the oftentimes very limiting parameters of the current federal, state, and local service systems available to children with differences. Instead they are becoming impassioned advocates, creating in-roads, shaping laws, and dictating what is and what is not acceptable for their children. As you've learned, parents have long established formal and informal local networks, accessible through state and county social service systems. A resource list, included at the back of this book, highlights some of the many online Asperger's syndrome groups organized to educate, enlighten, and entertain individuals, families, friends, and the community.

Your child, teenager, or young adult with Asperger's may feel isolated and estranged from others who share his similarities. Forging friendships with like others is a personal choice that may be of little to no consequence to your child, especially if he is comfortable with the number of healthy relationships in his life. Still others seek a kinship that may not be readily found in one's hometown. Computer technology and the Internet has revolutionized our world, and, in particular, has been a blessing for the person with Asperger's syndrome for reasons previously outlined. It is entirely possible for your child to communicate with others around the world that are also seeking a connectedness in learning about Asperger's syndrome and themselves. From the comfort of one's home, your child can converse with others; understand more about herself; feel joy and relief in comparing daily challenges others face; and vent about the general intolerance of the "big world." Through these relationships, your child may develop an enhanced confidence and comfort level about Asperger's—it's really *not* so different after all. Opportunities to meet in person, to make formal presentations, or to contribute to various online and hard-copy publications may available. It is a rare individual with Asperger's who does not desire to educate others.

Fact

We are still a long way from achieving a perfect system for individuals with mental retardation, autism, and other ways of being. In seeking formal and informal supports for your child, don't be surprised if you are both a recipient of service *and* an educator to others. Many traditional services are based on a medical or mental retardation model, and not an autism or Asperger's service delivery model. As always, encourage your child to be his own best advocate.

The Future

Ultimately, we are all temporary in the lives of the people that we know and love. After you have passed on, your wish for your child may include that she be surrounded with a circle of loved ones and friends, to be successfully employed, and to be well accepted—if not revered—in her chosen community. Hopefully, this introduction to Asperger's syndrome has provided you with philosophies and strategies that match well with your role as a parent. Use what makes sense and leave behind what does not. You may wish to use this book as a springboard to others that are more specific and technical, or you may wish to read about those who have encountered, lived with, or loved someone with Asperger's syndrome.

If you've enjoyed (and could relate to) the personal stories and anecdotes sprinkled throughout this book, you are certain to relish the unique and innovative perspectives of those who have so eloquently made written record of their experiences. Some such biographies are listed in Appendix A.

As we look to the future, we are seeing a growing acceptance in our culture of *all* people with different ways of being. Our language used to describe people's differences is no longer a matter of "political correctness," it is a show of renewed respect. In this day and age, no one can justly define "normal" or "typical." Not one of us can say we don't know someone with a difference or disability. This may include the woman who's had a mastectomy, the man who developed Parkinson's disease, the teenager with an eating disorder, or the child with Down syndrome. At some point in time, we will collectively recognize that *all* ways of being, including Asperger's syndrome, are simply a normal part of being human. After all, we're all more alike than different.

Appendix A

Further Reading

Aston, Maxine. *Asperger's in Love: Couple Relationships and Family Affairs* (London: Jessica Kingsley Publishers, Ltd., 2003).

Attwood, Tony. *Asperger's Syndrome: A Guide For Parents and Professionals* (London: Jessica Kingsley Publishers, Ltd., 1998).

Birch, Jen. *Congratulations! It's Asperger Syndrome* (London: Jessica Kingsley Publishers, Ltd., 2003).

Boyd, Brenda. *Parenting a child with Asperger syndrome: 200 Tips and Strategies* (London: Jessica Kingsley Publishers, Ltd., 2003).

Cohen, Shirley. *Targeting Autism* (Berkeley: University of California Press, 1998).

Faherty, Catherine. *Asperger's: What Does It Mean to Me? Structured Teaching Ideas for Home and School* (Arlington, TX: Future Horizons Inc., 2000).

Grandin, Temple. *Thinking in Pictures and Other Reports from My Life with Autism* (New York: Doubleday, 1995).

Gray, Carol. *The Original Social Story Book* (Arlington, TX: Future Horizons, Inc., 1994).

____. *The New Social Story Book: Illustrated Edition* (Arlington, TX: Future Horizons, Inc., 2000).

Holliday Willey, Liane. *Pretending to be Normal: Living with Asperger's Syndrome* (London: Jessica Kingsley Publishers, Ltd., 1999).

____. *Asperger Syndrome in the Family* (London: Jessica Kingsley Publishers, Ltd., 2001).

Jackson, Luke. *Freaks, Geeks and Asperger's Syndrome: A User's Guide to Adolescence* (London: Jessica Kingsley Publishers, Ltd., 2002).

Kephart, Beth. *A Slant of Sun: One Child's Courage* (New York: W.W. Norton & Company, Inc., 1998).

Lawson, Wendy. *Build Your Own Life: A Self-Help Guide for Individuals with Asperger's Syndrome* (London: Jessica Kingsley Publishers. Ltd., 2003).

Meyer, Roger. *Asperger Syndrome Employment Workbook: An Employment Workbook for Adults with Asperger Syndrome* (London: Jessica Kingsley Publishers. Ltd., 2000).

Moyes, Rebecca A. *Incorporating Social Skills in the Classroom: A Guide for Teachers and Parents of Children with High-Functioning Autism and Asperger Syndrome* (London: Jessica Kingsley Publishers. Ltd., 2001).

____. *Addressing the Challenging Behavior of Children with High-Functioning Autism/Asperger Syndrome in the Classroom: A Guide for Teachers and Parents* (London: Jessica Kingsley Publishers. Ltd., 2002).

Nash, J. Madelene, "The Secrets of Autism," *Time*, 6 May 2002.

O'Neill, Jasmine Lee. *Through the Eyes of Aliens: A Book About Autistic People* (London: Jessica Kingsley Publishers, Ltd., 1999).

Papolos, Demitri F., and Janice Papolos. *The Bipolar Child: The Definitive and Reassuring Guide to Childhood's Most Misunderstood Disorder* (New York: Broadway Books, 1999).

Pary, Robert J., MD, Andrew S. Levitas, MD, and Anne DesNoyers Hurley, PhD. "Diagnosis of Bipolar Disorder in Persons with Developmental Disabilities," *Mental Health Aspects of Developmental Disabilities*, vol. 2, no. 2, April/May/June 1999.

Pyles, Lise. *Hitchhiking through Asperger Syndrome: How to Help Your Child When No One Else Will* (London: Jessica Kingsley Publishers, Ltd., 2001).

Ryan, Ruth, MD. *Handbook of Mental Health Care for Persons with Developmental Disabilities* (Denver, CO: Omnipress, 1999).

Stanford, Ashley. *Asperger Syndrome and Long-Term Relationships* (London: Jessica Kingsley Publishers, Ltd., 2002).

Stillman, William. *Demystifying the Autistic Experience: A Humanistic Introduction for Parents, Caregivers and Educators* (London: Jessica Kingsley Publishers, Ltd., 2002).

Unok-Marks, Susan, Carl Schrader, Mark Levine, Chris Hagie, Trish Longaker, Maggie Morales, and Iris Peters. "Social Skills for Social Ills: Supporting the Social Skills Development of Adolescents with Asperger's Syndrome," *Teaching Exceptional Children*, November/December 1999.

Winter, Matt. *Asperger's Syndrome: What Teachers Need to Know* (London: Jessica Kingsley Publishers, Ltd., 2003).

Appendix B
Web Site Resources

www.aane.org
Asperger's Association of New England that fosters awareness, respect, acceptance, and support for people with Asperger's and their families.

www.aspennj.org
Asperger Syndrome Education Network, Inc., headquartered in New Jersey.

www.aspergersyndrome.org
Online Asperger's Syndrome Information and Support (OASIS), site created by parents.

www.autismservicescenter.org
The Autism Service Center, a national autism hotline and Web site.

www.autism-society.org
Autism Society of America.

www.ed.gov
United States Department of Education Web site.

www.feat.org
Families for Early Autism Treatment.

www.maapservices.org
Covers autism, Asperger's syndrome, and pervasive developmental disorder.

www.nacdd.org
National Association of Councils on Developmental Disabilities.

www.ninds.nih.gov/health_and_medical/disorders/autism.htm
National Institutes of Health autism site.

www.P2PUSA.org
National Parent to Parent Network Web site.

www.transitionmap.org
A Web site by Pennsylvania professionals for educators supporting high school students with differences who are transitioning to adult life.

www.unlockingautism.org
The Unlocking Autism Web site with a listserv to connect parents, teens, and adults with autism and Asperger's.

www.wrightslaw.org
The Web site of Peter Wright, Esquire, an expert on special education.

http://policeandautism.cjb.net/avoiding.html
A Web page about autism and law enforcement.

The Everything® Parent's Guides Series

Expert Advice for Parents in Need of Answers.

ISBN: 1-59337-043-1

How do I make sure my child is successful? What defines a successful child? Is my child already "successful"?

As parents struggle with these questions on a daily basis, *The Everything® Parent's Guide to Raising a Successful Child* helps put their fears to rest, providing them with professional, reassuring advice on how to raise a "successful" child according to their own standards.

This title walks parents through all emotional, intellectual, and physical aspects of development, including: building character, choosing—and limiting—extracurricular activities, disciplining effectively, ensuring a quality education, and instilling morals and values.

For parents of children with autism, daily activities such as grocery shopping or getting dressed can become extremely challenging. *The Everything® Parent's Guide to Children with Autism* offers practical advice, gentle reassurance, and real-life scenarios to help your family get through each day. Written by Adelle Jameson Tilton, the About.com Guide to Autism, this sensitive work helps you:

- Communicate effectively with your child
- Deal with meltdowns—public or private
- Keep your family together as one unit
- Find a school that suits your child's needs—integration vs. special education
- Learn about assistive devices, such as computers and picture boards
- Find intervention and support groups

ISBN: 1-59337-041-5

All titles are trade paperback, 6" x 9", $14.95 (CAN $22.95)

ISBN: 1-58062-978-4

The Everything® Parent's Guide to Positive Discipline gives you all you need to help you cope with behavior issues. Written by noted psychologist Dr. Carl E. Pickhardt, this authoritative, practical book provides you with professional advice on dealing with everything from getting your kids to do their homework to teaching them to respect their elders. This title also shows parents how to:

- Set priorities
- Promote communication
- Establish the connection between choice and consequence
- Enforce punishment
- Change discipline style to reflect the age of the child
- Work with your partner as a team

The Everything® Parent's Guide to Children with Dyslexia, by Abigail Marshall—manager of *www.dyslexia.com*—gives you a complete understanding of what dyslexia is, how to identify the signs, and what you can do to help your child. This authoritative book seeks to alert parents to the special needs associated with this learning disability and offers practical suggestions for getting involved in the classroom. You will learn how to:

- Select the right treatment programs for your child
- Secure an IEP
- Choose a school and reduce homework struggles
- Develop your child's skills with the use of assistive technology
- Maintain open communication and offer support

ISBN: 1-59337-135-7

Available wherever books are sold.
Or call 1-800-872-5627 or visit us at *www.everything.com*

OTHER *EVERYTHING*® PARENTING TITLES:

All titles are $14.95 unless otherwise noted.

Everything® Baby Names
ISBN: 1-55850-655-1

Everything® Baby Shower Book
ISBN: 1-58062-305-0 ($12.95 U.S.)

Everything® Baby's First Food Book
ISBN: 1-58062-512-6

Everything® Baby's First Year Book
ISBN: 1-58062-581-9

Everything® Birthing Book
ISBN: 1-59337-141-1

Everything® Breastfeeding Book
ISBN: 1-58062-582-7

Everything® Father-To-Be Book
ISBN: 1-58062-974-1

Everything® Get Ready for Baby Book
ISBN: 1-55850-844-9

Everything® Getting Pregnant Book
ISBN: 1-59337-034-2

Everything® Homeschooling Book
ISBN: 1-58062-868-0

Everything® Parenting a Teenager Book
ISBN: 1-59337-035-0

Everything® Potty Training Book
ISBN: 1-58062-740-4

Everything® Pregnancy Book, 2nd Ed.
ISBN: 1-58062-808-7

Everything® Pregnancy Fitness Book
ISBN: 1-58062-873-7

Everything® Pregnancy Nutrition Book
ISBN: 1-59337-151-9 ($14.95 U.S.)

Everything® Pregnancy Organizer
(Spiral Bound) ISBN: 1-58062-336-0 ($15.00 U.S.)

Everything® Toddler Book
ISBN: 1-58062-592-4

Everything® Tween Book
ISBN: 1-58062-870-2